Mental Health
and Religion

Kate Miriam Loewenthal

Senior Lecturer in Psychology at Royal Holloway University of
London, UK and Visiting Lecturer, Department of Theology
and Religious Studies, Kings College, London, UK

CHAPMAN & HALL

London · Glasgo~~~~~~~~~~~~~lbourne · Madras

D0257381

Published by Chapman & Hall, 2–6 Boundary Row, London SE1 8HN, UK

Chapman & Hall, 2–6 Boundary Row, London SE1 8HN, UK

Blackie Academic & Professional, Wester Cleddens Road, Bishopbriggs, Glasgow G64 2NZ, UK

Chapman & Hall GmbH, Pappelallee 3, 69469 Weinheim, Germany

Chapman & Hall USA, One Penn Plaza, 41st Floor, New York NY 10119, USA

Chapman & Hall Japan, ITP-Japan, Kyowa Building, 3F, 2-2-1 Hirakawacho, Chiyoda-ku, Tokyo 102, Japan

Chapman & Hall Australia, Thomas Nelson Australia, 102 Dodds Street, South Melbourne, Victoria 3205, Australia

Chapman & Hall India, R. Seshadri, 32 Second Main Road, CIT East, Madras 600 035, India

Distributed in the USA and Canada by Singular Publishing Group Inc., 4284 41st Street, San Diego, California 92105

First edition 1995

© 1995 Kate Miriam Loewenthal

Typeset in 10/12 Palatino by Saxon Graphics Ltd, Derby
Printed in Great Britain by Page Bros (Norwich) Ltd

ISBN 0 412 55140 3   1 56593 356 7 (USA)

A catalogue record for this book is available from the British Library

Library of Congress Catalog Card Number: 94-72659

♾ Printed on permanent acid-free text paper, manufactured in accordance with ANSI/NISO Z39.48-1992 and ANSI/NISO Z39.48-1984 (Permanence of Paper).

Contents

Preface

I sometimes think there are just two types of people in the world. Those who think religion drives people mad, bad or both – and those who think that religion is great and once you've got it, you can't go wrong psychologically.

This book is written for both types of people, and for people who wonder who is right, and for people who think that both are right and who wonder how.

I recall a young psychology student who decided to see who was right. Armed with several psychological tests measuring anxiety, happiness and other states of mind, he set off to test a group of religious people and a group of atheists. After a while, he was back. Atheists were quite hard to find, it turned out. He settled for agnostics. Presently he came back again with his results. He wasn't worried about the agnostics; some were happy, some not so happy – they were like the people he knew. But he was worried about the religious people: nearly all of those tested insisted that they were perfectly happy. He thought they were saying they were perfectly happy because they thought religious people ought to be perfectly happy.

Now here's a question: just because they said they were happy because they thought they ought to be happy, does that mean they weren't really happy?

That question is quite hard to answer, and it shows the sort of difficulties that are met in looking at the relations between religion and mental health.

Some people seem to have vested interests in asserting the panacea-like benefits of religion for mental health, and they may feel quite defensive about this. Helping professionals may be seen as threatening religiously valued practices and beliefs. For example Schloss (1993) quotes several warnings directed to the religious Jewish community against 'seeking professional advice for highly delicate issues from psychologists, psychiatrists and marriage counsellors'. These fears may be justified: this book quotes a number of examples of cases in which mental health professionals have been perceived as offering advice contrary to religious values, or have perceived religiously-valued behaviour as disturbed. A young woman seeking support from a counsellor as she in turn supported her husband through a difficult period claimed that the counsellor repeatedly advised her to seek a divorce. She felt that in her deep personal commitment to her marriage, she was being viewed as the victim of religiously-sanctioned chauvinism.

Others, regardless of their religious values, may be sceptical about the value of mental health professional services. These might be particularly those who have tried such services and perceived no benefits. One social services administrator claimed that all his department's clients who were receiving psychotherapy 'hate it, and say that it is useless'. They go along with it because they feel coerced by the welfare authorities.

Still others will believe that religion has mainly negative effects on mental health. For example many feminists believe that traditional religions bastion male power, enabling the exploitation and abuse of the weak, particularly women, children, the disabled and the politically disadvantaged.

But many people will appreciate that simplistic views require a tremendous effort to maintain. Dissonant facts get swept under the carpet, and single-minded antipathies or enthusiasms sound naive.

The history of world religions in their dealings with mental health is full of examples of fascinating beliefs on the interface between religion and psychiatry.

I have looked at different approaches to religion and mental health, and studies that have been made in a variety of different cultural-religious contexts. Ours is a pluralistic and fast-moving society, religiously. Virtually all the major traditional world religions rub shoulders with a variety of secularist and materialist philosophies and a plethora of new religious movements, all in the context of a society which is historically predominantly Christian and capitalist.

Mental health issues have hitherto been separated from their religious-cultural context. Professionals and clients are bemused. I hope that this book is a beginning at making some of the issues clearer.

Kate Miriam Loewenthal
London, April 1994

Acknowledgements

Many thanks to the following people for all kinds of help and support:

my family: my dear parents, husband, children, sons-in-law and grandchildren, and other relatives, especially to my husband Tali Loewenthal;

the Lubavitcher Rebbe Shlita, Rav J. Dunner, Rabbi S. Lew; Amelie, Lady Jakobovits;

my friends, neighbours, colleagues and all the others from whom I have learnt and by whom I have been helped, particularly a very good boss, Professor Michael Eysenck, and a very good editor, Rosemary Morris of Chapman & Hall.

To name a few more of the above:

Esther Cadaner, Leah Namdar, Yitzchok Loewenthal, Chana-Soroh Danow, Moshe Loewenthal, Rivka Loewenthal, Brocha Loewenthal, Freida Loewenthal, Sholi Loewenthal, Mendy Loewenthal, Zalmy Loewenthal – my children, who helped and never complained;

Tirril Harris, Dr Clare Bradley, Dr Bernice Andrews, Professor Chris Brewin, Dr Andy MacLeod, Rosemary Westley, Jean Richards, Maureen Collins – patient colleagues of Royal Holloway, London University; Professor L.B. Brown, Oxford University;

David MacIsaac of Reading University, my husband, and an anonymous reviewer, who read the manuscript and made many helpful suggestions;

Kerry Bak, Joyce Paley, Feigy Rabin, Evadne Stern – among the many friends who shared experiences and practical support.

Grateful thanks are due to the authors and publishers for permission to quote from the following:

Barnes, M., Doyle, D. and Johnson, B. (1989) The formation of a Fowler scale: an empirical assessment among Catholics. *Review of Religious Research*, **30**, 412–20.

Bragan, K. (1977) The psychological gains and losses of religious conversion. *British Journal of Medical Psychology*, **50**, 177–80.

Cochrane, R. (1983) *The Social Creation of Mental Illness*, Longman, Harlow.

Cochrane, R. (1993) Women and depression, in *The Health Psychology of Women*, (eds C.A. Niven and D. Carroll), Harwood Press, Switzerland.

Cunin, B., Cunin, B. and Cunin, S. (1993) Psychotherapy with orthodox Jewish patients: on clarifying distortions and conflicts. *Journal of Psychology and Judaism*, **16**, 123–31.

Finlay-Jones, R. (1989) Anxiety, in *Life Events and Illness*, (eds G.W. Brown and T.O. Harris), Unwin Hyman, London.

Gilbert, K. (1992) Religion as a resource for bereaved parents. *Journal of Religion and Health*, **31**, 19–30.

Gold, A. (1988) *The Marrano Prince*, CIS Press, Lakewood, NJ.

Greenberg, D., Witztum, E. and Pisante, J. (1987) Scrupulosity: Religious attitudes and clinical presentations. *British Journal of Medical Psychology*, **60**, 29–37.

Greenberg, D., Witztum, E. and Buchbinder, J.T. (1992) Mysticism and psychosis: the fate of Ben Zoma. *British Journal of Medical Psychology*, **65**, 223–35.

Kose, A. (1994) British converts to Islam. University of London. PhD thesis.

Levitz, I.N. (1992) The impact of the marriage imperative on Jewish life. *Journal of Psychology and Judaism*, **16**, 109–22.

Littlewood, R. and Lipsedge, M. (1989) *Aliens and Alienists: Ethnic Minorities and Psychiatry*, 2nd edn, Unwin Hyman, London.

Margolin, J. and Witztum, E. (1989) Supernatural impotence: historical review with anthropological and clinical implications. *British Journal of Medical Psychology*, **62**, 339–42.

Mordechai, T. (1992) *Playing with Fire*, BP Publishers, New York.

Noam, R. (1992) *The View from Above*, CIS Publishers, Lakewood, NJ.

Rizzuto, A. (1974) Object relations and the formation of the image of God. *British Journal of Medical Psychology*, **47**, 83–9.

Shain, R. (1992) *Dearest Children*, Feldheim, Jerusalem.

Shams, M. and Jackson, P.R. (1993) Religiosity as a predictor of well-being and moderator of the psychological impact of unemployment. *British Journal of Medical Psychology*, **66**, 341–52.

Spero, M.H. (1992) *Religious Objects as Psychological Structures: a Critical Integration of Object Relations Theory, Psychotherapy and Judaism*, University of Chicago Press, Chicago, IL.

1

Focus

People who identify themselves as religious are often invested in showing that religion makes people happy, and people who identify themselves as nonreligious are often invested in showing that religion makes people miserable and ill. This book is really about how and why both might be right.

The book is not meant to be a comprehensive review. It looks at some issues and trends, and tries to pick out some conclusions and directions for future discussion and research.

SOME VIEWS ON THE RELATIONS BETWEEN MENTAL HEALTH AND RELIGION

Here are several well-known and differing opinions.

- Happy is the man who trusts in the Lord (King David).
- Religion is the opium of the people (Marx).
- Religion is the universal obsessional neurosis (Freud).
- Religion makes and unmakes prejudice (Allport).

When we examine the many studies that have looked at associations between religion and mental health and illness (see reviews by Dittes (1969), Sanua (1969), Spilka and Werme (1971), Stark (1971), Argyle and Beit-Hallahmi, 1975; Batson and Ventis, 1982; Meadow and Kahoe, 1984; Paloutzian, 1983; Spilka, Hood and Gorsuch, 1985; Brown, 1987; Batson, Schoenrade and Ventis, 1993) there is some consensus that on the whole, religiosity goes along with greater happiness. But this could be for a large number of reasons, and there is a huge variety of complex and apparently contradictory findings.

In their book on the psychology of religion, Spilka, Hood and Gorsuch (1985), suggest four general types of effect.

- Religion allows or fosters mental illness, for example by encouraging guilt.
- Religion controls or suppresses mental illness, for example by encouraging happiness.
- Religion may protect from stress or its effects, for example by raising self-esteem.
- Religion may be therapeutically useful, for example by providing sympathetic counsellors.

A psychotherapist, Spero (1992), lists four causal routes by which – in his clinical experience – religion may be related to psychological illnesses in religious patients. With each of Spero's routes I have given an example (these are not Spero's examples).

1. Religious adherents may have a condition which is alleged to be unrelated to religion

> A., a married woman in her thirties with three children, was calm and friendly when she gave the research interview in her home. The children were in school and her husband out at work. She is devout and prays regularly, saying that it helps to give her strength to carry on. The family has quite major difficulties. A. keeps busy helping others, looking after her family and working as a teacher. She didn't report any clinical depression or anxiety but when she was asked about obsessional symptoms she laughed and said her weak point was locking doors and windows. She has to keep checking them, even when she knows they're really locked. She added that her mother was just the same and she thinks it came from the fact that they were burgled a few times. She's never looked for any kind of therapy for this problem, though she finds it quite a nuisance.

2. Patients whose religious beliefs and practices are outgrowths of their psychological disturbance

Phil was a 19-year-old Jewish student who was admitted to psychiatric hospital suffering from mutism and bizarre behaviour. He used to take several hours preparing his food to ensure that it was absolutely kosher. Phil feared that if he did not keep to all the religious rules he would be struck by a major physical or mental impairment. Levin and Zegans (1974), who described Phil's case, noted that Phil's mother was anxious about feeding him properly, since he always seemed finicky and underfed. When angry she would throw him into his cot and hit and kick him. After a difficult childhood and adolescence, including a previous psychiatric breakdown, Phil became preoccupied with orthodox Judaism (his parents had never been actively religious), becoming increasingly withdrawn from his family and preoccupied with food preparation rituals.

3. Patients whose disorder is produced by manipulation by the religious group or the leader

It is quite difficult to find clear examples of this, in the form of cases where there was no likelihood of a previous personality disorder, as for instance in Phil's case. It has been claimed that some cults and fundamentalist religious movements 'brainwash' their adherents and turn them into 'zombies'. However the meagre amount of 'hard' evidence available does not always support the idea that adherents of cults and new religious movements (NRMs) suffer from measurable psychological distress or illness caused by manipulation (Richardson, 1985; Galanter, 1989). Accepting the world-view of a religious group, and identity as a group member, is not necessarily distressing even if nonmembers of the group disagree with the world-view and disapprove of the members' lifestyle. The best-known examples of manipulation in contemporary times involve suicide incited in cult members by the group or leader, as happened with the inhabitants of Jonesville, some followers of Ananda Marga, and most recently, the events in Waco, Texas involving a breakaway branch of the Seventh Day Adventists. Much closer to daily experience, but less likely to indicate psychological illness, is this sort of statement (quoted in Staples and Mauss, 1987) by a member of an evangelical Christian group. Staples and Mauss suggest this is an example of 'suspension of analogical reasoning', indicating a 'willingness . . . to equate . . . beliefs or ideas with beliefs or ideas of other individuals or groups'.

> **Pete:** I also believe that it's the only true way to be happy on Earth: to feel like you are important, to feel like you mean something. To feel fulfilled while you are on Earth, you have to be a Christian.

Some psychiatrists may be hard-pressed to distinguish between delusional systems and world-views whose holders are able to lead useful and happy lives (Littlewood and Lipsedge, 1989). In Pete's case, although not everyone shares his world-view, we would be unlikely to conclude that he was deluded or otherwise psychologically ill.

Cunin, Cunin and Cunin (1993) describe how 'traditional religious concepts and practices can be distorted and exaggerated and linked to destructive family patterns that may be transmitted from one generation to another'. They consider, for instance, religious Jewish families in which the traditional emphasis on religious learning leads to

> a syndrome that often happens in families that are highly intelligent, where at least one member has some serious degree of emotional disturbance and where some relative is a Rabbi of some public acclaim and fame. The child as an extension of the father's self-image will be raised with the concept that whatever they will do 'it's never good enough'. They have to try ever harder and harder. The praise they will receive is praise solely for their performance and they may never feel good about themselves and who they are. They will lack self-confidence and self-esteem and remain dependent, attached and often attacked by their father for never being 'good enough'.

Cunin, Cunin and Cunin continue with a description of Mr A., father of several children, who was referred by a Rabbi who thought that Mr A.'s anxiety, depression and somatization were related to emotional difficulties. Mr A. said: 'I am unhappy with my life, and as a father and husband'.

Mr A. relayed that he had been brought up with the hope and expectation of becoming a *godol hador* (outstanding in the generation for learning and piety). He stated: 'My father said to me there's nothing for you but the highest honours – my father put that inside me. I was brought up with the unrealistic attitude not to deal with reality, but with the imaginary honour'.

This led to a damaged sense of self. Mr A., for example, reported: 'I have a judge, an incriminating father inside me. If I didn't make the 100 on a test, I was rejected and unprotected, a 90 wasn't good enough . . . Reality is not so reliable since my father was like a god and even though I knew he was wrong, he said he was right and I believed him, at least part of me did'.

Cunin, Cunin and Cunin comment that such children grow up with an introjected internal representation of a father which is malevolent. It has a split-off, autonomous life that eats away at self-soothing and self-calming functions. They can never feel 'good enough'. Mr A. could not

accept or trust the reality of his success, even when, at times, he did receive compliments or praise from others. And yet he also was plagued or consumed by a sense of jealousy or envy of the honours received by others. For example, at family events (or other functions), the roles and honours, or their lack could cause Mr A. to become severely depressed and experience somatic complaints, especially of the stomach or back. He would worry, ruminate and obsessively prepare for different roles or honours he might or might not receive. It is interesting that on several occasions, when he was welcomed at the head table, or to give a discourse, Mr A. sometimes would decline the honour if he thought the intent of the request was perverted or not genuine. In part, however, when Mr A. declined an honour, he did so because he thought he might be unworthy and guilty of having too much pride. After declining an honour, Mr A. subsequently felt depressed.

Mr A. also seemed to be continuing a destructive family pattern with his own children. He too hoped that his sons would become, at the very least, great *talmidei chachomim* (religiously learned). Harsh and critical of his sons' performance, he was rarely able to provide nurturance or express love. Neither could he take into account his sons' own abilities or interests. Mr A. was repeating and re-enacting the same script and interpersonal father–son psychodynamics that were extant in his own childhood.

Mr A's interpersonal world also was marked by a series of unhealthy relationships. This highly intelligent individual, who carried about a great sense of inadequacy and failure seemed to have developed a pattern of attaching himself in dependent relationships with authoritarian, pseudo-father figures who were strong and intelligent, but also cold, judgmental and intimidating. One result of these destructive, dependent relationships was that Mr A. seemed to be trapped as an adult/child in an inner world of chaos and mass confusion.

. . . therapeutic goals for Mr A. were to provide him with some ability for self-soothing, to mitigate the sense of failure, futility, anger and rage directed at his mother and father and especially himself for joining in collusion with his father.

A theme throughout this book is the difficulty that psychiatrists have in telling when a piece of behaviour which is sanctioned or prescribed by religion has become psychopathological. The case of Mr A. suggests that it is quite hard to say when a disorder has been (solely) produced by manipulation by the (religious) group or leader.

4. Patients with crisis-begotten symptoms, where crisis involves religious change

Witztum, Dasberg and Greenberg (1990) describe a young man who had an apparently happy and successful life until he lost his job. Shortly afterwards he became more religious and then got married. Thereafter he stopped sleeping and caring for himself, he became withdrawn and unkempt, and reported visions of angels. Although he improved somewhat under therapy, the visions continued.

DEFINITIONS OF MENTAL HEALTH AND OF RELIGION

Before looking more closely at relations between mental health and religion, we should look at definitions.

Mental health

This may be defined either 'negatively' by the absence of mental illness, or 'positively' by the presence of features said to be characteristic of mental health.

Mental health as absence of mental illness

This is an approach often taken in studies of religion and mental health. Obviously, definition of mental illness is crucial here. We exclude from our discussion mental illnesses of organic origin, where there is a physical cause (like Alzheimer's disease). Our discussion concerns the so-called functional mental illnesses, where there is no known organic cause. These are commonly divided into the **psychoses** and the **neuroses**. The psychoses are forms of madness such as schizophrenia, and they are, happily, less common than the neuroses. The main feature of psychosis is said to be that the sufferer is unable to distinguish between his or her beliefs, fantasies and visions, and reality: he/she really thinks, for instance, that he/she is Napoleon, or that his/her enemies wish to poison him/her with rays. Psychoses are sometimes classified as schizophrenias and mood disorders.

Most neuroses are really miserable illnesses. The two most common are (neurotic) depression and anxiety. Transient depressed and anxious moods are not illnesses; they are subclinical states. Clinical depression is characterized by a depressed, sad mood that is difficult or impossible to control and the presence of several other symptoms such as disturbances of appetite, sleep or libido, low self-esteem, feelings of physical slowness, brooding and suicide plans. Some of the symptoms are actually physical, belying the term 'mental illness', and others involve the person's thoughts. Clinical anxiety, as well as involving an uncontrollable fearful or apprehensive mood, involves bodily changes – again belying the term 'mental illness'. In anxiety the changes are those produced by arousal of the autonomic nervous system, which prepares the body for emergency action: they include palpitations, butterflies, sweating, trembling and dry mouth. Some sufferers from anxiety get attacks 'out of the blue' (free-floating anxiety), while others may get attacks precipitated by particular objects or situations not normally regarded as frightening (for example, agoraphobia – fear of being out in the open).

Depression and anxiety and related states and traits, including subclinical forms, can be assessed by questionnaires (i.e. psycho-metrically) or by psychiatric interview. Properly constructed questionnaires and well-conducted interviews should show acceptable levels of reliability and validity.

There are many other forms of functional mental illness. The varieties I have mentioned are both common and have often been looked at in relation to religion.

Mental health as the presence of features said to be characteristic of mental health

This approach recognizes that there is more to health than the absence of illness, and attempts are made to assess positive states or traits – usually psychometrically, by questionnaire-type meth-ods. Measures include positive wellbeing (e.g. Steinitz, 1980; Loewenthal, 1991), quality of life and life satisfaction (e.g. MacNamara and St George, 1979). There are well-developed attempts to include religious and spiritual aspects in the assess-ment of wellbeing. These include measures of spiritual wellbeing (e.g. Paloutzian, 1979) and religious maturity (Allport, 1950; Fowler, 1981; Batson, Schoenrade and Pych, 1985; Erickson, 1992). I hope to describe some of these measures in more detail in Chapters 6 and 7.

This is quite a long and varied-sounding list. Some people have suggested that we could distinguish between the feelings of wellbeing and satisfaction experienced by those who have not necessarily suffered and a suggested state of 'maturity' attained by some after negotiating serious difficulties. Another suggestion is that positive mental health might be indexed by any of the many measures assessing 'quality of life'.

Definition and assessment go hand in hand. In describing theories and findings, I will try to say exactly which definition or measure of mental health was used.

Definition of religion: religiosity

This is a harder task because of the variety of definitions and measures. For example, Brown (1987) spends over 100 closely printed, well-informed pages on the problems of defining, analysing and measuring religion and its many parameters.

The major religions concur on the existence of nonmaterial (i.e. spiritual) reality and on seeing the purpose of life as increasing harmony in the world by doing good and avoiding evil. The monotheistic religions additionally hold that the source of existence (i.e. God) is also the source of moral directives. All religions involve and depend on social organization for communication of these ideas. In theory, defining and assessing an individual's religion – religiosity – ought to be a straightforward matter. It isn't.

Glock and Stark (1965) pointed out that there are at least five aspects of religiosity and they could all be independent of each other – at least in theory! For instance a person who has frequent mystical experiences may not necessarily accept a lot of orthodox beliefs. Glock and Stark's five 'dimensions' are:

- experiential (to what extent the person has religious experiences);
- ritual (what religious practices the person actually engages in);
- belief (what the person actually believes in);
- intellectual (what the person actually knows about the teachings of their religion);
- a fifth dimension reflecting the extent to which the first four are actually applied in daily life.

In practice, three popular measures of religiosity are:

- affiliation: whether the person belongs to a religious organization;
- self-definition: whether the person defines themselves as religious, or Christian, or Jewish, or belonging to whatever category(ies) the researcher is interested in;
- belief in God.

Different measures of religiosity may yield very different results. For example in Britain in the 1960s, weekly church attendance was practised by less than 10% of the population, but over 80% believed in God (Argyle and Beit-Hallahmi, 1975). Nevertheless, Brown (1962) and Wearing and Brown (1972) and others have reported that people high on one measure of religiosity tend to be high on others.

A very important approach to religiosity was initiated by Allport (1950, 1966). He was trying to account for the fact that measures of religiosity tended to predict prejudice. He suggested that there were two types of religiosity. Intrinsic religiosity is supposed to be characteristic of a minority who are sincere, devout, and low on prejudice. Extrinsic religiosity is supposed to be characteristic of the conformist and self-centred majority, who are high on prejudice. There has been some controversy over the intrinsic–extrinsic distinction (Hunt and King, 1972; Watson, Morris and Hood, 1989), and Batson, Schoenrade and Pych (1985) in particular have initiated modification. Batson and Ventis (1982) and Batson, Schoenrade and Ventis (1993) claim that the distinction has been particularly useful in understanding the relationship between religion and mental health.

As with mental health, the definition or measurement method used for religiosity will be specified wherever possible.

Definition of religion: types of religions and beliefs about mental illness

In the Western world, there has been a growth in the number of active religions. A century ago, Christianity was not only the dominant religion in Europe, the United States and numerous colonial countries, it was also virtually the only religion in many of them. The social upheavals and changes in communication of the last century have given rise to new forms of traditional religion, interest in religions of other cultures and new religious movements.

As well as considering the psychological aspects of religiosity, we also have to bear in mind that the particular forms of religion may be important.

The predominant ethical systems in Europe and America are Christianity and materialism. Due to immigration and (to a lesser extent) proselytism and interfaith marriage, Islam, Judaism, Hinduism and Buddhism all have considerable numbers of followers in Europe and North America, but numbers are relatively small compared to numbers of affiliated Christians. The new religious movements, often based on Eastern religious philosophy, have attracted a relatively small number of followers, mostly fairly young and educated. It is thought that people tend to leave these new religious movements relatively quickly (Galanter, 1989). All the major religions have many different forms or denominations, often with considerable variations in beliefs and practices. All have been and are in a constant process of development and change. Here are some of the basic ideas and practices associated with some of the different religions (Dodge, Armitage and Kasch, 1964; Eliade, 1985; Gwinn, Norton and Gretz, 1989). I have also given estimates of the numbers of adherents of each religion, worldwide, and some idea of their representation in London.

Christianity

About 1000 million people worldwide are identified as Christians, mostly in Europe, the Americas and Australasia. Thus Christianity is the religion with the largest number of followers worldwide and in the developed countries. The Greater London telephone directory lists about 400 Roman Catholic and Anglican (Church of England) churches, with about a further dozen each for the major nonconformist denominations (Methodist, Baptist, United Reform); there are a number of smaller Christian denominations active in the London area as well.

The major divisions of Christianity are into the Eastern and Western churches and, within the latter, into the Roman Catholic and the Protestant churches. Of the varieties of Christianity, Roman Catholicism has the most clearly articulated doctrines and the most explicit rituals and practices. Roman Catholicism is the more prevalent form of Christianity in Eire, and many countries in southern and eastern Europe. The fundamental belief is in the unity of God. The doctrine of the trinity (Father, Son and Holy Spirit) is also central, as is the idea that the death of Jesus atoned for the sins of humanity. Jesus is seen as especially chosen by God. Roman Catholics also accept the 'ten commandments', involving belief in one God and prohibiting idol worship, murder, theft, envy and sexual immorality. Catholics are also religiously obliged to fast on prescribed days, attend mass and abstain from unnecessary work on Sundays and holy days, confess sins regularly, contribute to the support of the church and observe marriage laws.

In Britain and the USA, several varieties of Protestantism have overtaken Catholicism in terms of numbers of adherents, and in terms of political influence. The fundamentals of Christianity, as just described, are not disputed in Protestantism. The main differences between Catholicism and Protestantism lie in a less firmly defined set of specific religious obligations in Protestantism and less investment of authority in the church hierarchy. Among Protestant denominations, there are interdenominational differences in doctrines about sin, its origins and how sin is to be forgiven, and in emphasis upon love and joy, and on other matters.

There are a number of Christian groups distinguished by high degrees of active participation in group worship, including behaviours such as glossolalia ('speaking in tongues'), displays of grief at sinfulness, joy at being saved, and singing and dancing. Such evangelical/charismatic groups have a high proportion of Afro-Caribbean membership. One example of such a group is the African Methodist Episcopal Zion Church, which broke away from mainstream Methodism in the late 18th century as a result of race prejudice experienced by black church members. This style of Christianity is thought to be becoming increasingly popular among white people.

Important for mental health are Christian dogmas regarding sin. Dogma is less binding in Eastern Christianity and Protestantism, but still influential. There is said to be a legalistic flavour to Christian doctrine and dogma on sin, which is seen as the result of the misuse of human freedom. Human wilfulness is to have and to enjoy, to turn to self and to the things of this world and away from God. Suffering is the result of sin. Salvation involves justification, the removal of sin and its effects by one or more of penance, indulgence, confession, absolution and forgiveness. (Dodge, Armitage and Kasch, 1964; Solomon, 1965; Eliade, 1978–85; Gwinn, Norton and Goetz, 1989). It has been suggested that these doctrines may be associated with pejorative views of sufferers from illness and misfortune, including sufferers from mental illness (Lerner, 1980; Atkinson, 1993). However, although suffering is not seen as a desirable end in itself, it is seen as a gateway to renewal and rebirth. Historians of psychiatry have suggested that a widespread Christian view of mental illness, particularly during the 15th to 17th centuries, was that it is the result of demonic possession. This belief has largely been replaced by the view that psychiatric disorders are illnesses. A late 18th century British pioneer of more humane psychiatric treatment was Tuke, a Quaker, whose work is described shortly.

Islam

There are estimated to be about 350 million Moslems worldwide, most of them Sunnis. The most influential other group within Islam are the Shi'ites, while a third group, the Khawarij, is now largely confined to North Africa. Islam originated in the Middle East, where it is still the prevalent religion, but there are substantial numbers of Moslems in the Indian subcontinent and in some far eastern countries, and there are said to be growing Islamic minorities in many developed countries. Six mosques are listed in the Greater London telephone directory.

Islam is a monotheistic religion; therefore by definition belief in God is a central tenet. In Arabic, Islam means submission to the will of God. There is a clear core of religious duties which are relatively straightforward to specify. These include belief in God and the prophets, prayer, giving away a proportion of one's goods, fasting in the month of Ramadan and pilgrimage. Modern Islam is said to originate with the prophet Mohammed, who is however a continuation of a line of prophets beginning with Adam, the first man.

The central feature of the Islamic view of sin is that sin involves forgetfulness of divine unity. The root of sin is pride and self-sufficiency. Reason is seen as playing an important role in the choice of right.

An important Islamic view of the mentally ill is that they are the 'afflicted of Allah'. It is noteworthy that the earliest recorded psychiatric institutions – established over 1000 years ago – were in Moslem countries.

Judaism

Worldwide there are 10–12 million Jews, mostly living in Israel, the USA and the former USSR. About 250 000 Jews (most Anglo-Jews) are estimated to live in the greater London area. There are 77 synagogues and 45 communal organizations and cultural centres listed in the 1992 London postal area telephone directory.

Judaism is the oldest of the monotheistic religions, so by definition a central tenet is the belief in the unity of God. Jewish people are seen as the bearers of this belief. The Jewish people are obligated to practise a large number of different religious commandments, governing more or less the total lifestyle: diet, sexual behaviour, work, business ethics and worship are among the areas to which religious law applies. Different Jewish groups may vary in degree of observance and in specific customs. A Jew is defined as one born from a Jewish mother, or who has converted according to Jewish law. Judaism is unusual in that proselytism is generally not encouraged: non-Jews are said to be righteous and to merit heavenly afterlife if they believe in the unity of God and do not worship idols, are just, sexually moral and avoid cruelty and theft. In recent years, world Jewry has come into conflict with the Communist and Arab nations and is beset with problems of secularization. However there are signs of religious fervour in some sections and of widespread strong attachment to Jewish tradition and history.

Madness is mentioned in the Jewish biblical texts without clear attribution of its causes, though there is some suggestion of a distinction between spirit possession and insanity. Later Jewish sources of the Talmudic period distinguish a range of psychiatric conditions resembling those found in contemporary practice (Miller, 1972). The legal status of the insane with regard to their civil and religious obligations is a matter of discussion in works on Jewish law: for example whether the insane are valid witnesses (probably not) and whether insanity is grounds for divorce (probably yes, but the situation is complicated). The Hebrew term for madness (*choli nefesh*) means sickness of the soul, and there are rabbinic figures in Jewish communities who carry out counselling and therapeutic activities based on views that the rectification of spiritual–moral failings – such as pride – will improve mental health. Misfortune is seen as a warning to the individual to improve, and as a divine test of the individual; also as part of an overall divine plan in which everything is for the ultimate good. Misfortune is seen in Jewish mystical thought as part of a process involving reincarnation in which errors in previous incarnations are repaired – through this repair process Messianic completion will be achieved.

Hinduism

Hinduism is the religion of India, and in its broadest sense much of India's 500 million plus population may be said to be Hindu. There are also Hindus scattered around the Far East and many other countries where Indians have settled. The London telephone directory in 1992 lists one Hindu temple and two other centres.

Hinduism developed from earlier religions of the Indian subcontinent and has many varied manifestations. It is a pluralistic religion, tolerating a wide range of beliefs and practices. Its chief characteristics are its polytheism, overlying a fundamental monotheism wherein the lesser divinities are subsidiary aspects of one God. This infinite principle is truly the sole reality and the ultimate cause and goal. There is a rigid caste system, religiously sanctioned. Religious worship (*puja*) is carried out in a shrine in the home, usually by women.

Transmigration of souls and reincarnation are important aspects of Hindu belief. The ultimate goal is infinity (God), and the attainment of this goal is prevented by *karma* (rebirth); following death and a sojourn in heaven or hell, the soul is reborn into a physical form determined by actions in the previous incarnation. This process of rebirth (*samsara*) is seen as potentially endless, and not progressive in any way. Misfortunes are seen as an aspect of *karma*. *Karma* may be escaped by *marga* – emancipation. There are different types of *marga* suited to various types of individuals; the principal types are duty, knowledge and devotion.

Craissati (1990) states that mental illness in India carries a major stigma, and that consulting a psychiatrist and going to hospital are regarded as last and desperate resorts. In rural communities, where most of India's population (80%) live, tolerance for bizarre behaviour is very high. Psychotic symptoms are seen as the result of spirit possession or black magic, or as the consequences of a previous life. A mentally ill person will be taken to a healer within the community. If this is not successful, it is regarded as the family's duty to bear with the person. Craissati says that patients are only brought to the 'Western' psychiatric hospital where there is serious threat to the norms governing family life and sexual behaviour.

Buddhism

Worldwide there are about 150–200 million Buddhists, mostly in the Far East. One Theravada temple and six cultural centres or associations are listed in the 1992 London postal area telephone directory. Although images of saints and statues of Buddha are revered by Buddhists, this is not a polytheistic religion. In fact scholars debate whether Buddhism is theistic at all. Buddhism arose about 1500 years ago in India, as a reaction against the instrumental, formalized, caste-dominated polytheism dominant at that time.

The two main forms of Buddhism are Theravada, which is regarded as a more classical and orthodox form, and Mahayana. Zen (meditative) Buddhism is a variety of Mahayana first practised in China and then developed in Japan; this form of Buddhism is perhaps the most widely known to many Westerners due to its popularization in many English-language writings. The priestly life is esteemed in Buddhism. Most forms of Buddhism prescribe specific rituals and practices.

The fundamental teaching of Buddhism involves viewing an attachment to the world and its pleasures as the cause of pain. Self-mortification is also an extreme to be avoided; the founder of Buddhism, Gautama Buddha taught the 'middle path'. Life is fundamentally a process of suffering. As in Hinduism, transmigration and rebirth are not seen as progressive, and the central aim of religious belief and practice is to liberate. The eightfold path to freedom from suffering includes right thought, right speech, right action and right mental attitudes. These lead to the cessation of pain, and to enlightenment, and Nirvana (wherein the soul will not be reborn to further suffering).

Buddhist psychology is quite popular in the West (Valentine, 1989). It is suggested that religious practices and thoughts will promote the relief of many if not all forms of mental illness.

Other religions

Particularly since 1960, there has been a growth of 'cults': movements surrounding a charismatic leadership, often demanding total devotion from followers, and often requiring that they give up their connections with family and friends and many habits such as smoking, alcohol and promiscuity. Many of these movements involve communal living and dedication of earnings to the movement. There is frequently a strong emphasis on meditation, mysticism and spiritual 'highs' (Paloutzian, 1983; Galanter, 1989). These movements are sometimes known generically as new religious movements (NRMs). Examples include the Divine Light Mission, the Universal Church of the Rev Sun Yung Moon ('Moonies'), and Rashneesh. Many are based on the Far Eastern religions. Many NRMs are surrounded by strong controversies. Some claim that members are weaned off destructive habits (such as drugs and sex) and that there is no evidence that the members are psychologically unbalanced before or after (see e.g. Richardson, 1985). Opponents accuse NRMs of brainwashing their members and exploiting them, sexually, financially and otherwise.

A possible precursor of the newer religions is Baha'i, now well-established. Baha'i lacks the cult-like qualities I have described above, though it may have had them when it originated. This movement teaches the universality of all religious teachings of humanity. It started in the late 19th century in Iran, but by the early 20th century was well-established in many Western countries, and it currently has one centre in London.

Religious attitudes to and beliefs about mental illness

As may be seen from the brief review above, there are some similarities across religions. Beliefs about mental illness and its treatment may be closely tied to beliefs about sin and suffering, and quite widespread are views that mental illnesses may result from some kind of separation from the divine or even possession by evil. Psychiatry may be mistrusted, except as a last resort, and 'folk' healers may employ a wide range of symbolically loaded rituals and cognitive–behavioural techniques designed to facilitate spiritual healing and hence an improvement in mental health.

Many societies are reported to be tolerant of bizarre behaviour. It may of course be difficult for observers to distinguish between religiously driven behaviour – such as visions and speaking in tongues – and some symptoms of mental illness – such as hallucinations and schizophrenese ('crazy talk'). It probably isn't true, for instance, that in some societies **all** hallucinations are regarded as communications from spirits. We shall return to this problem later.

Attitudes to mental health change with time. In Western Europe and the USA, for example, the primary view of mental disorder until the 18th century was that it was caused by demonic possession. This may be associated with the preoccupation with witchcraft from the 15th century onwards. Fear, neglect, isolation and ill-treatment of the mentally ill was socially and religiously sanctioned. Bedlam in London and the Bicêtre in Paris chained up their unruly inmates. The aim of such institutions was simply to isolate the unruly from society. In some cases, the insane would be auctioned off to be 'cared for' (used as slaves) by farmers.

By the 19th century, medical opinions calling for more humane treatments were beginning to be less isolated. In the 1790s, Tuke, a Quaker merchant, founded the York retreat, where prayer and religious devotion were seen as central to the healing process. Charismatic reformers such as Pinel and Connolly contributed towards the movement to see the insane as people suffering from sickness, requiring treatment. Pinel abolished chains from the Bicêtre, and in the 1840s Dorothea Dix began a campaign to improve conditions in institutions for the insane.

Significant changes in psychiatric practice and thinking include the introduction of psychoanalysis in the early 20th century, the antipsychiatry movement and the introduction of cognitive–behavioural therapies in the latter part of the century.

Relations between religion and psychiatry have been very varied and the subject of controversy. For example, it is interesting that in Britain the Lunacy Act of 1890 ordered a church in every asylum, which the inmates had to attend twice a day, while in France, by contrast, Pinel insisted that the mentally ill should not be exposed to religious practices as it was felt that these might encourage delusions and hallucinations.

Specific religious practices and customs have not been described here. Quite often, the effort to maintain these may give the appearance of bizarre behaviour, which may be interpreted as mad, or unreasonable, or neurotic, or selfish, or heartless – and indeed some of these judgments may be quite fair on occasion. But sometimes they are judgments that evaporate as soon as the observer knows the religious motivations underlying the behaviour. It would be absolutely impossible to give even an outline of all the possible religious customs that might give rise to damaging judgments and misjudgments. Here is an example.

The concept of a 'good death' is very important to Hindus. A good death involves making spiritual preparation for the soul leaving the body and settling one's worldly affairs. One of the religious customs which many Hindus feel should be observed is that, when death occurs, the person should be lying on the ground, preferably in a certain orientation with respect to the north. This has led to many difficulties with Hindu patients in British hospitals. Many will make efforts to be at home if and when they feel the end is approaching. When the dying person is in hospital, they may manage to climb or roll out of their bed in order to be on the floor for the moment of death. This obviously requires tremendous effort, but it is often wasted, especially if there are no relatives or friends to explain the meaning of the behaviour. The horrified nurses rush over to replace the nearly moribund patient safely back in bed – much to his/her distress. Their sufferings are increased when their pleas and protestations are not effective and every time they manage to assume the religiously proper position on the floor, they are firmly bundled back on to the bed. The first time the patient appeared on the floor, the nurses might have thought it was a mishap of some kind, but after the third or fourth time, they think the patient is deluded, mad, or deliberately being a nuisance (Firth, 1991).

Other examples will appear later in this book.

A GENERAL FRAMEWORK FOR UNDERSTANDING SOME CAUSES OF MENTAL HEALTH AND ILLNESS

The views to be outlined below mostly deal with mental health as the absence of mental illness. Here is a brief synopsis of some opinions on the origins of the more common psychiatric disorders. The most widely investigated have been schizophrenia, depression and anxiety.

Psychoanalysts see anxiety as a reaction to threat of loss, and depression as a consequence of actual loss. Both conditions are painful and a discrepancy or threatened discrepancy between the perceived self and the ideal self. Psychiatric illnesses may be defences against underlying depression or anxiety (Freud, 1917; Horney, 1939; Joffe and Sandler, 1965; Brown and Pedder, 1979).

Cognitive psychologists and psychotherapists see that cognitions may play an important role in the maintenance and possibly the offset and onset, of depression and anxiety. For instance, anxious people estimate unpleasant events to be more likely than nonanxious people (MacLeod, Williams and Bekerian, 1991), and depressed people are said to suffer from attributional 'biases' whereby they see bad events as connected to their own permanent lack of worth and good events as flukes – nondepressed people, by contrast, show self-serving attributional 'biases' (Peterson and Seligman, 1984).

Some psychologists, notably Eysenck (1967) have stressed that sufferers from clinical neuroses such as depression and anxiety are likely to be temperamentally disposed; there is said to be a major hereditable component in many forms of psychiatric illness.

Others place emphasis on the person's view of themselves – the **self-concept**. Brown *et al.* (1986) suggest that low self-esteem may make a person more vulnerable to depressive illness when under stress. Higgins, Klein and Strauman (1985) suggest that when people see a discrepancy between what they ought to be and what they are, then they feel anxious. If however they perceive a discrepancy between what they are and what they hope or wish to be then they feel depressed.

Some medical sociologists have claimed that depression is usually preceded by an event or difficulty involving long-term loss, anxiety by an event or difficulty involving danger and schizophrenia by invasive occurrences (Brown and Harris, 1978; Finlay-Jones, 1989; Day, 1989). Various protective factors, some social and some temperamental, may however shield many people experiencing threat and stress from mental illness.

It has been suggested that several aspects of religion may have protective, stress-buffering functions. For example some people may feel a closeness to God during difficult times, or may keep going in difficult times by telling themselves that God sent this difficulty to them because they have the capacity to bear it. Aspects of religion may also be associated with threat and stress. For example adults may abuse children in very unpleasant ways for violations of rules the parents think are important; this often includes religious rules. When religious adherents try to adhere to some aspect of their religion, their behaviour may be misunderstood and interpreted in ways that can lead to unpleasant behaviour from other people. Religion therefore has protective, stress-buffering functions, and also stressful aspects.

These different views are not intended to be seen as in conflict with each other: all the factors suggested above are important.

The following framework (obtained by putting together the approaches above) may be helpful.

Stressful circumstances may be seen as original provoking agents, giving rise to characteristic emotions and cognitions, with a variety of social and temperamental factors affecting how the person copes with these feelings and thoughts. Some may become clinically ill, psychiatrically or physically, in a desperate attempt to deal with unbearable psychological pain. More fortunate others may find ways to change their circumstances so as to reduce loss, danger, or other aspects of stress. Others may find ways to control or bear their thoughts and feelings. Some ways may involve defences in which the self is seen as perfect and other people have to be put down.

Some psychologists, such as Allport (1950, 1961) and Jung (1958) see suffering as a means of reaching a mature understanding of self and sympathy for others. Suffering may be therefore the route to at least some forms of positive mental health.

In the scheme outlined above, a person who has not experienced severe loss, danger or other forms of stress might also be expected to be healthy; this may be the state referred to by William James (1902) as 'healthy-minded'.

There are a variety of scenarios in which religion may enter in one of many guises and play an important role in the scheme outlined above.

SUMMARY

Reviews of religion and mental health have generally suggested a positive relationship between the two, but there are complex and sometimes contradictory findings.

Some seeming contradictions may be due to lack of precision in definition and this chapter reviews some definitions of mental health and religion.

A brief summary of world religions and an outline of religious views on the causes and treatment of mental illness is included.

The chapter concludes with a summary of current scientific views on the causal factors involved in forms of mental health and illness.

2

The psychoanalysts: dealing with the heavenly father

Psychoanalysts have helped in many ways to understand religious feelings and their origins and how they might relate to neuroses, but they have also left some unresolved problems. An important contribution has been in attempts to describe psychologically healthy and unhealthy styles of religiosity.

There is a vast literature on psychoanalysis and religion. Here I want to focus on how some psychoanalytic theorists have dealt with religion in relation to the neuroses and also in relation to psychological health.

FREUD

Freud was born to a fairly assimilated Jewish family. His grandparents had been orthodox. He remained proud of his Jewish identity, had a fair library of Hebrew books and felt it important to have a traditional religious marriage ceremony. He was an involved husband and father – so in spite of professed irreligiosity, he was heavily influenced by a vast cultural and religious legacy. He had a Catholic nanny until he was four, and he was taken to Mass, so there was early contact with forms of Christian observance. But Vienna, where Freud lived, was quite anti-Semitic, in spite of legislation opening schools and universities to Jews, so Freud had few non-Jewish friends or followers. Freud pursued an only moderately successful career in academic medicine and physiological research. In his late thirties, he decided to switch to private practice, specializing in nervous disorders, and he started to treat neurotic patients with hypnosis. He discovered that the help and relief experienced by his patients could be got without hypnosis, simply by allowing the patient to talk freely about whatever came into their mind. Thus was born the 'talking cure' – psychoanalysis – and it was quite a breakthrough in the treatment of mental illness which hitherto had not been treatable. When a mentally ill person became unlivable with, they were simply socially isolated and if necessary confined so they could do no harm.

Freud's ideas developed during the 40 years he developed psychoanalysis. There are several important themes – and I shall pick these out and ignore the well-known controversies about the scientific status of psychoanalytic theories (Valentine, 1992; Eysenck and Wilson, 1973), the theories of infantile sexuality in relation to Freud's concealment of evidence of childhood abuse of some patients (Masson, 1984) and the question of whether psychoanalysis actually cures people (Eysenck, 1952).

The themes to be discussed here relate to Freud's view of God as a 'father-projection' and to his view of religion as a neurosis.

God as a father-projection

This idea derives from Freud's account of early family relationships. Among the powerful emotions experienced by the young child are fear of losing parental love, and grief and guilt when objects of love disappear or are harmed. Freud suggested that by the age of about five the child has identified with the same-sex parent, internalized a parent-figure, who thus continues to communicate with the child in the absence of the real parent. This internalization helps to assuage some of the painful emotions experienced by the child in early family relationships. The internalized parent is the foundation of conscience, of identity and of the God image. Freud asserted that God is nothing more than an exalted father-figure; instead of God creating man in his image, as narrated in Genesis, man has created God in his image (Freud, 1927, 1928, 1939).

It has always been recognized that there are problems in applying Freud's account of identification to girls, because Freud suggested that identification in boys was precipitated by castration anxiety. There is a further difficulty, in asserting that God is an exalted father-figure for a girl, when her internalized parent is female. Freud tried to get over these difficulties by suggesting slightly different details in the processes undergone by girls, culminating in the amazing suggestion that the female conscience is normally weaker than the male conscience (!) because female identification is not impelled by such a powerful anxiety as male identification. It's interesting that cognitive–developmental work on moral development does suggest gender differences: these are eloquently discussed in Carol Gilligan's *In a Different Voice* (Gilligan, 1977), but it is unlikely that many would agree that these differences are for the reasons suggested by Freud.

Leaving these difficulties with Freud aside, we see that Freud has made a very interesting suggestion, that the quality of the relationship with the father (and perhaps the mother) is reflected in the quality of the relationship with God, and in the perception of God. Put more specifically, a person with, say, encouraging or supportive parents would feel and see God as being encouraging and supportive, while a person with angry or critical parents would see God likewise.

This has implications for the links between religion and mental health. Put simply, the suggestion is that a person who is unhappy with their parents will be unhappy with God and, conversely, a good relationship with parents will lead to a good relationship with God. Thus the religious relationship may not offer much comfort if the parents have never offered much comfort.

There is rather mixed support for Freud's assertion that God resembles the father. Testing this idea has been problematic, since tests are done by asking adults how they see God, their father, their mother and any other figures the researcher is interested in (such as the self or the ideal self or spouse). By adulthood, the image of God may have been changed since it was first laid down, and so too may the relationship with the parents – so there is no strong reason to suppose that God and the father will be seen similarly. Nevertheless this method has been favoured by researchers.

Early research, reviewed by Argyle and Beit-Hallahmi (1975) showed rather weak relationships between the God-image and the father-image. Perceived similarities were stronger between God and the mother, and between God and the preferred parent. Later research, for example Vergote and Tamayo (1980) and Roberts (1988), continues to show only weak support for Freud's assertion about resemblance between God and the father. Vergote and Tamayo's collection of studies deals with the idea that there are maternal and paternal 'elements' in cognition.

They show that images of both parents are perceived to contain both paternal and maternal elements. For most of the people in most of the (mainly European) groups studied, images of God have more maternal than paternal elements.

Another study, by Krol (1982), on Polish teenagers, differentiated between 'good' and 'bad' fathers. 'Badness' in fathers was defined as the presence of alcoholism, coupled with a negative effect on their parenting behaviour. In this study, there was a general tendency for all subjects with 'good' fathers to have a more positive image of God than subjects with 'bad' fathers. In girls, the image of God and the image of the father were not very closely related. With boys, there were more similarities between God and father-images than with girls. The similarity between God and father-image was particularly marked in the case of boys with 'good' fathers. Krol concluded that boys were more likely than girls to associate the image of the father with the image of God. However, as stated, the research methods used are not ideal for testing the hypothesis!

It would be quite difficult to study young children's perceptions of God: Piagetians such as Elkind (1971) have had difficulty in this respect, and have not looked at the Freudian father-figure hypothesis.

Some retrospective material does give more encouragement to the idea. Both Rizzuto (1974) and Switzer (1976) use clinical material. Rizzuto suggests that the recalled relationship with the father is very like the described relationship with God. Switzer reported that many patients blamed their psychological problems on religion. In fact, however, Switzer believes that the root of the problem seemed to be a repressive, critical, punitive style of parenting going hand-in-hand with a repressive, punitive, critical parental religiosity. Anger at the parents is directed on to God.

Ullman (1982) used retrospective reports by converts to several different religions. Poor relationships at home, especially with the father, seemed to be associated with abandoning the parental religion. Kose (1994) reached similar conclusions. Studying British converts to Islam, he reported a higher proportion reporting poor relationships with their fathers than with their mothers.

On the whole, the retrospective material – which is methodologically more appropriate – does give some support to the Freudian proposal that the foundations of the God image and of religious feelings are based on early family relationships. The implications are that poor family relationships, especially with the father – criticism and punishment with little esteem and affection – will have a damaging effect on mental health as well as on views of and feelings about God.

Here are some pairs of statements by a young professional man, suffering from anxiety and hypochondriasis, presented by Rizzuto (1974). Though the statements are paired, they were made at different times, in the course of psychotherapy. Although it is possible that Rizzuto selected cases that made the point most clearly, the material does illustrate resemblances between feelings about God and recollections of feelings towards the father.

> **Father**: My father always insisted that I (make) the best use of my abilities.
>
> **God**: If there is a God, then I have dissatisfied him, because I have not made the best use of my abilities.
>
> **Father**: I was never close to my father.
>
> **God**: I have never experienced closeness to God.
>
> **Father**: I do not ask anything from my father.
>
> **God**: If I am in distress I do not resort to God, because I have no belief in God.
>
> **Father**: I do not express hatred to my father [Rizzuto adds that both parents said a number of times that the children hate their father].
>
> **God**: I never expressed hate for God but have felt exasperated at my situation or fate.

Rizzuto's account and analysis of Mr Brown – which follows – makes clear her approach in highlighting common features of the relationship with God and the relationship with the father, as well as showing how the relationship with the mother may be implicated in the formation of the God image.

> Mr Brown is a man who grew up in a religious family. He has always been faithful to his beliefs, practises regularly, and obtains self-esteem and a feeling of well-being from prayer and worship. He has a solid, dependent, well-defined relationship with his God. He holds God in deep respect. His obligations as a Christian are very important to him.
>
> My analysis of his image of God and his relationship to God prompted me to hypothesize its origins as follows: the image of God parallels his attachment to the parental couple.

His God image is alternatively and simultaneously made out of maternal and paternal traits. The maternal aspect of his God image awakens hope for love, acceptance, closeness and the ability to control dangerous inner tendencies. The paternal traits, integrated in most of the Catholic traditional teachings about God, represent a defence against the unconscious danger of excessive dependence which is implicit in the hopes for love and closeness. The paternal element is, in turn, integrated into his own mature, responsible fatherly care of others, which he perceives as a religious duty. At this level his ego ideal – to be as good as his father – and his religious duty converge to support his self-esteem as a man and deny the infantile dependent wishes reflected in the part of the image of God which is made out of maternal traits.

Mr Brown is a gaunt, 47-year-old truck driver, who had never been ill until his admission to a psychiatric unit. His symptoms were inability to work, anorexia, insomnia and weight loss. He was diagnosed as an obsessive-compulsive personality with a reactive depression. The depression appeared to be related to two events: 1) the return of his two oldest sons after two years of absence from home for a month's visit, and their subsequent departure; and 2) his having gone to the morgue to identify the body of a friend who had become an alcoholic derelict and died on the street. Exactly a month after the episode of identifying his friend he had an anxiety attack at night, while in bed with his wife. He thought he was having a heart attack. In his fear, he visualized his dead friend in the morgue. He described the event in the following words: 'I thought I was going to die; I was afraid I would lose them [his family] and that they would lose me. That was very scary. . . I prayed and asked God to help me.'

Mr Brown is the second oldest in a family of eight children. His father worked for the railroad and his mother took care of the home. The family lived in a rural area, and life throughout his entire childhood was remarkably uneventful. He was never sick but full of energy, which made him lead an active and adventurous life. He was 'not really well-behaved'; he was always 'scratching somebody's back or tearing somebody's things'. His mother was constantly worried that he would break his neck climbing trees or hills. In regard to his sexual development he claimed that until he was 14 or 15 he did not know the difference between 'drinking a glass of water and sex'. At 17 he dropped out of school, after having been a poor student all along. He was fully determined to improve his lot and 'be himself'. So, in spite of his parents' tears he left home, full of dreams, to join an uncle in a big city. First he became a fisherman; then tried out several jobs; and finally settled down to truck-driving, which he has been doing steadily ever since. He has not had a vacation during the last 23 years. At the age of 24 he married a girl seven years his junior; she was from his home town, and together they made a family that replicates in every detail his own family. Broadly speaking, the family, love, and mutual care were always the main concerns of both his and his parents' family.

The patient describes his father as a very hardworking, 'rugged' man, who tried very hard to make the family happy. He felt that his father was always right and admired him for his exclusive devotion to work and family. Physically, the father was a big man; emotionally he was very good and kind, but could not bring himself to show either positive feelings or anger. The only time when the father cried or expressed anger was when Mr Brown left home. At that moment, the father said to Mr Brown in anger, while crying: 'You may as well please yourself and go; do as you want; it is your life!' Significantly, the patient repeated his father's statement literally, when his own sons departed against his wishes.

Summarizing, his father offered to Mr Brown a respectable image of a reliable person, devoid, nevertheless, of emotional qualities.

Mr Brown described his mother as being very busy keeping house and minding the children. She loved the children and was totally devoted to the family. She was the 'boss' and the 'disciplinarian' in the family, because 'she was always there'. She was prudish and very shy about sex, to the point that, to the patient's indignation, she would never recognize that she bore children.

In summary, what the mother offered to Mr Brown was her constant presence, her affection and her control of his behaviour.

The patient hardly mentioned his siblings. From his overall description it seems possible that he managed to ignore them and felt lonely among them. The family was close and without overt conflict among its members. It functioned as a unit with well-defined parental roles. Both parents had a benign, protective approach; the children were loved and treated equally, and were expected to love their parents in return. The patient felt that his parents did indeed love the children and that he loved his parents. The basic expectation that coloured the family lifestyle was that each member would love every other member. This tended to discourage overt expressions of anger.

As regards religion, both parents were believers in the Catholic church. They attended church every Sunday and asked the children to pray every morning and night. Mr Brown learned to pray from his mother. The family religion was simple and ritualized. It was a reliable source of self-esteem. Though the patient thinks of religion as a serious matter, he remembers the major days of the church year as a joyful moment in the family's life and the occasions for the only parties they had. Mr Brown's parents believed in the devil and eternal damnation; accordingly their religion demanded watchfulness. As the patient put it, 'you got to stay holy'. The patient's present religious beliefs and practices are essentially the same as those of his parents.

Mr Brown belongs to the [category of] people whose God is an indisputable fact, a self-evident reality. Mr Brown relates to God as a real being and is deeply involved with Him. He finds it ridiculous to think that God may not exist. 'If God did not exist,' he says, 'there would be nothing'. In his perception, God is the background of all existing things as the unshake-able backbone of the universe.

These are the characteristics he bestows upon God:

1. God is love. Because he is love, he expects love in return. The failure to respond to God's love should be punished: 'Those who do not respect and love God should be punished.' The love of God should last forever because he wants us to go to heaven, 'where you love Him and He loves you, and that is the way you want it for you in the hereafter'. Meanwhile, the love of God is protection against fears, whatever they may be: 'If you love God, then you don't have much to fear'.

2. God is to be pleased, though his wishes are not easily known. The patient feels that 'I would have to pray to Him that I will please Him'.

3. God is helpful and rewards people by 'helping them to stay out of sin'. This helpfulness of God facilitates the task of pleasing him.

4. 'God is my maker and judge because he will judge us all'. As a judge He is well-informed because 'He sees all things'.

5. God is 'supreme', the universal ruler, bestower of cherished 'blessings', the giver of strength. He is also the forgiver of all sins.

As an individual, the patient is convinced that he needs God to be a person. In his perception, the process of becoming a person demands knowing God's wishes, responding to them, and renouncing one's own wishes if they are opposed to God's. God is always available to help to do both, obey and renounce improper wishes which stand in the way of becoming the person one is to be. The process has some important gratifications. It gives 'spiritual blessings', strength, inspiration, a feeling of well-being and, more than anything, the feeling that one is getting God's approval. This is what Mr Brown feels when he goes to church: 'I always get a comfortable feeling . . . Well, it makes you feel happy all over, as though you are close to God, for one thing. I feel it in all my being.'

Mr Brown feels that he needs God to be the person he ought to be, to escape from Hell and to go to Heaven after death, where he is to enjoy love for ever. For the time being he is to please God and needs to pray to learn how to please God. From God he receives a 'happy feeling' inside, which he greatly values. He is aware of his obligation to love God. The quality of the love he feels obliged to have does not allow for any negative feelings towards God or the right to rebel against Him. Besides, he finds no reason to resent or be angry with God. In spite of his conviction that God loves him, his feeling of closeness does not reach the level of intimacy. He experiences only happiness of certain wellbeing, like the inner experience of a protective presence whose warmth he feels 'all over'. The more personal and subtle exchanges which most people have with those they love is markedly absent. Thus his relationship with God, though positive and loving, is somewhat distant and intellectual, and remains mostly in the realm of obedience and duties. He likes the situation as it is, and although he is fearful of being separated from God, he is not interested in getting closer to Him. He feels that he became close to God at the age of seven, 'the age of reason', because 'previous to that, I did not understand too much about God.'

What life experiences have furnished Mr Brown with the materials for constructing his image of God?

At the level closest to the surface Mr Brown has used elements of his perception of his mother and father as a parental couple. Like his parents, God loves us all, makes clear that we are the children, demands obedience, does not tolerate anger, is protective and provides for necessary things. Besides obedience, Mr Brown's God demands to be loved, as also love of one's neighbour. He perceives God not as one person but as a Trinity, which coincides with his perception of father and mother together in charge of the children. In real life Mr Brown never doubted his faith and never stopped practising. In the same way, Mr Brown never separated emotionally from his parents, despite having left home at 17; he never mourned them after their death, but kept alive his relationship to them, praying for them every night. In his relationship with God he remains as much of a child as he is in his relationship to his parents.

At another level Mr Brown's way of perceiving God has earlier developmental roots, which, in my appraisal, grew out of his relationship to his mother. In responding on the questionnaire to the question whether or not he believed in a personal God, Mr Brown began by writing 'in God', then erased it and wrote 'in God, the Three Divine Persons'. Such revision reveals, I think, that at a deeper level, Mr Brown has an earlier image of God, which only later develops into a Trinity. In other words, the data strongly suggest that Mr Brown's earlier image of God was formed out of this relationship with his mother, and that at the 'age of reason' he became close to God the Trinity, which incorporated elements of his relationship to his father and mother as a couple. It was his mother who was 'supreme' throughout his childhood. She was there 'all the time' to 'see all things'; she was the boss, the disciplinarian, capable of punishing but also of showing overt affection and approval in a way that his father did not, partly because he was absent for long periods of time and partly because, when home, he neither punished nor expressed affection. It was Mr Brown's mother who worried constantly about his aggressive tendencies and constantly tried to help him restrain them. He remembers 'my mother chasing me around, seeing that I don't fall off a tree or something'. This behaviour of the mother appears in Mr Brown's God image as God 'helping people to stay out of sin'. The patient is convinced that his misbehaviour prompted his mother's crying: 'if I misbehaved she cried'. He tried his best to behave, to stop her crying and do as she pleased. This pattern has its reflection, it seems to me, in Mr Brown's God image where he maintains: 'I think that, in general, as a person, I have pleased God because I have tried my best to please God'. But he also feels guilty, in that the most important thing he expects from God is that 'He will forgive me and give me his blessings, because God is supreme'. Even at the present he is convinced that in the same way in which he could not be a good child without his mother's constant control, he could not do without God's: 'My love for God is important because I need God's love to live a decent life.' It was his mother, too, who offered him affection and tenderness, which surely translated into 'blessings' and 'a good feeling all over'. Asked what person he loved the most at each developmental stage, Mr Brown consistently said his mother. The moment he married, however, Mr Brown's love went to his wife. He was very careful to say: 'But I love my father, too'. This statement, I believe, represents the same type of emotional defence that Mr Brown used in erasing the word 'God' and replacing it with the 'Three Divine Persons'. In real life, he had a deeper attachment to his mother than to his father. Full acknowledgement of this, however, was distressing. Accordingly, he clarified that he also loved his father. Similarly, the earliest attachment to God reflects internalized elements of his relationship to his mother. In writing in 'God' he became close, I believe, to that earliest image. Distressed by it, he moved from God to the Trinity, which includes paternal elements.

Mr Brown fights against his longings to be more dependent by reaction formation. He makes others – his children and his wife – extremely dependent on him, working very hard and being completely in charge. In so doing he identifies with his father, whom he holds up as his ego ideal. In his real life this patient is a responsible man, a reliable worker, a good husband and father. At heart he has remained a child. His drawings betray the child in him: they are quite infantile and naive. Both the drawing of his family and the picture of God look like the work of a five-year-old. The figures are composed of very simple lines; they are sexually undefined. So is God, who, 'If I have to draw', he explained, 'I think of Him as a person'. In his relationship with God, Mr Brown wishes for dependence, protection, and help to be the person he is supposed to be. This wish, I submit, is an internalization of Mr Brown's infantile interaction with his mother, which provides him with a 'happy feeling', but also accounts for his continued attachment to the pleasurable experiences he shared with her. Mr Brown did not, however, create a God out of his internalizations alone. His family and church offered him a well-defined God, clearly paternal and trinitarian. At the moment of encounter with this God – at the age of seven (probably receiving instructions for the first communion) – Mr Brown experienced closeness to God and claimed that 'previous to that I did not understand too much about God'. This official image of God allowed him, I suggest, to retain his earlier God-image with its maternal traits, without betraying to himself the nature of the needs this image embodied. It also seems possible that the paternal God of the church facilitated his developing identification with his father. At any rate, the God the church offered to him was a masculine figure, which he gladly accepted. In this way, Mr Brown could permit himself to experience longings for the dependent relationship he had with his mother, in the context of religious practices that provided him with social and parental approval and personal self-esteem. To please God as well as to respond to the demands of adulthood, Mr Brown had to be a man in real life. Through the complexities of his God-image, however, Mr Brown is able to re-experience the child without having to feel ashamed.

Rizzuto's main case is that the image of God has its main source in early ('object') relations, and a grasp of the adaptive and maladaptive potential of internalized God-images would be useful to clinicians, pastoral workers and religious counsellors and educators. We will return to this suggestion later in the chapter, when discussing the contributions of the object-relations theorists to the understanding of relationships with God.

Religion as a neurosis

This view was derived by Freud from the same set of ideas as his notion of God as a father-projection. Religion is based on identification, as described above. Identification – the internalization of the parent and the foundation of the God-image – is the result of attempts to defend against the pain of fear of losing love, and assuaging grief and guilt over loss and damage to loved ones. Freud saw mental illnesses as attempts to defend against painful emotions, and in his view the processes involved in the formation of individual religiosity were similar to those involved in the formation of neuroses. Additionally, religion involves social organization and consensus of beliefs and feelings – so Freud's view, colourfully expressed, was that 'religion is the universal obsessional neurosis. It spares the individual the task of forming his own neurosis'. In an early paper, Freud (1907) had spelt out the similarities between religious rituals and obsessional rituals. Guilt is created when rituals are not carried out, and assuaged when they are, so a self-perpetuating 'ritualaholic' cycle is set up. Freud (1927) also argued that religion, by repressing impulses, may give rise to neurotic illnesses.

It is widely suggested that the Freudian view of religion as neurotic is limited. There are healthier forms of religiosity, it is suggested.

There are a number of studies which have looked at correlations between religion and neuroticism. Notice that 'neuroticism' is a much more general term than 'obsessional neurosis'. Neuroticism is a trait, a tendency to emotional lability and to suffer from worry, sleeplessness and so forth. It is not an illness as such. Obsessional neurosis is a specific illness, in which the sufferer is driven by a need to repeat certain thoughts or behaviours. So these studies on religion and neurosis only relate in a general way to Freud's ideas.

I know of no studies specifically on religiosity and obsessional neurosis – except that in the Eysenckian view neurotic introverts are more likely to suffer from obsessional and compulsive disorders, and as we shall see there is work which looks at religiosity in relation to introversion–extraversion, as well as neuroticism.

An active worker in this field is Leslie Francis, whose work has mostly been on adolescents in schools, mostly from Christian backgrounds. He has used the EPI (Eysenck Personality

Inventory) which assesses neuroticism and introversion–extraversion as well as the tendency to give socially desirable answers. Here are some items from the EPI:

Neuroticism: Are you moody?
Have you often lost sleep over your worries?
Do you suffer from 'nerves'?
Introversion–extraversion: Do you mind selling things or asking people for money for some good cause?
Do you like cracking jokes and telling funny stories to your friends?
Do you often get into a jam because you do things without thinking?
Social desirability ('Lie' scale): As a child, did you always do as you were told immediately and without grumbling?
Have you sometimes told lies in your life?
Do you sometimes laugh at a dirty joke?

Francis's measure of religiosity is favourability of attitudes to religion (Francis, 1978). Francis, Pearson and Kay (1982) found in a sample of about 1000 15–16-year-olds that religiosity did indeed go along with both neuroticism and introversion. Presumably that would agree with Freud's views, if you argue that people with the personality potential for obsessionality would be drawn to religion. If the subjects were divided into four groups (Eysenck's 'personality quadrants') then the order of religiosity was:

- neurotic introverts (most religious);
- neurotic extroverts;
- stable introverts;
- stable extroverts (least religious).

However – there is a big 'but'! It is known that on the EPI women come out as somewhat more neurotic and introverted than men. They also tend to emerge as more religious than men. Francis, Pearson and Kay's analyses went on to show that the associations between religiosity, neuroticism and introversion were the result of the effects of gender. If you look at the associations between religion and personality in the two genders separately, then there are no associations between religion and personality. The relationships between religion and social desirability (saying that you are a good person) also complicate the interpretation of this kind of study.

Taking this along with the mixed results of other work on religion and neuroticism, anxiety and introversion, we may conclude that there is no clear indication that the religiosity goes along with anxiety, neuroticism or obsessionality.

A last word on Freud

There is an important difference in implications between Freud's father-projection hypothesis and his view of religion as neurosis. In the former, mental and religious health are seen as resting on the quality of early parental relationships. In the latter, religion is seen as a collective and neurotic defence against the painful emotions of fear, grief and so on. The installation of a permanent, on-site, loving God is a wonderful solution to the painful let-downs experienced in dealing with real parents and real life. This style of religiosity is ambiguous: for some it may involve a belief that God will not let anything bad happen to the believer. William James's (1902) 'healthy-minded' religiosity and Allport's (1950) 'immature' and (1966) 'extrinsic' religiosity are brought to mind. But some believers may trust God after great difficulties, often with a greater depth than before, which brings to mind James's 'twice-born' and Allport's 'mature' and 'intrinsic' styles of religiosity. If you have followed this argument through, it's quite difficult to see how this last-mentioned style of religiosity could resemble a neurotic illness.

Many religious authors have taken exception to Freud's views on religion on a number of counts (e.g. Amsel, 1969). Some have suggested that Freud was describing an unhealthy or neurotic style of religiosity (Lee, 1948). One prominent Freudian, Bruno Bettelheim (1983) has however blamed the mechanistic view of Freudian theories on Freud's translators; in Bettelheim's view, psychoanalysis is by definition a totally spiritual exercise. There is ambiguity in Freud's ideas and in the relevant evidence, but I feel we are left with a residue of important suggestions about religion and mental health.

JUNG

Jung is better liked by religious commentators than Freud has been. Jung was the son of a Swiss pastor and, after embarking on a career in medicine and psychiatry, he found himself the psychiatrist in charge of a Swiss mental hospital while still a comparatively young man. An admirer of Freud's writings, he began a close correspondence with Freud, terminating after 10 years following a disagreement on a seemingly trivial technical point.

In fact there were profound differences between the two men. One was from a nondevout Jewish background, the other from a devout Christian home. Freud dealt with educated neurotic patients. Jung's were generally hospitalized, generally psychotic and generally less intellectual. Jung disagreed with Freud's ideas on the importance of sexuality and he was much more positive about mysticism and religion than Freud. Freud's popular writings are very readable, Jung's are a bit obscure – I find!

However his views on religion and mental health are not difficult to summarize (see Jung, 1958). As I understand it, Jung sees the journey towards 'true' belief or knowledge as a process which is simultaneously one of psychological and of religious exploration. By confronting the paradoxes within oneself – the wish to be good and perfect versus the 'dark side' and its very socially undesirable suggestions, and by acknowledging and harnessing the 'dark side' – one is engaged in a religious process. This is identical, psychologically and religiously, with confronting and dealing positively with the paradoxes in life – the simultaneous possibilities of good and evil, the fact of human suffering. Jung is said to have undergone a 'mid-life crisis' from which he emerged with a profound mystical understanding of his place in the universe. In Jungian terminology, this process, which is ongoing, is called 'individuation'.

Jung identified at least two styles of religiosity, though without nice catchy labels. The 'good' style, which is synonymous with psychological health, involves acknowledging, confronting and dealing positively with pain and evil. Jung sometimes called this 'true' belief. The 'bad' style, Jung sometimes labelled 'blind' belief. It involves a passive, unquestioning acceptance of dogma, an indifference to suffering and evil, which are denied and swept under the carpet. Because evil is not acknowledged and controlled, wrote Jung in the Europe of the 1920s, the floodgates of Hell will burst open . . . Jung is rightly praised for his foresight, though we could wish he had been less accurate. He would claim that he was trying to forestall trouble.

Jung's views on the confluence of psychoanalysis and the mystical path represent important insights for those interested in religion and mental health, and he may have been helpful to many trying to bear suffering and to use it in a positive way. He was also one of several psychological theorists to identify psychologically healthy and unhealthy styles of religiosity.

Levi Meier (1991), a chaplain and psychotherapist, gives the following examples of healthy styles of religiosity and dealing with suffering:

> X. was diagnosed as having a depressive neurosis, which she associated with her parents who were emotionally abusive. Her heroic attitude was expressed by her disentangling herself from her abusive parents and individuating on her own path.

> One patient . . . dialogued with God regarding his cancer. He claimed that he and God together would not be the victims of cancer, but rather, they would courageously and valiantly fight the disease together. Although he eventually succumbed to the illness, he maintained the vigour of his mind until the end. He was not fighting with God; he was allied with God in fighting the cancer.

Hill and Mullen (1992) have articulated four aspects of Jungian psychology which they believe are valuable for pastoral care:

- his mode of treatment which takes a broad view over the whole lifespan, rather than focusing on psychopathology;
- the process of individuation, 'a dynamic process of coming to selfhood';
- the theory of personality types: the way a person deals with life and reacts to events;
- the concept of synchronicity, involving the importance of the need for meaning.

Jungian psychology is reported to be helpful in pastoral work. This may be because it deals with adult development, and with concerns that clients find more relevant and acceptable than the Freudian framework. The Jungian framework does not place such over-riding importance on dealing with early relationships. It does take account of spirituality, and of adults' concerns with direction and meaning in life.

Empirical work on the validity of Jung's theories has been focused on his theory of personality types. Here, validity is reported to be good (Ryckman, 1993). There has been no empirical work on Jung's theories dealing with spirituality and psychotherapy.

FRANKL

The distinction between healthy and unhealthy styles of religiosity was made by a number of other writers in the psychoanalytic tradition. Erich Fromm (1950) distinguished between authoritarian and humanistic religion, while Victor Frankl (1959) identified a 'foxhole' religion – God's function is to keep troubles away from me, and I only bother with God when there's a danger of me being let down – to be contrasted with a process of discovery of meaning in life and of the inner strength to live and to do good. Frankl says he arrived at his ideas on psychotherapy when, following a Freudian training in Vienna, he was imprisoned in a concentration camp. As is known, these camps were places of unthinkable horror, but Frankl claims that even there, there were people who were still free – free to choose to do a kindness to another, to give away a crust of bread, to bear themselves with dignity. Even in these unthinkable circumstances, there were people who felt purpose and meaning. Frankl survived, and developed a system called 'logotherapy', popular in the USA but little used in Europe, which embodies a number of innovative therapeutic techniques. Frankl became known as 'the father of existential therapy'.

Rather like Jung, Frankl saw the process of psychotherapy as involving a search – a search for meaning and a discovery of inner strength. Frankl claimed that the majority of clients were suffering from a neurosis so common that it had become normative in civilized 20th-century America. Frankl called it **noogenic neurosis**, and its symptom was simply a lack of meaning and purpose in life. Most people were – and are – suffering from a feeling that they don't know why they are alive, that they have no worthwhile purpose in life, and are not even aware that they would feel better about themselves and others if they were to try and discover a worthy purpose. Frankl saw the therapist's task as facilitating the initiating and hopefully the completion of this search. Frankl's views on religion (a word he seldom uses) and psychological health are somewhat similar to Jung's, but the terminology is different. For Jung, the religious–psychological search has a mystical goal. For Frankl, the goal of the search is meaning and purpose.

Based on Frankl's work, Crumbaugh and Maholick (1969) developed a Purpose in Life test, which has been used to look at the impact of changes in religious belief. Paloutzian (1981) looked at students from Christian backgrounds and found that Purpose in Life was higher among converts than nonconverts. Paloutzian's data suggest that purpose in life may rise in an initial period of postconversion enthusiasm, waver and then stabilize. This is particularly interesting since other work on conversion and mental illness (Bragan, 1977; Witztum, Dasberg and Greenberg, 1990) also supports the idea of a postconversion honeymoon period, followed by a period of 'returning to earth'.

Here are some examples of the kinds of feeling characteristic of purpose in life:

- usually enthusiastic;
- see life as exciting;
- enjoy facing daily tasks;
- feel prepared for and unafraid of death;
- see life as worthwhile;
- see a reason for existence.

Frankl's work is hardly known in Europe, but is better-known in the USA. His ideas on purpose in life have been applied in the understanding of religious change and its effects on mental health.

OBJECT-RELATIONS THEORY

The last decades have seen increasing sophistication by psychoanalysts in dealing with the complexities of people's relationship with God. There is a growing recognition that theorizing is possible and even improved if the theorist does build the existence of God into theory (Watts and Williams, 1988; Spero, 1992). On the psychological front, many theorists have found object-relations theory helpful (Oden, 1967; Rizzuto, 1974; Spero, 1992). Object-relations theory derives from the work of Melanie Klein (1932), Winnicott (1958) and others and is concerned with the way in which from babyhood onwards we lay down internal 'objects'

and 'part-objects' – both good and bad – as a result of our feelings and experiences with other people.

Rizzuto (1974) looks at feelings about God. She proposes that
most adults can be located in one of the following four categories:

1. having a God to whom they relate in various ways – 'I have a
   God';
2. wondering whether to believe or not in a God whom they are
   not sure exists – 'I might have a God';
3. amazed, angered or quietly surprised to see others deeply
   invested in a God who does not interest them – 'I do not have
   a God';
4. struggling with a demanding harsh God they would like to
   get rid of if they were not convinced of his existence and
   power – 'I have a God but I wish I did not'.

Rumke is a Dutch psychiatrist who has proposed seven stages in
the development of faith. Although not an object-relations theorist it is interesting to see – apropos of Rizzuto – that Rumke has
concluded that **unbelief** represents a psychological disturbance
(Rumke, 1952).

Spero (1992) proposes an elaborate scheme to explain how
God is represented internally. Spero believes that in psychotherapy, religious and psychological healing are linked, and
improvement includes an improved relationship with God.

He describes the analysis of a Roman Catholic nun, with a
narcissistic character disorder; more details appear in Chapter 8.
Themes emerging in the analysis included envy of men, sexual
identity, sinfulness, other religious issues and the relationship
with the therapist. Spero writes: 'It became increasingly evident
that religious themes and resistances were inextricably tied to
basic aspects of sexual identity and the emerging transference
relationship.'

> The eventually successful analytic journey revealed a religious
> woman who, for the first time in her life, felt an especially
> close relationship with God, one no longer mediated by theo-
> logical understandings which happened to cater to her narcis-
> sistic, concretistic view of reality and her constricted sexual
> identity . . . If until now she felt she recognized God, it was
> only because he was an extension of familiar object experi-
> ences from home. She now began imagining what started as a

kind of healthy, girlish relationship with his image and gradually grew into a trusting investment in his newly identified capacity for caring and activity.

Object-relations theory has been useful in psychotherapy, enabling exploration of the relationship with God in the context of exploration of all relationships. This is reported to be helpful but scientific exploration of the validity of the theory has been confined to theoretical speculation and the reporting of clinical case material.

ATTACHMENT THEORY

Attachment theory derives from the work of Bowlby (1969, 1973, 1980) who has been very influential in psychotherapeutic thinking, and whose work has had some influence on psychology generally. Bowlby's interest lay in the attachments formed by children to parents and others. Kirkpatrick (Kirkpatrick and Shaver, 1990; Kirkpatrick, 1992) has applied the Bowlby framework to a useful understanding of some ways in which relationships with God may be related to family relationships. Unlike the other speculations we have discussed in this chapter, Kirkpatrick's are not focused on psychotherapeutic practice, and they are directly translated into empirical validation. Attachment theory suggests three broad types of mother–child relationship:

- secure, in which the emotional tone is generally warm, and independence is allowed;
- avoidant, in which the emotional tone is cold and distant, but there may be a degree of over-control;
- anxious/ambivalent, involving a mixture of the two above styles.

American college students reporting secure relationships with their mothers tended to follow their mothers in religiosity. They were less likely to report an intense personal relationship with God, and were less frequent church attenders than those with avoidant mothers. Those reporting avoidant mothers tended to be high on religiosity, were more likely to report a sudden conversion, and a close, personal relationship with God. A suggestion is that God may serve as an attachment figure for those who have not had the framework for the development of basic trust. Those who have probably developed basic trust appear to have a more relaxed relationship with God.

The work on attachment theory and religion uses retrospective methodology, but the findings so far are certainly more promising than those based on other approaches.

SUMMARY

Freud saw God as an internalized father-figure. The evidence on resemblance between perceptions of God and of the father is mixed, and some of it is methodologically doubtful, but it does give some support to the idea that people's views of God could be coloured by their experiences of their parents. Thus happy relationships (with the parents) may lead to a happy relationship (with God).

Freud also saw religion as a form of collective neurosis, a defence against anxiety and other painful emotions.

Although Freud is generally viewed as antireligious, some commentators do not agree, and many feel that Freud's view of religion as psychologically unhealthy was a description of one style of religiosity.

Psychologically healthier, non-neurotic styles of religiosity were described by Jung, Fromm, Frankl and others. The object-relations approach to describing the origins of religious feelings and representations has been developed and applied in developing the religious dimension of psychotherapy, and attachment theory has been applied to assist the understanding of the way the relationship with God might be affected by family relationships.

The recurrent theme in applying psychoanalytic theory to understanding religion and mental health has been the individual's relationship with God.

3

Communities where no-one goes mad?

So far we have looked at ideas about individual religion and mental health. But culture, religion and mental health are – as I used to find myself writing in my psychology final exam papers – inextricably inter-related.

Forms, incidence and prevalence of psychiatric illnesses vary in different societies, partly because psychiatrists vary in diagnostic criteria, partly because clients and families vary in what they refer to psychiatrists for help, and partly because different societies have differing rates and types of stress and encourage or suppress different types of response to stress (e.g. Littlewood and Lipsedge, 1989). Stress symptoms may be different in different cultures, which makes the process of comparison of referral and prevalence rates difficult.

Dunnigan, McNall and Mortimer (1993) illustrated the point that different metaphors are used to describe mental illness in different cultures. Among the Hmong from Laos, the following are some of the terms used for psychological distress: *nyauj siab* = difficult liver; *ntxhov siab* = obscured liver; *txhawj siab* = worried liver; etc. The first term ('difficult liver') is characterized by chronic fatigue, sleep and appetite disturbances, agitation, lack of concentration and other symptoms characteristic of major depression, but these symptoms sometimes occur with other dysphoric conditions in Hmong vocabulary, and 'difficult liver' can result from chronic illness or debility – perhaps therefore with the connotation of physical exhaustion. Dunnigan, McNall and Mortimer's point is that cultural variations in forms of psychological distress are closely associated with translation difficulties, making the process of cross-cultural comparison difficult.

So when looking at the relations between culture, religion and mental illness, results are difficult to interpret. But they can be surprising. Here are some examples.

HUTTERITES

The Hutterites are small, self-contained farming communities of descendants of a Protestant German religious sect who came to the USA in the 19th century. The men dress rather like orthodox Jews, with black hats and coats and patriarchal beards. The women dress very soberly in long dark undecorated clothes, wearing no make-up. Contact with the outside world is limited, and modern machinery is disapproved of.

The Hutterites were studied by Eaton and Weil (1955). During the 1940s someone in the American National Institute of Mental Health was scrutinizing statistics for different mental illnesses. These statistics were obtained by looking at the rate of hospital referrals, and it was observed that the Hutterites appeared to have very low (zero!) referral rates.

The questions were: are the Hutterites an ideal community, who by virtue of their way of life found a way of escaping psychiatric breakdown? Or are the Hutterites as prone to psychiatric illnesses as other Americans, but they are just not going along for psychiatric help?

Both these questions could be answered by getting prevalence estimates based on psychiatric assessments of a community sample. The results were surprising in that the overall prevalence of psychiatric illness was similar to that of the general American population.

Eaton and Weil's team assessed about 8500 Hutterites; about 200 were judged to be clinically ill, psychiatrically, and of those about 50 were judged to be psychotic. So far, the prevalence rates were said to be similar to those for the general urban population in the USA at that time. However the pattern of mental illness was quite different. Among the psychoses, the mood disorders (basically involving depression) were twice as common as the schizophrenias, which is the reverse of the normal American pattern. Among the neuroses, depressive illnesses were also very common.

One explanation of this is that mental illness will out, whatever the society. The influence of culture is simply on the forms of mental illness – with the Hutterites the story was said to be that the favoured and valued style of religiosity placed a strong emphasis on sin, unworthiness and guilt, so that somewhat depressed attitudes were encouraged and valued. Another influence of culture, of course, is that clinically depressed and other psychologically ill Hutterites were not going for psychiatric help, and it is interesting to speculate what effect this was having on the prevalence rates.

There are several questions arising from this research. I am not particularly content with the idea, sometimes expressed in cross-cultural psychiatry books, and concluded from this research, that there's nothing we can do to affect the basic rates of mental illnesses – it's only the forms that vary with culture. The Hutterites weren't going for psychiatric help – so that could mean that fewer people were becoming ill, but they were staying ill for longer because they weren't getting help. Or, it could mean that Hutterites were becoming psychiatrically ill as often as other people, and that the Hutterites were using methods of supporting or curing their psychiatric invalids that were at least as effective as those being used by psychiatrists!

Other interpretations are possible. One will be looked at in the next example.

HEBRIDEANS

George Brown and Tirril Harris (1978) had studied the social circumstances, life events and difficulties of women in Camberwell, South London. They were interested in the social origins of depressive illnesses. They showed that if a woman did not experience an event or difficulty with severe long-term threatening consequences (a 'provoking agent'), she was very unlikely to become depressed. Women with 'severe' events or difficulties were much more likely to become depressed, and the likelihood was increased if their social circumstances made them more vulnerable – having several young children to care for, or having no-one to confide in, for example.

Following the Camberwell study, the team turned its attention to some really rural communities on the Hebridean islands. It was thought that the 'repressive' type of strict religiosity might imply that more religious women would be more neurotically ill. The analyses of Brown and Prudo (1981), Prudo et al. (1981) and

Prudo, Harris and Brown (1984) showed that the more religious women (religiosity was assessed by church attendance) were the less likely to be depressed. Church attendance and crofting (living in a sheep-farming smallholding) were taken as indices of integration into the traditional community. The less integrated were more likely to be depressed, though less anxious. Lower rates of depression among the more integrated women were the result of lower rates of provoking agents, and also of the protective effects of religiosity. Religiosity may exert its effects partly by the closer supportive family and social networks, partly by the favourable effects of belonging on self-esteem and partly by feelings of spiritual support in adversity. In this series of studies, the effects of religion on depressive disorders were thus operating in two ways: one via indirect effects on the rate of provoking agents, and one via the protective effects of religion in adversity. However, the crossover effect that anxiety appears more likely as depression is less likely may not be an effect of religion as such; it appeared to be related to loss of the mother in women integrated into the traditional community.

Analogous effects may have been operating in the Hutterite communities studied by Eaton and Weil, but comparable data were not collected.

The Brown and Harris team did not study depression in men in Camberwell and the Hebrides, so as yet we know little about the ways in which religion may be implicated in the social factors involved in depression in men.

HASIDIM

Hasidism is a style of orthodox Judaism emphasizing joyful service of God and mystical contemplation, as well as scrupulous adherence to the details of Jewish law. Different groups of Hasidim follow different leaders, said to possess 'general souls'.

Jeanette Kupferman (1979) stayed with a group of Hasidim in North London. She thought the women were less likely to be depressed than women in the general population, partly because of the emphasis on joy, and partly because the veto on sexual contact between husbands and wives during and after the wives' menstruation meant that the women had space for themselves. However no assessment and quantification were reported. By contrast, Goshen-Gottstein (1987) thought that the repressive norms and socialization practices of strictly orthodox Jews in Jerusalem (including many Hasidim) involved 'mental health risks', especially for boys. This study again involved no sampling and measurement.

Loewenthal *et al.* (in press) randomly sampled quotas of 'middle' and 'strictly' orthodox Jewish in Britain, and used a mood checklist to assess depression and other states. Lower levels of depression went along with higher levels of religiosity (as indexed by orthodoxy of synagogue affiliation), but this could have been an artefact of confounded variables. Loewenthal *et al.* (1993) found lower levels of depression in orthodox Jewish women than in women in the general population and than in orthodox Jewish men. This latter finding is the reverse of the picture in the general population, where women are more likely to be depressed than men. These studies (which included many Hasidim in the strictly orthodox groups) showed that depression in orthodox Jewish women was associated with factors associated with loss of the wife and mother roles, both very highly esteemed in Judaism. Bart (1970) made a similar suggestion for American-Jewish women; she thought the 'empty nest' syndrome (depression) in mid-life Jewish women was the result of the loss of the valued mother role.

Very large family size is valued and often attained among Hasidim and other strictly orthodox Jews. You may recall that having several young children to care for was found to make Camberwell women more vulnerable to depression in the event of depressing circumstances (Brown and Harris, 1978). In the light of cultural values, we might not expect family size to be related to depression in the same way among orthodox Jewish women. Indeed, Loewenthal and Goldblatt (1993) reviewed a number of studies that suggest a complex relationship between family size and depression and its symptoms. Both religion (indexed by affiliation) and family size went along with lower likelihood of depression symptoms, and the effect could not be explained by stress levels, which did not differ by religiosity, and which were actually **higher** in women with larger families. One way in which family size relates to mental health in religious Jewish women is thought to be via self-esteem, affected by tangible evidence of fulfilment of the valued mother role. The Loewenthal and Goldblatt study showed that although family size and religiosity were strongly associated, there were specific and distinct effects of family size and of religiosity on depressive symptoms. Family size went along with lowered likelihood of:

- hopelessness;
- early waking;
- loss of concentration;
- brooding.

These effects were interpreted in terms of changes in lifestyle, time-budgeting and expectations resulting from parenting. Religiosity went along with lowered likelihood of:

- depressed mood;
- loss of interest;
- suicide plans;
- early waking;
- retardation (slowing).

These effects relate to a lower level of disillusion and a higher level of purpose in life among the more religious. However in a preliminary analysis of material from a similar study three years later, after the onset of the 1990 recession, many of these effects had disappeared, as the economic difficulties of coping with a large family became more salient.

Loewenthal (1992) also reports some evidence of the use of religiously based antidepressant cognitions and practices in Hasidic and other strictly orthodox women: 'I just go through everything I have to be thankful for'; 'It's so important to have *bitachon* [trust that everything God does is for the best]'. These strategies are based on the value placed on joy, valued particularly in the teeth of adverse circumstances.

We have seen so far from these studies of religion in society that there are many routes by which religion and mental health can be related.

EXPLAINING AND MISUNDERSTANDING OTHER PEOPLE'S BEHAVIOUR

The question has often been raised whether behaviour which is valued or at least tolerated in one society may be considered mad or bad in other social groups.

Here are a few introductory examples. They all have to do with the general problem of how we explain other people's behaviour.

One of the first complaints I heard about mental health professionals dealing with members of the orthodox Jewish community in which I live was of the following type:

Mr and Mrs B had a son who was having some difficulties in school. He wasn't keeping up with the class, was very restless and disruptive, and was being difficult at home. The school suggested they should take their son to see a psychologist. They were very indignant at this suggestion because someone else that they knew had done this, and had met with a total misunderstanding of the behavioural norms and values of the community. They said the psychologist had come to watch this other boy and saw him swaying backwards and forwards over his book. (This is normative behaviour, encouraged particularly in boys, when praying and studying religious texts.) The psychologist was reported to have said that she thought the boy was disturbed because of the way he was swaying. When the parents pointed out that all the boys do it, the psychologist was alleged to have said, 'Perhaps they're **all** disturbed'.

A poignant example of misunderstanding arising from failure to understand the religious norms of another person is offered by Tova Mordechai (1992). Tova Mordechai was a student minister in a Christian group who had their own way of observing the Sabbath, as will be described. Mordechai went to stay with an orthodox Jewish family, arriving shortly before the Jewish Sabbath began:

'Would you like to take a shower now and wash your hair?' Sandy [the hostess] inquired.

'It's all right,' I said, taking a look around the kitchen, which was still in an untidy state. 'I don't mind helping you a bit more'. I had always taken a long hot bath after the Sabbath came in and was planning to do just that as soon as the Sabbath came in and things had settled down a bit.

The minutes ticked by, and Sandy asked me again, 'Are you **sure** you don't want to take a shower? The bathroom is empty now – it's really no problem'.

She must have thought I was a dirty little pup! 'No thank you, it's quite all right,' I answered politely.

We were still pottering around the kitchen, taking care of a dozen odd jobs, when Sandy finally declared, 'Okay children, time to light candles.'

Excitement filled the air as little people came running from all directions to congregate in the dining room.

'Well, I don't think much of this,' I said to myself. 'How can I light a candle? I'm still in my dirty clothes and we've worked right up till the last minute! And this is a religious home?' In the [Christian] college we'd always stopped work completely an hour before sunset on Fridays to have time to unwind. We'd change into our good clothes and sing soft songs, slowly entering into the Sabbath spirit. There was a conscious effort to separate ourselves from the physical environment and to enter a state of spirituality. The abrupt change in this household did not suit me at all. How did they truly expect to prepare for the Sabbath in a split second?

I followed Sandy into the dining room . . . The table was extended, draped with a beautiful white linen tablecloth, and set with gleaming china and silver. Dotting the settings were several embroidered velvet covers which hid loaves of freshly baked bread . . . The sideboard was covered with silver candelabras and candlesticks. The children scrambled on and off the chairs taking turns saying the blessing over the candles and lighting them. Sandy pointed to the candle that was to be mine, and the children argued over who was to help me say the blessing. Sandy instructed me to wave my hands three times over the light and then cover my eyes until I'd finished the blessing. In embarrassment I repeated the meaningless and strange-sounding words as best I could.

'Good Shabbos', she said, and kissed me on the cheek. I smiled gently. So little ceremony, so little intensity – the Jews did nothing more than light a candle, and they had Sabbath! Very odd.

'Is it all right if I take a shower and wash my hair now?' I asked. Sandy looked at me open-mouthed. 'I'm sorry, but I thought you understood. We don't do that on Shabbos. That's why I asked you beforehand if you wanted to wash your hair.'

I was devastated. Why hadn't someone told me? I couldn't believe this. I was filthy! . . . There was no way I was going to spend the next 25 hours walking around like that!

I stomped up the stairs, grumbling to myself that I was going to take a shower anyway. It wasn't my fault, they should have explained it, and if they thought I was going to set foot out of the house with my hair reeking down the block, they had better think again, and –

I was so angry! Images of the Jewish women in the [synagogue I had visited once] flashed through my mind, and it dawned on me that I would have to face another crowd of fancy Jews in the synagogue the next morning. I thought of them, all dressed up in the latest fashions, inching away from me in disgust as I sat there with dirty hair in my frumpy borrowed clothes that were two sizes too large. My father's words rang in my ears: 'First impressions are very important!'

'I can't, I can't,' I screamed inside. 'I just can't! This is awful. Oh, God . . .' My eyes filled with tears. I opened the door of my room and stood back, somewhat startled. I couldn't go in. Something was in that room . . . Peace.

Tova Mordechai's anger was quite quickly replaced by a sense of peace, but not all such misunderstandings have such satisfactory conclusions. They often give rise to negative emotions, and involve negative judgments of others which may have long-lasting and devastating consequences for the self and for relationships with others. Mordechai's example mentions her feeling that the other people were 'odd', her feeling that they 'must' consider her 'a dirty little pup', expecting that other people (described as 'fancy Jews') would 'inch away from her', feeling 'devastated', very angry and screaming inside. There is a lengthy angry inner tirade directed against more or less a whole cultural–religious group.

MacIsaac (1992) describes two examples of misunderstandings in the context of health care. In both cases, the misunderstanding was removed by discussion and clarification:

I nursed a Hindu who was asking for a blood transfusion (for which there was no medical need). It turned out that he had been masturbating and his religion had taught him that each drop of semen contained so much blood. If I had not been aware of his religious beliefs he might have been misdiagnosed as a schizophrenic.

Another patient, a girl of Evangelical [Christian] faith was admitted with beliefs of devil possession. It turned out she was having sexy thoughts of a man of her acquaintance and had convinced herself that spirit possession – a belief of her religion – was the cause of her sexual feelings.

Health and mental health care is beset with mismatched perspectives. One of my favourite examples – favourite because it epitomizes and highlights the poignant situation of the carers and the sufferers – is the study of Bradley, Brewin and Duncan (1983) of women in childbirth, and the midwives who cared for them and delivered their babies. The midwives consistently underestimated the amount of pain that the mothers reported experiencing. One can easily see how this kind of mismatch leads to damaging and nonconstructive judgments of patients, such as demanding, inadequate, neurotic or paranoid.

Very often, misunderstandings can be removed by asking the right questions, and listening to the answers. Working conditions do not always allow the time for this, and helpers are not always inclined or trained to do this. Unsolicited attempts by patients to explain their feelings or the causes of their behaviour are open to misunderstanding.

LITTLEWOOD AND LIPSEDGE: MAD, BAD OR HOLY?

Littlewood and Lipsedge (1989) are troubled by the difficulties of practising psychiatry on members of minority groups. Hence the title of their book: *Aliens and Alienists*. The general story is one of misunderstanding and damaging stereotypes. They write:

Frantz Fanon eloquently describes the immigrant in Europe who, lonely, bewildered and cut off from his cultural roots, appeals to the initially sympathetic white doctor. A vague series of physical symptoms seems to evaporate with the doctor's questioning and probing; the patient grows more nervous and the doctor more irritated. In despair the patient seeks different doctors, anxiously trying to convince them of **something**. The medical community builds up its picture of the inarticulate black malingerer: the 'North African Syndrome'. In Britain, Asian women are allocated the similar 'Begum syndrome'.

They continue by observing that depression was not diagnosed in such patients because they do not complain of it by name, or mention guilt – both highly culture-bound values.

Their main question is whether one culture's manners are another culture's symptoms. It's a good question.

Littlewood and Lipsedge offer the case of M., a young Hasid, the only child of Holocaust survivors (see Chapter 8). M. had failed to become a religious scholar (*talmid chocham*) and his marriage had failed because of his impotence. He turned to excessive religious scrupulosity, fasting and immersing himself for long periods in the ritual bath. M.'s mother believed he was mad. M.'s father suggested that he was just very religious. One psychiatrist suggested he was suffering from anorexia nervosa. A social worker suggested that M. was trying to gain self-esteem and status: after failing to become a scholar or a husband, he was gaining a reputation as very pious. A nurse suggested he was schizophrenic, since he heard divine commandments to fast and purify himself during prayer. Another psychiatrist suggested M. was depressed but had to deny it because depression is not culturally endorsed. It was truly difficult to decide whether M. was ill or simply engaging in culturally sanctioned behaviour.

Littlewood and Lipsedge encourage the attempt to distinguish healthy and unhealthy religiosity. In the end, they concluded that M. was probably suffering from unhealthy religiosity.

Similar dilemmas arise in the case of B., the punitively-reared daughter of a black Jamaican Baptist minister. Torn between her desire to be femininely attractive, and family pressure to be 'born again', she left Jamaica and came to London and enjoyed life for a while. Life became tougher when B. was left as a single parent to bring up her son. She became a Catholic, but then left the church when the local priest declined to carry out an elaborate exorcism in her front room, which had been polluted by a neighbour who was, B. said, a witch. B. said the priest was not really white, he was black inside. After B.'s father died, she began to beg for gynaecological operations 'to clear all that away'. After an argument with her son in which she maintained the rightness of obeying the white police and government she was found naked on her balcony shouting down into the street that God had told her to kill herself. Littlewood and Lipsedge felt B. to be the victim – to an extreme degree – of the cultural convention that black is evil and dirty, and white is good and pure. She was much more attached to the white nurses and doctors than the black and insisted that she herself was not really black. Is B. mad? This is what the neighbours think. Or is she bad? This is what B. is afraid she is. Or is she just black? This, suggest Littlewood and Lipsedge, is certainly a very important feature of B.'s misery. B. is certainly the victim of physical and possibly sexual abuse, and racism, some of it perpetrated in the name of religion.

It is possible that the attribution and expectancy theories of cognitive social psychology (founded on Rotter, 1966 and Kelly, 1967) – which will be discussed in Chapter 9 – could contribute something to the understanding of the general problems being discussed here. These theories deal with our explanations of other people's behaviour: under what conditions do we decide that someone standing on a balcony threatening to kill herself is mad, or bad, or the victim of circumstances? These analyses are obviously important because, when they are done by helping professionals, they affect the kind of treatment and help that is offered.

There has been some work done on the explanations that various groups of helping professionals, carers and patients have for different psychiatric conditions. There has also been some study of the ways a given piece of behaviour is differently understood when it is enacted by members of different cultural groups. For example Hunter, Stringer and Watson (1991) studied Catholics' and Protestants' explanations of Catholic and Protestant violence in Northern Ireland. Confirming Pettigrew's (1979) suggestion, they found that own-group violence was generally seen as externally caused (i.e. provoked; 'it was done in self-defence'), while out-group violence was seen to be internally caused ('they are brutal').

However this approach has not been extended in the direction of looking at the ways religious and cultural factors contribute to the explanation of a given piece of behaviour, or a particular person, and mental illness. Hopefully there will be such work, but for the moment it must remain as a gleam in my eye – and hopefully the eyes of others.

SUMMARY

Several studies of religion and mental health in different societies are reported.

Eaton and Weil showed that although virtually no Hutterites were being referred for psychiatric treatment, the rate of disorder was as high as in the general population, though forms of disorder differed.

Brown, Harris and Prudo showed that, in a rural British community, religion could operate as a protective factor against the onset of depression, as well as in other ways. Loewenthal and others reported comparable findings in orthodox Jewish women, as well as showing some positive effects of family size on some aspects of mental health – in some circumstances.

Littlewood and Lipsedge raise the important question of how readily a psychiatrist can diagnose a psychological illness in someone from another culture, when what s/he sees as symptoms may be reasonable and appropriate behaviour in the patient's own culture. Some examples of perceptions and misperceptions are given. There is a need for the application of cognitive–social–psychological theories in this field.

These studies of religion in society show some of the ways in which religion is related to mental health. Further chapters will return to some of the issues raised here.

4

Conversion: a turn for the better?

Religious conversion involves a transformation of identity, affiliation with a religious organization, new friends and new ideas, values and attitudes.

There are two common ideas about religious conversion in relation to mental health. One idea is that it's usually unhappy and neurotic people who turn to religion. Another idea is that religious conversion solves lots of problems and makes people happier. This chapter looks for any truth in these ideas.

The following illustration suggests that – at least in J.'s case, there is truth in both ideas.

Bragan's case-study, reported in 1977, illustrates both features:

J. is a 25-year-old student minister. He was born in England, to working-class parents. He was and is fond of both of them, but it seems to have been a rather drab and cheerless home. J.'s father wanted J. to improve himself, and he showed some promise in school, but after leaving school he led an aimless life, taking a manual job. J.'s family emigrated to New Zealand, and eventually he followed them after finding life too lonely. He found a rather menial job and still felt aimless and lonely. He took up music, and became a drummer in a jazz group which eventually became famous. However he became disenchanted with the group's lifestyle and left the group shortly before its real success. Shortly afterwards he read the New Testament, became gripped by this and became a Christian. This term had particular meaning for him: he thought the liberals were doomed to hell, but enjoyed destroying the fundamentalist position in debate, at which he was very good. He was welcomed and acclaimed in the church, and was happy for the first time in his life. He was encouraged to go to college to study for the ministry, and found a girlfriend. However, his girlfriend returned to her home country and he found himself increasingly depressed by the intellectual cynicism of university life. He began to feel the world as cold and cruel. A professor taunted him: when J. challenged his nihilistic views, the professor told J. to find a girlfriend. J. suffered a depressive illness through which a new girlfriend stood by him, and at the time of writing, J. seemed to be working through psychological therapy with some success.

J.'s story has many features characteristic of conversion narratives. The discovery of a meaningful religion follows a period of aimlessness and feelings of need; the honeymoon following conversion is followed by a period of downs and ups. J.'s story, like many conversion narratives, remains unfinished.

CONVERSION PROCESSES

With real life and real religions, simple truths are hard to find. Religious groups vary enormously in terms of their investment in conversion activity and in the kinds of methods favoured. The Anglican church, for instance, is pretty laid-back about conversion; it's happy about the decade of evangelism, and the vicar is always happy to welcome new faces. But the average Anglican doesn't spend hours traipsing about the streets and knocking on doors spreading the gospel. Nor does the vicar. He has enough to do looking after the flock he has. Less established religious groups, by contrast, actually need new members. Olson (1989) in a study of Baptists in the USA found that newer churches were seen as more friendly and attractive. The older churches' members were seen as 'cliquey'; the older churches' members had been around a long time and had as many friends as they could cope with. So religious groups vary in how much they need new members and how much they engage in outreach.

Religious groups also vary in the methods they use, and in the kind of conversion process or experience that is seen as acceptable. To be accepted in some revivalist groups, you would probably have to stand up and tell everybody else, very enthusiastically, what the Lord had done for you – witnessing. But if you wanted to be accepted as a worshipper in a rural

English parish church, flamboyant witnessing would definitely be out.

Since Starbuck (1899) and James (1902), psychologists and sociologists of religion have defined many different kinds of conversion. Scobie (1975) in a study of British male Christian ordinands found 20% had undergone sudden conversion experiences, 50% had undergone a more gradual transformation, and 30% had been converted unconsciously by remaining in the religion of their family of origin. Some would call this latter type of conversion **commitment** (Snow and Machalek, 1987). Loewenthal (1988) in a study of Hasidic women found somewhat analogous types: **inspirational**, where the women reported having been inspired to increasing their religious observance by an inspirational experience usually involving some practical aspect of Judaism, **resisting**, where the woman's increased observance was initiated by someone close to her and initially resisted by the woman herself, and **affirming**, where the woman affirmed her commitment to the observant Judaism of her family of origin in the face of pressures to lapse. More elaborate typologies have been proposed to include conversion to new religious movements and cults. Lofland and Skonovd (1981) suggested six 'motifs' in conversion, depending on the degree of emotional arousal, whether the process is sudden or gradual, and other features. Robbins (1988) points out that of Lofland and Skonovd's six motifs, **revivalist** conversion appears to be decreasing, while **experimental** ('try it and see how good it is') and **intellectual** ('read and explore your options before getting involved') conversions are on the increase. Kose (1994) found marked differences between men and women converts to Islam in the types of motifs reported. Women, for instance, are more likely to report **affectional** motifs – a conversion involving a lead from someone close to the woman.

Our discussion of religious conversion in relation to mental health must therefore be set in the context of variations in the types of conversion undergone.

Here are some examples of different types of conversion experience. In these excerpts I have concentrated on what were seen by the converts as the turning points.

M. was happily married, with two children, a comfortable home and a good relationship with her husband. One morning, her husband complained that he didn't feel well. M. thought that he didn't look too good, and since he never normally complained about his health, she decided to ask the doctor to come. By the time the doctor arrived, M.'s husband was in great pain. The doctor called an ambulance immediately, but M.'s husband was dead before he arrived at the hospital. It was a heart attack. M. said that it was like one of those cartoon films where you see a character running along, and they run off the edge of a cliff, but they are still running on the same level. Then they finally realize that the ground has gone, and they go crashing down. M. said she felt just like that: she just carried on with her life as normal, until she realized that the ground wasn't there any more. Then she crashed down, and she stayed down for a long time.

She'd always been a lukewarm person about religion. She thought it was a good thing but had never done much about it except go to church on a few occasions like weddings or funerals. During her low period a friend suggested that she went to a prayer meeting in someone's home. She went along, and felt as if she had been helped, so she kept going back, and eventually became a member of the charismatic Christian group in whose members' houses the prayer meetings were held. Some members of the group had the 'gift of tongues' (glossolalia) in prayer meetings, and M. had once or twice been granted this. She began to study, both the Bible, and reading about Christianity generally. She gradually began to feel her life picking up, and assuming a new meaning and purpose. She felt more cheerful, and though she was approaching retirement age, she plucked up her courage and resigned from the safe but boring job she had for many years, and began studying for a new career, which she hoped would enable her to put her Christian beliefs into practice in a more direct way.

M.'s turning-point seems to have been the feeling of being helped that she experienced when she went along to the prayer meeting.

B.'s religious career, as reported to Ali Kose (1994) is a colour-ful one:

> B. said that his parents were Church of England simply because he knew they weren't Catholic. The only religious content to his childhood was the knowledge that his parents were not Catholic – and therefore, by default, 'C. of E.'! He left school at 15, and got mixed up with some motorbike gangs for two years. These gangs were into black magic and witchcraft. At that time he also drank a lot, and smoked hashish.
>
> Then he met a girl who was Hindu, and dropped out of the gang, and began reading the Hindu scriptures. He thought all religion was senseless, and the engagement came to an end, partly because B. did not like the religion, and partly because of difficulties with B.'s fiancee's parents. Until he was about 20, B. said he did not care about life, and he enjoyed being different from other people. He enjoyed that fact that he could walk into a pub where there were all very ordinary people, respectable-looking, and he would be dressed in a leather jacket and filthy jeans, looking real nasty. He felt that everything was just a game, and everything he did was just to project an image, and to cause a stir among other people.
>
> When he was 20, B. went on a trip to the USA, and while he was there the Iranian revolution took place and some Americans were held hostage in Iran. B. always used to find Americans very cocky and arrogant. Concerning the hostages, B. used to ask his American friends: 'Are you getting some justice back now? That little country over there is giving you a kick in the teeth.' He used to have long discussions over the whole issue. While the hostage business was still going on, he came back to the UK and decided to find out what sort of reli-gion it was that had brought the USA to its knees. He bought a copy of the Koran and read it all the way through. B. felt that the things written there were directed at him. He felt almost as if whoever wrote it had been watching him for the last few years and knew what he had been doing. 'It was saying, don't do this, don't do that . . . it was all written down, what I had been doing wrong. It was really a shock. Things that I had been doing quite privately were all there, all in the open.'
>
> At first, B. rejected what the Koran was saying, but then the more he thought, the more it made sense. The fact that it

mentioned all the Prophets was appealing because he felt he was not losing anything. He told his friends that there was something in that book. But they started teasing him. After a few weeks, B. decided to go to a mosque to find out more. He spoke to an Imam who gave him some books. He read them and thought that some were silly and some were sensible. From the mosque, he met quite a few people, and one invited him home, and he stayed with him for about two weeks. The way this Moslem man was treating him had an enormous effect upon B. The following week, B. was praying in the mosque just by copying everyone, and after the prayer the man who had hosted B. said that if he wanted to become a Moslem, he could now do the *shahadah*. B. acquiesced and thus became a Moslem.

Although in Lofland and Skonovd's terms, the main motifs at the time of B.'s conversion were intellectual (his curiosity about Islam which led to him finding a mosque and an Imam, and doing some reading) and affectional (the friendship and kindness shown by his Moslem host), B. is sure that the original impetus was his rebellious feelings. First he rebelled against his father, then against his immediate social group by joining the motorcycle gang, and then against wider society by joining a religion which was obviously hated by the people of the West. B. says that rebellion was the 'prod' that led him into Islam, but not what kept him there.

The turning-point in N.'s life came when she was at college in the 1970s. The student culture supported experimentation with consciousness-altering drugs, and N. and her friends were no exception. One of N.'s friends was Jewish, and although he was not otherwise into religion, he used to stand a *menorah* (eight-branched candlestick) in his window and light it during the mid-winter festival of Chanukah. N. thought this was 'cute', being particularly struck by the contrast with her friend's lifestyle, which she saw as oblivious to social and religious convention. She decided to learn more about Judaism, and after several years of study, experimentation and discussion, she converted and married a religious man (described in Loewenthal, 1988a).

Note that neither, M., B. or N. show any obvious signs of psychopathology, apart from M.'s depression following the loss of her husband. This latter is not strictly speaking a psychopathological reaction, as a temporary depression is a 'healthy' response to loss, and it is clear that M.'s depression was temporary. Like most and perhaps all religious converts, M., B. and N. report feeling happier and more purposeful as a result of their conversion. Victor Frankl (1965) has suggested that a state of 'noogenic neurosis' – a feeling that life has no aim and purpose – is endemic in secularized Western society, and it is not normally regarded as a cause for psychiatric concern. It is quite likely that M., B. and N. were suffering from the condition identified by Frankl, along with several million other members of Western society. They are described because, apart from feelings of aimlessness, they have no obvious psychopathology and we would guess that this is probably true of many converts.

THE CULT CONTROVERSY

Since the 1960s there has been a rise in the USA and to a lesser extent in some other countries, in the number of cult-type 'new religious movements' (Galanter, 1989). They are all actively involved in recruitment, and all claiming to offer spiritual enlightenment and psychological wellbeing. Do they? Or do they brainwash, tear young people from their families and from society, exploit and enslave, causing misery to converts and their families?

In case you have trouble telling the difference between a religion and a cult, Paloutzian (1983) offers several guidelines. Cults, he says, will show most or all of the following features to a marked degree. Traditional religions may show some of these features, but the features may be lacking altogether in traditional religions:

- charismatic and dogmatic leadership;
- total dominance of converts' lives;
- total separation from former lives;
- economic and other exploitation;
- bizarre or unusual doctrine, often only revealed to the convert when s/he is felt to be 'ready'.

Batson, Schoenrade and Ventis (1993) offer a more succinct definition of a cult. It

- is a religious group, which
- is new, and
- involves total commitment.

Meadow and Kahoe (1984) suggest an important feature of cults. They involve a sense of 'oughtness' in which the sense of what is just and good may become difficult or distorted.

Cult converts may be often deliberately sought out. Favoured methods include looking in local papers for small ads of recent bereavements and street-selling focusing on young, aimless-looking people (who are likely to be unattached). The 'victim' is thus likely to be without strong ties (Robbins, 1988), and may be looking for something which life is not yet giving them. Sociologists of religion have suggested social factors which may be associated with successful cult activity, such as weakening of traditional religion (Stark and Bainbridge, 1980).

Cult conversions may be followed by improvements in employment status, a drop in measures of distress, and reported drops in drug-taking (Richardson, 1985; MacPhillamy, 1986). However Kirkpatrick (1988) has questioned the inferential statistics used in some studies showing therapeutic effects of cult membership. Kirkpatrick's own analyses do not show such effects, and they do show some support for the Conway and Siegelman claim (see below) of harmful effects of cult membership.

Critics of cults would concede that cult conversion must have some (perceived) advantages, otherwise – in an open society – nobody would join. However the critics claim that the costs in terms of loss of intellectual and other freedoms, pain to the converts' families and exploitation of members are not worth the gains.

The best-known scientific 'attack' on cult membership appeared in Conway and Siegelman's (1982) provocatively-entitled paper, 'Information disease: Have cults created a new mental illness?' Their study of 400 ex-cult-members suggested that information disease was the result of programming undergone by cult converts. The principle symptoms are:

- floating feelings/altered states of consciousness;
- nightmares;
- amnesia;
- hallucinations/delusions;

- inability to break mental rhythms of chanting;
- violent outbursts;
- suicidal/self-destructive tendencies.

Critics of Conway and Siegelman's conclusions include Lewis and Bromley (1987) who studied 105 ex-cult-members; they found that the presence of information disease symptoms was not related to length of membership or time spent in ritual, as Conway and Siegelman might claim. The presence of symptoms was, however, related to the 'dynamics of the exit process'. Symptoms were rare among those defectors who had not sought (or received involuntarily) counselling or deprogramming. Cause and effect are hard to disentangle here. Lewis and Bromley think that it is leaving the cult, and changing social and symbolic worlds, that produces emotional turbulence. But other explanations are possible.

Whatever the merits and demerits of cult membership, cult members may be voting with their feet. There are reports that some cults may have difficulty in holding on to their membership (Long and Hadden, 1983). Jacobs (1987) has proposed a two-stage descriptive model of individual disaffiliation from cult-like religious movements. She suggests that members first loosen bonds with other members and then become disenchanted with and disengaged from the charismatic leader.

Some cults disintegrate, for example following quarrels among leaders, or perceived failures in leadership. For example Festinger, Riecken and Schachter in *When Prophecy Fails* (1956) describes the partial disintegration of 'the Seekers', a religious group led by a Mrs Keech, who prophesied that the whole world would be destroyed by a flood, but that she and her followers would be saved by extraterrestrial beings. When the predicted date arrived, no flood and no extraterrestrial beings were forthcoming. Mrs Keech closeted herself, and then emerged to say that it had been revealed to her that the world had been saved by the faith of the Seekers. Although those closest to Mrs Keech became more ardent proselytizers, many others left the group, disillusioned.

It is quite difficult to evaluate research on mental health in and around cults, because of the vested interests of those engaged in the cult controversy. Right at the beginning of this book, I said that the religious were invested in demonstrating the benefits of religion for psychological health, and the new religions don't seem to be any different in this respect from the old.

Here is an account by a British convert to a group of Sufis active in Britain. Kose (1994), to whom this account was given, suggests that K.'s conversion illustrates how membership in such a group can help a person overcome depression, and can make life bearable.

K. was born in a working-class home where religion was never discussed. His mother rarely went to church and father was indifferent to religion. He was given elementary religious instruction at school and sent to Sunday school where, he described, the atmosphere was secular. In his twenties, K. felt he did not fit into this society and did not accept the usual social values such as working. This led him to join [what he called] an anarchist group where he wanted to get rid of any kind of social conditioning. By doing so, he thought he found freedom, peace and happiness, and he started experimenting with marijuana and LSD. By the age of 26, K. felt disillusioned with anarchism, coming to the conclusion that 'it will not go anywhere', and he developed an interest in a sort of Buddhism through a philosophy of a macrobiotic diet, which he described as 'almost making your religion out of diet'. He felt that man had become artificial and if he could return to natural living, like growing his own food and living on basic things, then the problems of the world would be cleaned up.

Having been involved with macrobiotics, K. had a girl-friend who was also involved with macrobiotics. He got her pregnant and she chose to have an abortion against K.'s wishes, about which K. felt that it destroyed the love between them and they drifted apart. Then he felt upset and depressed for quite a while, drifting aimlessly through life looking for something, not knowing what it was. He was still interested in macrobiotics for a few years, but he did 'anything he came across', and then he became interested in New Age philosophies. As an extension of his involvement with New Age thinking, he went to California. He thought 'all the cults are here'. He also thought that if he went to another country and started again, he could have a better life. There he met a girl and they lived together for two years, and got married for the papers so that K. could stay in the United States. But it did not work out and she 'took up with another guy'. Losing two girl-friends one after the other led K. to involvement with a Rashneesh group which renounces sex and advises celibacy. Yet K. was still not happy. After staying three years in California he felt even more rootless than he did in England. So he decided to come back to London in 1982, when he was in his mid-thirties. He said of this time: 'I could never under-stand what used to bother me. It seemed to me all these other people seemed to be finding things but I did not. Life gener-ally did not seem to have any kind of purpose'.

When he came back, he took an interest in Buddhist medi-tation, but still did not depart from New Age. He was mixing with them. He also started going to church, feeling that perhaps the best thing for him to do would be to go back to his original tradition, since he was a Westerner. But he soon felt that it was a kind of class activity, a middle-class thing. K. now concedes that perhaps he was deluding himself by being an eclectic, but he felt: 'To me it really did not seem to matter what people believe as long as it worked. That would have been sufficient. If I had found something that worked, even if the beliefs had been absurd, I would have accepted it. I was looking for something that worked, something that gives you integration and strength. That was what I was looking for. Whatever it was I did not care what kind of mad beliefs. But if it worked as far as I was concerned that must be true, because it works'.

Three years after his return from California he happened to meet a convert follower of S. [the leader of a Sufi group], who invited him to a Sufi meeting. K. was curious and he thought he would go, as it was something he had never looked at. It was a *dhikr* (contemplation of the divine) ceremony, and he felt the atmosphere was very peaceful. He also enjoyed the food served afterwards and thought 'it is even worth coming here just for the food', and he decided to go along again. 'It seemed better than any other things. I was going to go because I was always going all the time from one thing to another. I was looking for something. I did not know what it was. And then I kept going every Friday night and just started to understand a bit more about it.

The same night when he first went to the *dhikr* meeting K. had a dream which suggests how strongly he was craving to overcome his problems: 'In the dream I was Muslim and I went to a house. And there was a room with some people in this house. And I felt that I had these problems in this room and I sorted out the problems. I felt or I knew that I was Muslim and I was the only one who was Muslim in the house. They seemed to be in confusion whereas I was not because I was a Muslim. That was the dream, but it was very clear. It was not vague or weird. When I woke up I thought about it and I said "I don't have any intention of being a Muslim. Come on, I am not going to be Muslim"'.

K. was also attracted to the friendliness of the people in the group: 'I liked people to talk to. They seemed nice people. The feeling was very good. If I had any questions, they were willing to talk to me about things. I just started to get interested in Islam. They were not trying to convert me. They were not saying I should become Muslim. They just suggested that I meet S. [the leader] when he comes.

When S. came in four months' time, K. accepted him as his master and took the *shahadah* (Islamic profession of faith) then.

As his involvement with the group and his relationship with S. improved, K. gradually felt that life had become manageable: 'It feels like now I am in control of my life. Whereas before it had always seemed that somehow there was always something I was missing. I don't know exactly what it was. But now it brings everything into equilibrium and balance. That is the best thing about it.'

Kose concluded that this particular religious group served a consciously psychotherapeutic function, and collected several reports of members who had recovered from depression and other distressed and psychiatric states. K. had been a member of the group for seven years at the time of interview, and reported no return of his feelings of aimlessness and need for something.

A rather more cautious conclusion could be drawn from the benefits of L.'s involvement with a Seventh Day Adventist group.

I met L. about 10 years ago, when he was living in a commune near London run by the group. He had been getting on badly with his family, who lived in South Africa, and had decided to travel and see the world. He was wandering, aimless and lonely, soon after arriving in London, and had been picked up by a group member. His day involved rising early for prayers and bible study, followed by breakfast. The group laid on a bus into London, where members were dropped off to work in various shops and restaurants run by the group. They returned to the commune in the evening, after working a 12-hour day. L. said that he had been depressed, aimless and lonely, and he welcomed the structure, friendship and purpose provided by the group. On the other hand he felt trapped, and the group was not providing answers that were satisfying to him. His family said they didn't mind what he did: he had been aimless for some time, and it was quite a relief to them to know he had something to do with himself. L. said that he really wanted to leave the group but he was afraid to return to his former aimless and lonely life. He continued to develop contact with friends from outside the group, and finally he felt able to leave the group and to go to college, while continuing to develop his lately-discovered religious interests, this time in Judaism, the religion of his origin.

CONVERSION: FOR BETTER OR WORSE?

The relations between religious conversion and mental health have been studied in the traditional and new religions, though sampling methods sometimes seem a bit vague and haphazard.

Bragan's (1977) case-study of a Christian convert entitled 'The psychological gains and losses of religious conversion' was described briefly at the beginning of this chapter. This case highlights many of the important general mental health features of the convert's career. The start of the career involves a period of lack of purpose and dissatisfaction with life, especially in terms of relationships, work and religion. No positive identity has been established (Marcia, 1966; Loewenthal, 1989). Contact with a religion – its literature or its members – leads to a sudden or gradual appreciation; a tentative new identity is consolidated by increasing or continued involvement with the religion – its ideas and teachings, its members, its activities. Conversion in the sense of ideological and attitudinal change alone may be rare. Relationships and occupation are affected: sometimes the convert is helped to see purpose and fulfilment in existing relationships and work, sometimes these may be changed in the light of new values and morality, and sometimes the religious group may encourage or help the development of new relationships (Loewenthal, 1989) or occupation (Bragan, 1977).

One implication of this simplified account is that we might expect converts to be less happy and perhaps more anxious and depressed prior to their conversion. However there aren't any studies that I know of reporting the capture and testing of converts just before their conversion, apart from a study by Wilson (1976), described in Meadow and Kahoe (1984), in which 533 young Americans were tested and then followed-up after about four months for re-testing. Just 11 were found to have converted, nine of them to a soft-sell Christian evangelistic group called Young Life. These converts were not significantly different from the nonconverts on any of the measures of personality and adjustment that Wilson used. Among the converts, there were differences in between some pre- and postconversion test scores. These were taken to indicate changes in personal adjustment, in the direction that there was a shift from 'relative' neuroticism to healthy adjustment.

There are some retrospective data on pre- and postconversion states. Clark (1979) reported that 60% of cult converts were substantially disturbed and chronically unhappy prior to conversion. Bragan's (1977) subject reported feeling miserable, Buckley and Galanter (1979) report 'significant' depression in one subject. Ullman (1982) compared converts with lifelong adherents in several different types of religious group. The converts reported 'unhappier' childhoods and adolescence, and more stress prior to conversion. Ullman's analyses suggested the importance of relations with the father in religious biographies, as do the analyses of Kieren and Munro (1987). Kirkpatrick and Shaver (1990) found that those who had reported a 'cold' relationship with their mothers were more likely to have undergone a sudden conversion and were more likely to report a close personal relationship with God than those whose relationships with their mothers were described as warm and secure. These latter subjects showed a more laid-back type of religiosity (or lack of religiosity), usually following in their mothers' footsteps without undergoing any obvious crises. Cult and religious converts show a high proportion reporting having sought psychological help prior to conversion (Levine and Salter, 1976; Galanter *et al.*, 1979).

A rare prospective study was enabled by the occurrence of good data on preconversion state. Witztum, Dasberg and Greenberg (1990) found that *baalei teshuvah* (BTs) (returners to observant Judaism) were over-represented in referrals to a Jerusalem psychiatric clinic, of whom the majority (66%) had been psychiatrically unwell prior to conversion. In this study the assessment of pre-'conversion' state **had** been preserved in the form of a summary of previous treatment. Current state was assessed by two independent psychiatrists using DSM-III criteria. Schizophrenia and affective disorders were the most common diagnoses. However the catchment area of this clinic contained a high proportion of BT *yeshivot* (institutions of religious learning) so although BTs were over-represented in the clinic in relation to their proportion in the general population, they may not have been in relation to their proportion in the catchment area.

All in all, it does sound as if converts were not happy prior to their conversion. But this seems to be relative to their post-conversion state, not relative to the state of other people in their social milieu. The studies reviewed here are generally short on data comparing converts to lifelong adherents and to the non-religious. Moreover the data are generally retrospective. Snow and Machalek (1984) and Staples and Mauss (1987) point out that converts' accounts of conversion may be more than just descriptions; they are actually part of the conversion process and play a role in the reshaping of identity. In William James's (1902) view, conversion turns the self into one that is 'consciously right, superior and happy', so converts are by definition likely to produce accounts of prior selves who were 'wrong, inferior and unhappy'.

If we follow the simplified account of conversion given above, we might expect there to be a rise in wellbeing and a drop in distress following conversion. Bragan (1977) stresses the importance of the attainment of identity by conversion in promoting wellbeing. Stanley (1964) found theology students who had undergone sudden conversion were lower in neuroticism scores on the Maudsley Personality Inventory than gradual developers and lifelong adherents. Allison (1967), however, found sudden converts higher on manifest anxiety than gradual developers and lifelong adherents. Since neuroticism and anxiety measures normally intercorrelate very highly, there seems to be a contradiction in Stanley's and Allison's findings. However, Witztum *et al.*'s data suggest that conversion is followed by a 'honeymoon' period, with a rise in wellbeing and a drop in distress. Stanley's subjects, youngish students, may have been caught in this period, while Allison's subjects may have been generally at a later stage in life. Witztum *et al.* suggest a resurgence of earlier problems following the postconversion 'honeymoon'. Bragan's report makes a similar suggestion.

However, Shaver, Lenauer and Sadd (1980) found converts reporting themselves as happier than nonconverts. The subjects in this study were volunteers replying to a questionnaire in a women's magazine, so the sampling method is likely to have given rise to biases. Bergin's (1983) conclusions are that conversion significantly reduces pathological symptoms, but the timescale to which this conclusion applies is unclear. A study by Paloutzian (1981) looked at college students and compared converts and nonconverts on the Purpose in Life test. Converts scored higher than nonconverts. Students one week and six months from conversion scored higher than those one month after conversion. This bears out the general suggestion of postconversion improvement in wellbeing followed by downs and ups, but with wellbeing being generally somewhat better postconversion than preconversion. Bear in mind, though, that the majority of converts are unlikely to be in a serious psychopathological state before or after their conversion.

Overall, I would like to stick to the simplified scheme outlined at the beginning of this section, wherein converts start off in a sad way (or so they say), get helped by their conversion, but may possibly relapse under the pressures of assimilating to the new social world and new beliefs, and working out a viable lifestyle.

The available evidence is a bit shaky. Poor sampling, over-reliance on retrospective accounts, lack of really long-term follow-up and lack of adequate comparison groups are the chief problems. Apart from the differences between sudden and gradual converts and lifelong adherents, differences between different types of conversion experience have been overlooked. So a nicely designed study might give quite a different picture.

CONVERSION OR CHANGE?

We conclude this chapter with some more examples. They suggest that by focusing on one single conversion episode in a person's life, we may overlook the more fundamental fact, that there are ongoing lifelong processes of religious and personal change. Religious and personal change are interlinked and continue throughout life.

Our first example involves some dramatic religious and personal ups and downs, and is described by Greenberg, Witztum and Buchbinder (1992).

Greenberg and colleagues describe four men, Jewish Israelis, in their mid-twenties. All were born to Sephardic families (oriental-Jewish, in which the study of mysticism is normative and respected). Upbringing was nonreligious. All had become religiously observant during or just after their army service. There was no reported family psychiatric history, and the adolescence of all appears to have been generally successful, with all four being promoted to officer status during army service, indicating superior level of functioning. Three reported deaths of close friend or family members, and all seem to have been depressed just prior to their subsequent involvement in mystical, cabbalistic study and practice. The dreams and hallucinations precipitated by their mysticism were at first taken as signs of saintliness, but as they became withdrawn, apparently paranoid, neglectful of self and religious observance, they were deemed to be in need of psychiatric help. Two were improved and two unchanged. Greenberg, Witztum and Buchbinder compare their fate to that of Ben Zoma (a second-century mystic described in the Talmud), who became mad as a result of esoteric religious practices. They point out that many study mysticism without psychological harm, and discuss factors that might lead to the damaging effects reported. The underlying cause for breakdown in Greenberg, Witztum and Buchbinder's cases is suggested to be possibly unresolved depression resulting from the death of a close other. Here is the history of one man, as described by Greenberg and colleagues:

A 23-year-old single man, religious penitent (i.e. became religiously observant) for four years, complained of worsening concentration, sleep and appetite as he was disturbed by voices that gave him instructions. Of Iranian origin, he was an unruly child, although he successfully completed his matriculation. He served in the army as a parachute instructor, and witnessed the death of a close friend in a terrorist border ambush. He became depressed and irritable and at that time he became increasingly interested in Bratslav Hasidism and aged 21 he began studying in a Bratslav academy (Greenberg, Witztum and Buchbinder, 1992). Shortly before referral, he started having a recurrent nightmare: soldiers on patrol fall one by one, including his dead friend. The patient also falls and is lifted on to a stretcher. On examination he was neatly dressed. He appeared depressed, spoke in a monotone and with an air of despair. He described hearing voices which instructed him to kill himself and others.

He received low doses of neuroleptic medication. At his second visit he disclosed the following: for some months he and a friend had been studying Jewish mystical texts, including the Zohar and works by Vital such as the *Book of Visions* and the *Book of Transmigrations*. After reading the section in the *Zohar* interpreting the biblical text: 'When you go out to wage war with your enemy' (*Deut.* 21:10) as dealing with the Satanic forces, the two decided that they too would go to war against the forces of evil, and attempt to hasten the redemption. Trained as a scribe, he wrote out God's name on parchment as dictated by the Zohar, one text written in the shape of a sword. The pair intended using these amulets to call up the Lord and Lady of the 'other side', Samael and Lilith, in order to destroy them.

On the night appointed for the 'battle', the two friends recited the devotional prayers and went to sleep in a state of tense anticipation. A frightening vision appeared before him: pursued by a figure of fire surrounded by flames, he tried to wake up. A second vision followed: a column of men dressed in ancient bizarre clothing, some blind, others totally bald. All stood and stared. Then came the figure of fire, shouting: 'You thought to destroy me; it is I who will destroy you!' 'The sword', he added with a groan while telling his story, 'it was double-edged'. Since then, demons have pursued him day and night. Their form is constant: blind, hairless, ugly and hatted, telling him to kill others and himself, that they will make him mad and that he will go to hell. His partner suffered similar visions, became psychotic and was hospitalized. Leading kabbalists whom they consulted around the country were appalled that the two had attempted what great Rabbis had not dared and they offered no advice, except the ancient remedy of fasting, for which he felt too weak.

He explains what befell himself and his friend as what happens to the weak 'who glimpse and are damaged' (the Talmudic description of Ben Zoma's fate). 'The vessel was too weak to hold so much light; it cracked and was then smashed to smithereens'.

This patient was diagnosed as suffering from 'depressed mood, sleep and appetite changes, mood-congruent hallucinations, which gave him instructions, good recovery, suggestive of schizo-affective disorder'. His psychotic partner in study was the more active of the duo, but the continuation of our case's symptoms for months after the two friends separated rules out 'folie a deux'. Greenberg, Witztum and Buchbinder find it hard to decide whether the patient's behaviour and symptoms represented psychosis or theurgy. They outline the mystical background to the patient's behaviour, including the use of amulets, and the nature of evil:

in Jewish mystical writings, evil is a necessity without which there would be no free will for choosing the good path. In kabbalah, the realm of evil, called 'the other side', is distinct from holiness, yet is produced by God. Acts to call upon God and destroy the forces of evil are described in the lives of mystics and particularly Hasidic leaders (Buber, 1947), although discouraged in the general population by religious authorities.

Witztum and colleagues's dilemma about whether the 'patient' was really ill or not is reminiscent of the difficulties discussed in Chapter 3. For the present, we could note that whatever we decide about the source of the patient's demons, it is clear that they were making him unhappy and ill. It also seems clear that they were somehow the result of a misguided religious enthusiasm arising from a combination of his new-found religiosity set in the context of traumatic war experiences.

Fowler, in *Stages of Faith* (1981), devotes a chapter to the pilgrimage of M:

M. described her mother as giving, but always demanding and critical. Her father was affectionate and a good provider, but always uninvolved, and M. felt distant from him. The family were churchgoing, without being real believers. M. had felt suicidal from a very early age, sitting alone in her room brooding about her mother's treatment of her. M.'s memories of school were fairly happy, however, in spite of some ups and downs with teachers and friends. Towards the end of her schooldays, M.'s family moved, and this resulted in changes of school to which M. never really adjusted, so she took the opportunity to go to college early. Then followed five years of 'Eastern religions, pop psychology, the occult, illicit drugs and sex, and all that kind of stuff' and dropping in and out of college. A disastrous affair with a man, attempted suicide, a car crash and arrest for shoplifting followed.

M. began to wonder whether she was doing something wrong and began a religious search, at first through Eastern religions, the occult – and occasional Bible reading.

M. became a Christian after reading some biblical sources suggested by a recently converted brother. She felt that the biblical passages were really relevant to her situation. She got involved with a commune, became disaffected and then got involved with another group. Eventually she left this group after the failure of a romantic involvement with a fellow-member. M. felt rejected, and soon afterwards she was expelled from another group after having 'locked horns' with the leader who demanded 'submission' from M. M. then moved to another ministry, where she met and married a man with a similarly chequered history. The marriage had ups and downs, with the husband less steadfast in his religious commitment than M. The marriage finally broke up shortly before the birth of the couple's second child, and M. returned to live with her parents. M.

maintained a strong religious sense of meaning and purpose in all the ups and downs of her postconversion involvements with different Christian groups, and with the failure first of her engagement and then of her marriage.

Fowler interviewed M.'s Christian brother three years after interviewing M. Her brother said that although M.'s relationship with her parents continued to be difficult, there were some improvements, and the parents were showing more interest in religion than before. M. had become engaged, and was also working steadily and successfully in computer programming. This had been a great boost to her low self-esteem. She was described as moving towards great progress in her personal growth, and 'has never been happier in her life'.

I and my fellow-researchers, who include Vivienne Goldblatt, John Brown, Simon Gibson, Shirley Firth, Hanifa Khan, Ali Kose, Tessa Gorton and Guy Lubitsch, have spent several years interviewing people in Britain from most of the traditional religions: Christianity, Islam, Hinduism and Judaism. Our work has had a strong focus on religious development and personal change, and we have included measures of psychopathology or distress in most studies. Much of the published literature on conversion has a strong emphasis on psychopathology – it is often produced by clinicians who deal with psychological casualties. Our work, by contrast, has been in the community, and psychopathology is at least as infrequent in the religious groups studied as in the general population.

Conversion episodes as such seem less important than ongoing processes of religious and personal change. John Brown, for instance, is looking at the structure of belief systems in relation to crises, while Simon Gibson is looking at life strategies in Christians. Hanifa Khan is looking at life-events and depression in Moslems, while Shirley Firth is looking at how mourning is affected by religious change in Hindus adapting to life in Britain. Ali Kose is studying conversion to Islam, and Vivienne Goldblatt, Tessa Gorton, Guy Lubitsch and I have been looking at depression among orthodox Jews. What is striking is that even where we have focused on psychopathology, the people studied have thrown up evidence of vigorous attempts to lead kind, responsible, caring and useful lives, in accordance with religious teachings. My last example is from one of many interviews among orthodox Jews.

Mrs N. is in her 50s. She is happily married, with several children, all now married and living nearby. She gets a lot of pleasure from her grandchildren. She is extremely hospitable and active, taking particular pleasure in caring for a huge range of people whom life has not treated kindly. Now her children no longer need full-time care, she is on the lookout for more people to help. She is a popular and beloved figure, with a ready listening ear, and a kind word for all.

When she was six years old, her parents said good-bye to her. She had been brought up in a warm and loving religious home in Germany. It became obvious in the 1930s that all Jews were in great danger, and when the opportunity came for children to be selectively rescued, far-seeing parents took the heart-breaking decision to send their little ones to Britain on a 'children's transport'. All Mrs N. can remember of the war years is how she and the other little children cried all night. As the years went by, they adapted and hoped for the end of the war when they would be together with their families again.

As a young teenager, the frightful truth began to be apparent. She would never see her family again. She became embittered, morose, and gave up all her religious faith and practice, angry with God who could allow such things to happen.

She married, and one day a friend of her husband's suggested that they go to visit a great Hasidic Rabbi (the Lubavitcher Rebbe). Her husband was curious to go, and she went along for the trip. She decided she would shock the Rabbi by telling him how she had become irreligious and was very angry with God because of the family she had lost in such terrible circumstances. She carried out her intention, but instead of any kind of reproof, the Rabbi smiled and said he was very glad to learn that she was angry. She was very taken aback at this. The Rabbi said that her anger at God was a very strong connection. He suggested that she tried to thank God on any occasion which seemed to warrant it, and also to continue to give charity generously – 'I know you like to give', he said.

None of this made sense to Mrs N. How could thanking God and giving charity help her, or heal her wounds? But Mrs N. did find that it helped, and her outlook on life became more positive.

All this was over 20 years before the interview, and Mrs N.'s life since has been one of continuous learning, questioning, discovery and growth.

Mrs N. had turning-points in her life, and one of them might be described as conversion. The features of Mrs N.'s life that I wish to draw attention to are the lifelong changes and the 'outcome' state, which at the time of the interview was positive.

It would be useful if more attention could be paid to defining and assessing such positive outcomes of religious change.

SUMMARY

This chapter looks at some different types of conversion and briefly reviews the cult controversy. The underlying questions are whether the people who convert into a religion do so because they are unhappy (either by disposition or because of experience) and whether conversion can help resolve some psychological ills.

There is evidence to support both these views, though there are problems with methods of investigation.

The chapter concluded with examples drawing attention to the need to study lifelong change processes, and for more attention to be paid to positive outcomes.

5

Women and men: happy to watch the kids?

The roles of women and men in modern society are frequently discussed. As social conditions change, ideologies change, and so we have seen different ideas about the roles that could and should be played by women and men.

The last few decades have seen a proliferation of feminist ideologies. The 1970s saw frustrated women, who felt they could do as good a job as men, particularly in the professions. They saw they were often denied a fair chance to do so. They pointed to the eloquent occupational statistics, where there was a majority of women at the bottom of any hierarchy and a majority of men at the top. They argued for equality of opportunity in employment and promotion. At the same time, they argued that many women are not cut out for a life of home management and childcare. Sexual liberation – in various forms – was also on the agenda: at its most radical, sexual liberation meant *ad lib* promiscuity, lesbianism, contraception and abortion – 'the woman's right to control what happens to her own body'. I've simplified what are really a number of different feminist and related philosophies. Ann Oakley, in her book *Subject Women* (1981), identifies several different forms of feminism. Later, some strands of second-wave feminism put a positive value on 'feminine' but unvalued activities: childbirth, loving and caring for children, homemaking – other feminists, however, discount this move.

By and large, then, many feminist ideologies are antithetical to some of the values and behaviours prescribed or esteemed in many religions. A recent feminist anthology on women in religion carried the title which says it all: *Refusing Holy Orders* (Sahgal and Yuval-Davis, 1992). In practice as well as in theory, feminist ideologies are often associated with antireligious attitudes.

Himmelstein (1986) studied two key antifeminist attitudes: anti-abortion and anti-equal rights amendment. Himmelstein's work was done in the USA in the 1980s. It had been suggested that antifeminist attitudes were related to rural living, dependency on men and lower socio-economic status. In fact, in the sample studied, there was no sign of these effects. Antifeminist beliefs were related only to 'lack of rootedness in religious networks'. One explanation of Himmelstein's finding is that lack of positive experience and social support from a religious group leads to feminist and antireligious attitudes.

Men's and women's roles in religions are very different. The traditional religions have on the whole valued marriage and childbearing, although all have an ascetic tradition in which detachment from family life and asexuality are valued for a minority. Sexual activity is regulated in basically every religion, with home and family fairly central in most. In many societies this is often associated with the almost total disempowerment of women. For example Chang (1991) records that in China until the 1920s women were regarded as the absolute chattels of their husbands. Her grandmother's first marriage was as a concubine to a police general, and she was unable to leave her home, waiting many years for her husband to pay a visit, spied on by the servants. Her grandmother's second husband was more enlightened, allowing her more freedom, but until the 1920s there were absolutely no economic opportunities for women other than domestic service. (Chang, 1991). During the reformation, Luther tried to add some dignity to a similar situation which prevailed in Europe: Bridges and Spilka (1992) write that Protestantism, through Luther, was to re-establish marriage as an honourable state ordained by God, which by absolute prescription confined women to the home, childbearing and childrearing.

Some new religious movements have found that encouragement of the traditional family is a worthwhile selling point, while others have fostered asceticism and still others sexual promiscuity or exploitation especially of women members by male leaders. The issues of sexuality, marriage, family, childbearing and childrearing are central in all religions and have an enormous impact on the lifestyles and identities of women.

Here follow some illustrations of the impact of religion on women's lifestyles.

THE COSTS AND BENEFITS OF THE RELIGIOUS LIFE FOR WOMEN

In this section we shall look at the types of stresses associated with religion, as it relates to women and their lifestyles.

First some Christian examples.

> Mrs R. is a lukewarm Roman Catholic. She married young and had five children quite quickly. They are quite a handful, and there is not a lot of money coming into the house. She is not employed as she has enough to do to see after the children, and Mr R., a labourer, is not bringing in a lot of money. Both Mr and Mrs R. drink 'a bit', and Mrs R.'s doctor has warned her to cut down because of her liver. But it is very difficult: drinking is really her only solace in an uneasy marriage amidst the endless drudgery of seeing after the house and children. She would not leave her family, so the 'little drop, now and then' is a way of opting out without giving up on her obligations.

And this case study is the stuff of the agony columns in the 1950s and 1960s.

> My boyfriend and I have been going out for nearly a year now. We really care deeply for each other and hope to get married in two years when we have enough to buy our own home. Marriage just isn't possible at the moment. He says that if I really cared for him I would do more than just kiss him. I am not sure what to do. I am frightened of losing him, but I have been brought up to believe that sex before marriage is wrong. What should I do?

The agony aunts of the 1950s and 1960s were able to tell their correspondents that if their boyfriends really loved them, they could say gently but firmly 'no' – and the boyfriends' respect for them would grow. By the 1970s the agony aunts couldn't see why a nice girl couldn't say 'yes', and by the 1980s the agony aunts apparently weren't getting that sort of letter any more. Premarital sex had become acceptable, it would seem.

There are estimated to be 2–3 million Moslems living in the UK. A few thousand native British people are said to have converted to Islam (Kose, 1994) but most are first- or second-generation immigrants, mainly from the Indian subcontinent. The majority wish their children to be good Moslems, and mosques and communal organizations are proliferating. Khanum (1992) suggests that boys from Moslem families are not seen to be under serious cultural, religious or sexual threat in state schools, and these schools are seen as necessary for boys to achieve the qualifications they need for success in life. For girls, however, state schools are seen as involving threats to the ideology and sexual purity of Moslem girls. Wealthy Moslems send their daughters to English public and private schools. Others are seeking to establish private single-sex schools to ensure that Moslem girls do not stray very far from orthodoxy. Standards of secular education in these schools are not very high, and the schools are short of money and facilities. Customs differ in different sections of the Moslem community, but the open, bantering or flirtatious encounters between the two sexes that are normative in Western society are strongly discouraged, and many parents will seek suitable marriage partners for their adult children – sometimes carrying out searches in their country of origin.

Here is a Moslem woman, described by Hanifa Khan (unpublished).

Mrs P. is a fairly devout Moslem lady living in West London. She is in her late forties and has a son and a daughter, both in their twenties. Her daughter did not go to a Moslem school as there were none available. As a teenager she became very discontented, saying that she wanted to be free to choose her own friends and grumbling that she had no freedom. About a year ago, she made it clear that she wasn't very interested in her parents looking for a nice boy from a similar background for her. There were frequent arguments. Mr P. blamed it all on Mrs P., saying that she wasn't religious enough when the children were younger. Mrs P. is worried about the effect of her daughter's attitudes on her son, whom she sees as a very good boy. The daughter is now talking about looking for a flat to share with friends.

Here is a young Asian Moslem man, living in the UK (from Grant, 1992).

> H. is a 22-year-old university student. He hopes to study next for a PhD next year. He lives a modern life, and for two years between the ages of 14 and 15 he drank [alcohol, forbidden by Moslem law]. His hair is long and curly, in protest against his family's wishes, and he is sexually experienced. His father wanted him to marry a girl from Pakistan, and found a suitable girl for him, but he didn't want to go along with his father's wishes. The family argued over H.'s future for two or more years. Finally, his father called in a professional mediator. The mediator managed to persuade H. to compromise by pointing out the loss of status and respect H.'s father would have to endure if H. persisted in living a modern life without marrying a suitable wife. H.'s compromise is that he will go through a marriage ceremony in name only. His wife will remain in Pakistan while H. returns to the UK. When immigration is arranged for the wife, she will live with her in-laws, while H. carries on with his modern life, and 'if she is very beautiful' he may fall in love with her. H. feels strongly that 'a man has his needs' and that his future wife should not be allowed to imperil their fulfilment. It remains to be seen whether H. will climb down from his high horse, but meanwhile the prospects for his future wife's happiness seem very dim.

In the Jewish community there is considerable pressure put on women (and men) to get married – to a Jewish partner – and to have children. The more strictly orthodox tend to get married younger and to have more children, but the 'pressures' are reported right across the religious spectrum. Here are some examples.

Ms Z. is enthusiastic about her Judaism. She goes to a lot of adult education groups, and she is quite observant. However she is nearly 30 and still not married. Her mother 'drives her mad', asking her when she is going to settle down with a nice boy. But Ms Z. is not interested in any of the Jewish boys she knows, and she thinks they are not interested in her. She feels more interest from her non-Jewish men friends. But she would not consider marrying a non-Jew, because she feels that would be wrong, and it would 'kill her mother'.

Mrs O. was proud of her Jewish identity, but never really had much to do with Judaism. In fact she prided herself on her emancipation. She tried to bring her daughter up to share her feelings of pride in her Jewish identity, together with her attitude that the actual religious observances were generally unnecessary in contemporary life. Mrs O. was surprised at her bitter disappointment and chagrin when her daughter married a non-Jew and converted to Christianity. It was a double betrayal and a rejection of everything that Mrs O. stood for. Many of Mrs O.'s friends were non-Jews, and marriages between Jews and non-Jews were common in her social circle, and she was not particularly bothered by her daughter's 'marrying-out' – but she was troubled by the conversion.

Levitz (1992) describes the origins of what he calls 'mating-anxiety' in the orthodox-Jewish community.

Several years ago I treated an outwardly cheerful but clinically depressed *yeshiva* [institute for Jewish learning] student who would consciously force himself to smile whenever he was in public, so that when the time would come for *shidduch* introductions [to prospective marriage partners] he would be friendly and affable. For him, mating-anxiety began at age 15, when, after years of observing his parents' anxiety over the difficulties of an older sibling to marry, he began to obsess over his own marriageability. Impression management became his strategy for coping with an anxiety whose resolution was several years away.

For the ninth-grade students of a prominent girls' *yeshiva* who during school breaks would go down to New York's diamond district in order to look at wedding rings, mating-anxiety became a conscious psychological phenomenon at about the age of 14.

For another group of sixth-grade girls in a prominent Brooklyn elementary *yeshiva*, there were symptoms of mating-anxiety at the age of 11. These were the girls whose poor school performance kept them in the lowest of three academic tracks. Since the window of their classroom faced the street, the girls covered it with paper drapes, specifically not to be identified as students in the lowest class, a potential stigma for a future *shidduch* [prospective marriage partner].

It is conceivable that mating-anxiety begins perhaps at an even younger age, particularly for girls. A popular children's story relates the story of two chickens, Bayla and Kayla. Bayla, whose characteristics are both dutiful and compliant, listens obediently to each of Mama Hen's requests. She helps her cook, bake, clean their coop, wash the dishes and tend to the other chicks. Kayla, on the other hand, portrayed as selfish and ungenerous, never finds the time to help out. The story concludes with a rather pointed message: Bayla, the obedient daughter, claims her just reward by getting married to the best rooster in the yard, while Kayla remains unwed and alone. The theme of marriage as reward, and singlehood as reproof for past behaviours is made clear and unmistakable to even the very young.

But marriage itself imposes behaviour expectations that are too difficult for some. The following case, described by Fisch (1992) is of an ultra-orthodox young Jewish man.

X was 21 and in good health apart from mild obsessive personality traits up to the time of his wedding. There was no psychiatric family history. One week after the wedding he began to express odd obsessional fears concerning contact with rust, avoided any contact with iron, walked in a bizarre, unnatural, ritualized way and spent hours in the bathroom washing and cleaning himself . . . He expressed psychotic guilt while his mood was elevated, and his behaviour was expansive, irritable and negativistic. Drug treatment . . . did not change his condition over the next two years. He did not make any comments about his marriage except for worry about retarded ejaculation in the first few days after the wedding. He was eventually diagnosed as a chronic undifferentiated schizophrenic.

Fisch describes several cases of psychosis precipitated by marriage in the ultra-orthodox Jewish community, seeing this as a largely culture-bound phenomenon.

Many of the examples I have given are to do with boundary maintenance: people having difficulties over maintaining standards of behaviour. Is boundary-maintenance worth it? Does it cause more stress, more distress and more illness than the absence of boundaries? Here are some examples of scenarios cited by Finlay-Jones (1989). The stressful events and difficulties were experienced by women recruited from general practice attenders in the Regents Park area in London. Only one-third of the women interviewed were currently married. Three of the nine 'severe' events cited by Finlay-Jones appear to involve stress resulting from living without some of the traditional religious boundaries surrounding sexual behaviour.

A young woman became pregnant despite using contraception. The boyfriend's family had opposed their earlier attempt to become engaged. His elderly parents were relying on him to support them financially, and opposed his marriage.

A woman in her twenties began an affair with a married man who taught at the college where she was a student.

A divorced woman in her thirties was thrown out by the man she'd been living with. He was also her boss, so she'd lost her man, her job and her home.

No systematic study has been made of the question as to whether boundary-maintenance is worth it. The methodological and conceptual difficulties would be considerable. My impression is that lack of boundaries may give rise to different and possibly more frequent and severe stresses than boundary maintenance. This is borne out by the following observations.

Among social anthropologists, Kupferman (1979) for instance discusses the practice of restricting sexual intercourse between married couples to times when then the wife is not menstruating. This practice is almost invariably bound to an edifice of religious justification. Kupferman concludes that wife-beating is more likely in societies which do not practice menstrual taboos, concluding that boundary maintenance may be associated with a decreased use of violence.

Another study which has looked at religion in relation to marital violence is described by Brinkerhoff, Grandin and Lupri (1992). This was a Canadian study, using questionnaire measures. The overwhelming majority of the respondents were at least nominally Christian. The study provides valuable data on the relations between religiosity and physical abuse, in one religious–cultural context. Religiosity was assessed by a question on affiliation, and another on frequency of church attendance. Violence was assessed from answers to eight questions on the Conflict Tactics Scale (CTS). Other questions on the scale look at nonphysical violence, such as verbal abuse. The eight questions to do with physical violence were:

1. threw object at another;
2. pushed, grabbed or shoved the other;
3. slapped the other;
4. kicked, bit, or hit the other with a fist;
5. hit or tried to hit the other;
6. beat up the other;
7. threatened the other with a knife or gun;
8. used knife or gun on the other.

Husbands and wives were asked how often they had committed each of these violent acts against their partners in response to conflict during the past year. There are several problems with the CTS. The main one is that it doesn't take account of the damage done, which is usually greater in the case of male violence. It also doesn't take account of whether the violence was self-defensive, which is usually the case with female violence. With these reservations in mind we can record some of Brinkerhoff, Grandin and Lupri's conclusions. These were that spousal violence in men is unrelated to religious denomination; the religious denominations were categorized into Catholic, mainline Protestant, conservative Protestant, other and none.

However, conservative Protestant women appear to abuse their spouses more often than do women from other denominations. It appeared then that strong beliefs in religious patriarchy do not appear to generate spousal abuse in men. However, religious activity does not appear to mitigate violence either, particularly among the moderate attenders.

Argyle and Beit-Hallahmi (1975), in a review of work up till the mid-1970s, concluded that the more religious were the more likely to be maritally adjusted and to report greater happiness in marriage. Religion and agreement about religion were among the most important factors predicting marital adjustment. Argyle and Beit-Hallahmi conclude that religion may draw people together in a context where the ideals of love and family life are prominent.

A most detailed examination of religion in relation to forms of stress has been reported by Brown and Prudo (1981), Prudo *et al.* (1981) and Prudo, Harris and Brown (1984). They compared women in a rural community (the Hebrides) with women in an inner-city environment (Camberwell). Of the Hebridean women interviewed, 63% were churchgoing, while only 14% of Camberwell women were churchgoers. Prudo, Harris and Brown distinguished three different types of life-event:

- **regular events** – these are standard transitions, found and expected in all populations, such as illnesses, examinations, marriages, births, deaths;
- **irregular events** – these are less standard transitions, such as moving house, changing social ties, changes to do with work;
- **disruptive events** – these are transitions in which the social fabric is threatened through neglect or disruptions, such as burglaries, assaults, divorces, suicides.

City women were more likely than rural women to experience severe irregular and disruptive events. Among rural women, the less 'integrated' (nonchurchgoing, noncrofting [farm smallholding]) women were more likely to experience irregular and disruptive events. Regular events were as likely in rural as in urban women, and in 'integrated' women as in less 'integrated' women.

All in all, then, the evidence suggests that religiosity may be associated with perhaps lower levels of some forms of stress, in spite of the problems which may be associated with maintaining religious standards (Loewenthal, 1993).

GENDER, CHILDCARE, RELIGION AND MENTAL ILLNESS

In this section I shall looks at the patterns of mental illness as they relate to gender, particularly in Western Europe and North America. A key theme that emerges is the question of tradition. There are several ideas about which suggest that traditional women's roles in contemporary modern society, and women's roles in traditional societies and religions, may impact upon women's mental health. A particularly popular idea is that traditional societies and religions are patriarchal: social organization is such that power is vested in the male head of the family unit. Women are powerless.

Gender and mental illness: referral studies

In Western society, women and men show different patterns of different mental illnesses. Women are more likely to seek treatment for psychological illnesses than men, especially depressive disorders. Men are somewhat more likely than women to seek treatment for schizophrenia and alcohol or other drug dependency. Cochrane (1993) quotes the age-adjusted rates of admission (per 100 000) to mental hospitals in England in 1981 (Table 5.1).

Table 5.1   Rates of admission to mental hospitals in England in 1981 (adapted from Cochrane, 1993)

Diagnosis	Male (per 100 000)	Female (per 100,000)
Depression	101	200
All other diagnoses	245	255

These conclusions are based on studies looking at rates of referral for psychiatric help. The true rate or prevalence of different mental illnesses in the community may not be mirrored in the proportions of people actually seeking treatment. Those who behave violently, and their victims, may not seek help and we know little about the prevalence of such behaviour. Depressive illnesses in men may be more common than the referral figures suggest. Many men are not willing to reveal details of depressed mood and symptoms. The 'true' rates of different mental illnesses (prevalences) may be different from the referral rates, which of course are based on those who seek treatment.

Cochrane concludes that in England the high referral rates of women for depression and related disorders are probably due to two effects. One is that the relatively powerless position of women in society makes them develop styles of coping that are already akin to depression; Jones and Cochrane's (1981) study found that people's concepts of a 'normal woman' and a 'mentally-ill woman' were much more alike than their concepts of a 'normal man' and a 'mentally-ill man'. The second effect is that women are more socially isolated than men, which makes them more vulnerable to psychological disorder when under stress and more likely to have to seek professional help. Married men are more likely to be supported emotionally by their wives than wives by husbands; men are more likely to be in employment and thus have a second system of social support outside the family.

Thus the gender differences in mental illnesses are explained by Cochrane as due to the differential situations of women and men in marriage and in employment.

Cochrane quotes Carmen, Russo and Miller (1981) as follows:

> Since men hold the power and authority, women are rewarded for developing a set of psychological characteristics that accommodate to and please men. Such traits – submissiveness, compliance, passivity, helplessness, weakness – have been encouraged in women and incorporated into some prevalent psychological theories in which they are defined as innate or inevitable characteristics of women. However they are more accurately conceptualized as learned behaviours by which all subordinate group members attempt to ensure their survival . . . behaviours such as inhibition, passivity and submissiveness do not lead to favourable outcomes and play a role in the development of psychological problems.

Another suggestion is Gove's (1972) view that women are more likely to become depressed than men because they have only one principle source of satisfaction: their homemaker role. This role is often devalued: unstructured, invisible and of low status. Men by contrast have a work role and a domestic role. Gove suggests that difficulties in one role may be lightened by the other, which can provide support and self-esteem.

Paykel (1991) considers that gender differences in ways of expressing distress, in social situation and in biology, all combine to make women more likely to be depressed than men. Paykel concludes that gender differences in depression show up in community studies, as well as in referral studies. But do they?

Gender and mental illness: community studies

Studies of mental illnesses in community settings, where representative samples of populations are interviewed and assessed, should give a better idea of the prevalence of different disorders. Brown and Harris's (1978) work, discussed above, is an example of a community study. They suggested that class differences in prevalence of depression could be explained by differing social factors. Working-class women, who are more likely to suffer from clinical depression than middle-class women, are also more likely to suffer from stress: a 'severely' threatening life event or major long-term difficulty. They are also more likely to be vulnerable to depressive illness when under stress: to have experienced loss of a parent in childhood, to have three or more young children to care for, not to have a confidant in their husband or other friend, and not to have paid employment outside the home.

But what do studies of mental illnesses in the community tell us about gender differences in patterns of mental illness? Unfortunately Brown and Harris's work did not examine gender differences – either in prevalences or in causes of depression. Cochrane's studies of self-reported symptoms in different communities in Britain do not appear to examine gender differences. There are a number of community studies which look at gender differences in prevalence of depression in different communities, and which also look at gender differences in the causes of depression and in the handling of depression, including seeking help. Some work looks at specific samples and compares men's and women's scores on psychometric tests.

Table 5.2 lists some means for a mood checklist (the Usual Mood Check List: UMCL) that we administered to groups of University applicants, students and adolescents in secondary schools in the UK in 1991–2.

Table 5.2 Mean scores of males and females on a checklist measure of mood (1991–2).

	Male (n = 28)	Female (n = 110)	Significance of difference (unrelated t)
Anxiety	2.8	2.9	*n.s.
Depression	2.7	2.0	$p < 0.025$
Hostility	2.7	2.4	*n.s.
Low self-esteem	2.4	2.5	*n.s.

* n.s. = non significant

The means are the numbers of poor-mood words that subjects said usually applied to them, plus the numbers of good-mood words that subjects said did not usually apply to them. The samples are samples of convenience and there were more women and girls than men and boys, and more single than married people. There is no reason to suppose that the people tested were not representative of potential and actual students and adolescents. There are slight differences between males and females on anxiety, hostility and low self-esteem, but none of these are statistically significant. The difference is significant in the case of depression, and it is in the direction that the men and boys are more depressed than the women and girls.

Table 5.3 gives the correlations between a well-known measure of depression (the Beck Depression Inventory: BDI) and gender.

Table 5.3 Correlations between scores on the Revised Beck Depression Inventory and gender, in six samples of patients (from Beck and Steer, 1987)

	Mixed diagnoses	Major depression	Major depression (one episode)	Dysthymic disorder (recurrent)	Alcoholic	Heroin-addicted
n	248	113	168	99	105	211
Correlation with gender	0.11	0.04	0.06	0.05	0.16	0.17*

* $p < 0.05$

In the BDI, subjects·are asked to say which depression symptoms they have recently been suffering from, for example, sad or depressed mood, pessimism (no hope for the future, belief that nothing will work out well), and/or a sense of failure.

The correlations with gender are low, and (with the exception of heroin addicts) nonsignificant. Another study from the same stable (Steer, Beck and Brown, 1989) again showed no gender differences in number of symptoms reported and BDI scores. Again the subjects in the study were psychiatric patients, so it could be said that no gender differences would be expected in groups of people who have already been diagnosed as psychiatrically ill.

Another well-known measure, the Eysenck Personality Inventory (EPI) measures neuroticism, as a trait rather than as a transitory state. Some of the items, at face value, are about depression (others are about anxiety). The authors (Eysenck and Eysenck, 1964) say that, although they eliminated items that showed major differences between the sexes from the test, there were still significant gender differences in that women generally score higher on neuroticism than men. However we do not know whether this is due to differences on the 'depression' items, the 'anxiety' items, or both.

Some work suggests that the relations between gender and depression vary with age or cohort, and with whether the community is 'traditional'. A study by Carta *et al.* (1991) involved psychiatric assessment of nearly 400 adults from two mining villages in Sardinia. This community study showed no gender differences in depression, though women were more likely to be anxious.

Another study in a traditional community, by Gonzalez de Rivera *et al.* (1991), however, found women higher than men on several self-reported indices of subjective suffering, including depression. This study was in the Canary islands, and tested 570 adults on the SCL-90-R.

Another study in a traditional community, on older traditional and orthodox Jews in London, showed somewhat similar effects, with women tending to be higher than men on self-reported anxious mood. However, in this study, the men were significantly higher than the women on depressed mood (Loewenthal *et al.*, 1993). We were able to compare married couples with each other, and found that husbands were significantly more depressed than their wives. The correlates of depression were different in men and women. Women tended to be more depressed when they were not at the hub of a family network, while men were more depressed if they were not economically active, that is, if they were retired or unemployed. The men in this study might have been more depressed than the women because the sample was of fairly old people (the average age was over 50), and men were thus more likely to be retired or unemployed than women and to be isolated from a family network. I must confess, though, that when the results first started to come in, I was pretty startled. I had accepted the prevailing idea that depression was a woman's problem – and I thought all the things that I suppose people think when 'the experiment doesn't work': maybe there's something wrong with the sample, the measure or some other aspect of the method. Gradually I began to talk to other researchers about this problem, and to look at more of the published research. I began to come to the conclusion that the view that women are more depression-prone than men is by no means the sacred truth that it's sometimes given out to be.

There are community studies that report depressive illness as more likely in women than men. Such findings tend to occur in nontraditional societies: Finland (Lehtinen *et al.*, 1990), Sweden (Rorsman *et al.*, 1990), New Zealand (Joyce *et al.*, 1990) (however in this study, in the youngest cohort, men had a higher prevalence than the women), the UK (e.g. Bebbington *et al.*, 1989) and the USA (e.g. Murphy and Leighton, 1989).

Notice that in the New Zealand study just mentioned (Joyce *et al.*, 1990), there was a suggestion that there might be generational, age or cohort effects in the differential prevalence of depression among men and women. Women had higher prevalence of depression than men in the older cohorts, but the younger men were more likely to be depressed than the women.

A study which takes this further was reported by Silverstein and Perlick (1991). They looked at historical changes in gender differences in depression in the USA. They conclude that gender differences in depression among people 40 years of age and older were high among cohorts that reached adolescence during periods of increasing opportunity for female achievement. Among cohorts that reached adolescence during periods of stable or decreasing opportunities for women, gender differences in depression were not significant at any age.

An Australian study may be an illustration of this effect. Hong and Grambower (1986) looked at gender differences in approximately 500 college students on a number of factors including depression-proneness, self-efficacy and self-concept, and found no gender differences on any factor except belief in human benevolence. Hong and Grambower suggest that this finding is a reflection of the values of this cohort of college students.

Cochrane (1983) concludes that sex differences in mental health are not universal across time and place. He suggests that

> although reliable runs of figures over a long time-period are not readily available, it appears that the excess of female over male rates of mental hospital admissions is a relatively recent phenomenon. Lowe and Garratt (1959) cite figures which show that early in this century men were somewhat more likely to be admitted to mental hospital than women and that substantially higher female rates have only been recorded since the Second World War. Equally there are societies, and indeed ethnic groups within our own society, where the pattern is reversed and in fact men have higher rates of mental illness than do women. This is true in the Republic of Ireland and in Scotland.

Cochrane's arguments here apply to referrals, and to all mental disorders warranting hospital admission, but they may equally apply to specific diagnostic categories.

We can see, then, that in community samples there is by no means a universal tendency for women to emerge as more likely to be depressed than men. The best generalization that can be made is that gender differences in depression (and possibly anxiety) are related to whether or not the society or group under study is 'traditional'; in nontraditonal societies there are age and/or cohort effects. In traditional societies there are less likely to be gender differences in depression. Where there are differences, these may be in the direction that men are more depressed than women. One explanation for age/cohort effects is that women are more likely to be more depressed than men in eras of increasing opportunity for women.

One way of understanding this might be through Higgins's (1987) suggestions about the relations between perceptions of self and mood. Higgins suggests that depression is characteristic of disappointment, a state which comes about when there is a discrepancy between the hoped-for self and the actual self. Anxiety comes about when there is a discrepancy between the self as it ought to be and the actual self. We could see from this that depressed mood and possibly depressive illness might be more likely in conditions of social change – both economic prosperity and recession would be associated with disappointments and losses, for instance. In prosperity, with career opportunities for women, the expectation is set up that a woman can be economically active and successful, and women may perceive any lack of success as more disappointing because of normative expectations. In terms of recession, perceived disappointments and losses would be the result of actual events of the kind that are unfortunately common in times of economic depression and recession.

Sociologists sometimes distinguish between complex and simple societies. Complex societies are characterized by social change and a good deal of fluidity in roles, and a corollary of this is not only social advancement but disappointments when advances are not made and disappointments about losses of role and status. Simple societies are characterized by fixed roles. Everyone knows their station in life, and most of us (if we live in such a society) feel obliged to do our bit. The sense of obligation is likely to be higher in conditions of social stability, with anxiety at the possibility of failure to meet obligations.

All this is very *post hoc*, but it goes some way to account for the conclusion that gender differences in mental illness might be to do with social conditions rather than something intrinsic to gender.

In this discussion of gender and mental illness I have dealt at some length with the literature on depression, and also touched on the issue of anxiety. Both are unfortunately very common and very unpleasant conditions. I am conscious that I have said little about schizophrenia, another very common and unpleasant condition, or about any other psychiatric illnesses. I believe that the general conclusions that I have reached so far may be equally applicable to psychiatric conditions other than depression and anxiety.

Gender and mental illness: explanations

Before leaving this long discussion of gender and mental illness, I would like to review some of the explanations of gender differences in mental illness, in view of the conclusions I have reached so far.

The first explanation of gender differences in mental illness has to do with biology. An eminent supporter of this view is Paykel (1991). He points out that referral rates for depression are

about twice as high in women as in men. No-one is really disput-
ing this. One explanation is that women are more likely to seek
help and that therefore there are large numbers of men in the
community who are untreated because they have not sought
help. This is possible and I should like to return to some variations on this shortly. Paykel also points out that depressed men
are more likely to kill themselves or to become alcoholic than are
depressed women. In both these scenarios, the men would not
appear as depressed in either referral or prevalence statistics. In
spite of this latter argument, Paykel goes on to assert that the 'sex
ratio . . . applies equally in studies of community prevalence'. I
don't think that all the evidence reviewed here supports this.
Paykel, however, accepts that there are cohort effects on gender
differences. It is hard to accept the assertion that the sex ratio of
depression (2:1 women:men) applies **equally** in the community
(as in the clinic). Paykel goes on to suggest that biological explanations are plausible, although hard to test. Social-situational
factors, and gender differences in the way distress is expressed,
together with biological differences, all may account for the fact
that most of the female excess in depression occurs in women
who are aged 25–40, who are married and who have children.

A second explanation of gender differences in depression rests
on the assumption that women are in a less powerful position
than men. Cochrane's discussion of this position has already been
quoted. Rosenfield (1992) provides some evidence supporting the
view that housework has a lowering effect upon the wellbeing of
both men and women. Rosenfield also suggests that relative
income (whether one is earning more than one's spouse) also
relates to wellbeing. Rosenfield suggests that unemployment is
associated with lower power: less resources and less prestige. This
is often the lot of women, but the argument applies equally to
men when they are unemployed. Rosenfield's data and conclusions however may not apply to all societies. In Israel, for
instance, Hobfoll (1991) reported that women were more likely
than men to report depressed mood under stress (child's illness),
but this was due to women being more overloaded than men, not
to a difference in personal or social resources. Prestige and
resources may be available to women in traditional societies, even
if they are not gainfully employed. The whole argument rests on
the universality of the association between gainful employment
on the one hand and power (prestige and resources) on the other.

Traditional religions often accord at least lip service to the idea that homemaking is valuable and prestigious. However, scientific scrutiny needs to be made of acceptable indices of the prestige and resources of homemaking women in traditional religious groups and societies.

Let us look at some other explanations of gender differences in mental illness. Another possibility is that women and men differ in their habits of thinking. One suggestion is that episodes of depression may be prolonged and possibly more severe if the sufferer engages in **ruminating**. Nolen-Hoeksema (1991) says that rumination involves focusing on symptoms and their possible causes and consequences. This inhibits behaviour and thinking distracting the sufferer from their depression. Rumination also inhibits problem-solving thinking and behaviour, and has a negatively-biasing effect on thinking. Women are more likely to ruminate than men. One possible reason for this may be powerlessness, particularly lack of resources, but clinicians, particularly cognitive therapists, would be keen to try to encourage the sufferer to seek solutions to their problems and/or ways of seeing things more positively.

A popular explanation of gender differences in mental illness, particularly depression, is that distressed men may develop psychopathologies other than depression. Men who attempt suicide are more likely to actually kill themselves than are women who attempt suicide. This leaves more depressed women to be diagnosed as suffering from depression. There is a psychoanalytic view that schizophrenia – which is a little more likely to be diagnosed in men than in women – may be a response to an underlying depression. There is a lot of evidence suggesting that in contemporary 'Western' society, alcohol consumption is more likely among men than in women as a response to stress and distress. Golding, Burnam and Wells (1990) found that drinking among white and Mexican-American men in the USA was associated with depressive symptoms. There was no such association for women. Berger and Adesso (1991) looked at men and women, depressed and nondepressed, in a 15-minute drinking session. All subjects were 'social drinkers'. The main feature of the rather complicated findings was that depressed men drank more – this included taking bigger sips! – than other subjects – and drinking had more anti-depressant effect for depressed men than for nondepressed men or depressed women. Ball and Clare (1990) suggest that a high incidence of depression in London Jewish men compared to men of other groups is because men from other groups who become depressed are more likely to take to drinking, and would be more likely to get a primary diagnosis of alcoholism than of depression. More men than women may have learnt that an appropriate response to distress is 'I need a drink'.

To return to Paykel's suggestion that women are more likely to report depression than women, the evidence just mentioned adds up to the picture that depressed men are more likely to develop symptoms that will lead to diagnoses other than depression. There is also the possibility that men are simply 'macho' and unwilling to disturb a competent or tough self-image by admitting to depressed mood or illness.

> Mr M. is a jolly, lively, life-and-soul-of-the-party type. He has plenty of friends, but relations with his immediate family are strained, probably because of his volatile temper. He has a number of business and family problems, and has been sleeping poorly and losing weight. But he says he is not really a worrier because he likes to get on and take action when things worry him. He is not depressed, definitely not, because he enjoys life and doesn't let things get him down.

Mr M. could not be diagnosed as depressed since, in spite of some depressive symptoms, he does not think his mood is depressed. Perhaps Mr M.'s state is typical of that of many men. Mr M. would be reluctant to admit to depression. Vredenburg, Krames and Flett (1986) found that depressed men were more likely to report sex-role-appropriate symptoms such as work-related problems and somatic concerns than inappropriate symptoms like crying. The effect is heightened by the likelihood that doctors and psychiatrists are reported to be more likely to diagnose depression in women than in men. In a North American study, Potts, Burnam and Wells (1991) examined 500-plus clinicians' diagnoses of 23 000-plus patients. The patients also had a standardized assessment of depressive disorder, the Diagnostic Interview Schedule (DIS). The main finding was that among the patients who met the DIS criteria for depressive disorder, the clinicians were less likely to diagnose depression in the men than in the women.

So depressed men may be more likely than depressed women to develop a syndrome that is not primarily depressive in its presenting symptoms. They may be less likely to seek help, and they may be less likely to be recognized as depressed by mental health professionals.

Sorenson, Rutter and Aneshensel (1991) suggested that the higher prevalence of depression in women in the community may be due to the fact that women tend to become depressed at an earlier age than men.

One more suggestion is that stress levels differ in women and in men. Women may suffer more depression-inducing stress. Women may have suffered more from certain types of abuse in childhood (Cutler and Nolen-Hoeksema, 1991). Hobfoll (1991) found Israeli women more likely than men to report depressed mood, and this did not seem to the result of poorer resources or poorer use of resources; Hobfoll thought the women were suffering from role overload. When under stress, they were more likely to find they could not meet the demands seen to be placed upon them. Newman (1986) in a North American study, looked at stressors (hardships) in women and men in relation to depression. Stress (hardships) had an equal effect in both men and women, in leading to depressive syndrome; women were found to report more of certain hardships than men. These were:

- absence of a spouse;
- social isolation;
- financial difficulties;
- chronic health problems.

This view would explain sex differences in depression in terms of sex differences in amount of stress. Thus women are not more 'prone' to depression. The argument runs that if men were in women's shoes, they would also be depressed.

I believe that all this suggests that psychological illnesses are related to social and cultural factors – this is not to exclude a contributory role for constitutional factors. Thus sex or gender as such may not be related directly to mental illness. The relationship is indirect. It is mediated by the different roles and expectations of men and women in different social groups.

I conclude this section by repeating that the widespread view that women are more depression-prone than men seems to be a great over-simplification. We certainly cannot conclude that in traditional religious groups women are more depressed than men, and that this is because of the patriarchal nature of traditional religion. We cannot draw the first conclusion because there is no evidence to support this. If anything, the evidence suggests that in conditions of modernity (and postmodernity), women are more likely to be depressed than in traditional societies. We cannot draw the second conclusion because, while it is likely that many traditional religious groups are patriarchal, the evidence suggests that this may not be more depressing for women than for men.

The anxiety disorders and the psychoses deserve more investigation, in the context of gender differences in relation to the incidence and prevalence of mental disorders in different cultural and religious contexts.

Marriage and mental illness

Marriage is said to have more of a 'protective' effect for men than for women (Cochrane, 1983). Table 5.4 shows rates of mental hospital admission for men and women, by marital status, in the early 1970s for England and Wales.

Table 5.4 Rates of admission to mental hospital per 100 000 population by sex and marital status, England and Wales, 1973 (from Cochrane, 1983)

Marital status	Males	Females	Ratio M:F
Single	663	623	0.93
Married	257	433	1.68
Widowed	752	720	0.96
Divorced	1959	1596	0.81
Married:single ratio	0.39	0.70	

Note that marriage appears to be 'protective' for both men and women, but considerably more so for men. A more recent study of hospital admissions, reported by Bebbington (1987), looked at first admissions for affective disorders (depressive neuroses and affective psychoses) in the UK for the 1982–5 period. The widowed and the divorced showed higher admission rates for all disorders studied than did the single and the married. In other words, marriage as such did not appear to be as 'protective' as in the figures quoted by Cochrane for a decade previously (however Cochrane is quoting figures for all admissions, for all psychiatric conditions). A more recent community study looked at prevalences of depression, anxiety and other symptoms in 299 women and 271 men (Gonzalez de Rivera *et al.*, 1991) in the Canary Islands. It was found that separated people and the widowed were more likely to suffer from the symptoms studied than were the single and the married. This study used a Spanish version of the SCL-90-R and assessed a wide variety of psychiatric symptoms including psychoticism, hostility, paranoid ideation, obsessionality and phobia as well as the familiar enemies depression and anxiety.

However, causality is hard to determine. For example, higher referral rates and prevalence for mental illnesses in single and divorced people may reflect a greater difficulty in getting married and staying married in people with psychological problems. For widowed and divorced people, the effects of bereavement and divorce on mental health are likely to be adverse, and could precipitate psychological illness. It may be a bit misleading to think of marriage as 'protective', partly because there are other factors associated with nonmarried states that may have little to do with protection and social support.

Much of my own research has been in the orthodox Jewish community in Britain, where marriage is religiously encouraged and childbearing – especially among the more orthodox – is also religiously encouraged. Goshen-Gottstein (1987), in a discussion of ultra-orthodox communities in Israel, suggests that the 'repressive' socialization practices of ultra-orthodox Jews in Jerusalem carry different mental health risks for men and women. Men and boys are encouraged to devote almost all waking hours, when not in prayer, to the study of Torah. Women are to devote themselves to caring for (usually) very large families. However no quantification or comparison with other groups is offered.

Witztum, Dasberg and Greenberg (1990), in a study in the ultra-orthodox Jewish community in Israel, suggest that marriage among orthodox Jews may precipitate psychological breakdown, especially in men. This observation may apply specifically to the types of men in Witztum and colleagues's catchment area, who may feel it is very important to be devoted to religious study, and who find this a little difficult to reconcile with the provider role. Fisch (1992) reports similar findings to Witztum, Dasberg and Greenberg.

Biale, in a historical paper (1983), looks at the effects of marriage in Eastern European Jewish men. Traditionally, parents of marriageable daughters would try to find religious and scholarly husbands for their daughters, and would then offer to maintain the young couple for a specified number of years while the son-in-law continued with his religious learning. It was often expected that the son-in-law would bring prestige to his in-laws by becoming a rabbi or other important communal figure. Sometimes the son-in-law or the daughter would help in the family business, or start their own business. Marriage was contracted at a relatively early age. Girls are considered adult, in Jewish law, at 12 and boys at 13, and couples would often be married as soon as they attained religious maturity. Biale suggests that the arrangement could work well, for it licensed adolescent sexuality while providing a sheltered environment from which the young couple could slowly emerge and find their feet, socially and economically.

However the arrangement could prove disastrous. Biale's discussion deals with 19th-century *maskilim* – those who were disaffected with traditional Judaism and who worked to spread the 'enlightenment', encouraging secular learning and the adoption of a more assimilated dress and lifestyle. The primary rebellion was against the *heder* (school). In memoir after memoir, both the *heder* and the *melamed* (teacher) are presented as the very antithesis of (warm and loving) home and parents: the boy is beaten and abused and his love of learning squelched. When the young boy married, his in-laws may have given him a home which matched his parents' for warmth, love and care – or it may have matched the memory of school.

Biale is interested in the probably less common case of an unsatisfactory relationship between the newly married man and his in-laws. He quotes memoirs of early marriage which indicate a considerable degree of both anger and depression: 'honey mixed with poison', 'the kiss of death', 'adolescence is portrayed as premature old age', 'the feeling that one has failed at the very outset of life'. Biale's argument of course is not focused on the distress and psychopathologies engendered in these particular cultural/religious conditions, but on the ideological activity which Biale sees as a consequence of the particular forms of distress described. Nevertheless, Biale provides us with a vivid description of traditions and their associated mental health risks and benefits which to an extent are perpetuated in the communities studied by Goshen-Gottstein and by Witztum, Dasberg and Greenberg: parents of marriageable daughters may expect to provide substantially for the married couple, even though they are unlikely to live under the parental roof, and relatively early marriage, in the late teens, is often regarded as desirable.

These examples show that in a religious-cultural context where marriage is a valued state, normatively associated with a high degree of various forms of social support, there are still mental health risks.

However, one would expect that the married state would generally be associated with less distress and psychopathology in minority religious groups that value the married state, to at least the same extent as in the general community. In the Jewish community, Fernando (1975) and Loewenthal *et al.* (1993) found this to be the case for women, but there was no association, in either direction, for men between being married and any of the distress measures used. The latter study used checklist measures of depression, anxiety and hostility, and looked at community samples of women and men. Samples were from two types of Jewish community, the strictly or 'ultra'-orthodox, and the more moderately or traditionally observant. Women who were functioning as wives and mothers, and men as providers, were less depressed. Single and widowed Jewish women and unemployed and retired Jewish men were the more depressed. In the groups we studied, divorced people were fairly rare. A few years ago, we were trying to interview orthodox Jewish women and noticed that widows seemed particularly prone to say that they felt they couldn't be of any interest. Single Jewish women feel their lack of role, and perceive their status as transitional: 'when I got engaged I really began to feel I was somebody'. Childless women may also feel at a loss: 'people don't know what to say to me'. This marginalization is the downside of the coin in a society which accords esteem to the normative married women who is producing many children.

We have seen that in contemporary general society, where especially in cities the explicit influence of traditional religion is low, marriage has been shown to be not as good for women as for men. Men are more 'protected' from psychological illnesses by marriage than are women. The lack of esteem given to the mother role may be reflected in the greater vulnerability – reported in some cohorts – of the mother of young children to depression (Brown and Harris, 1978). However the general tendency for the married state to be associated with better mental health is certainly true for men, and – with some qualifications – also holds for women.

In Islam, marriage and childbearing are highly valued. However men appear to have more powerful sanctions against their wives than in Christian and Jewish societies. A woman is compelled to accept a divorce, and once divorced, may be in a very weak position, economically and socially (Khan, unpublished). The implications of this for mental health still have to be explored. One possibility is that women may accept conditions of married life that could be quite distressing, rather than face the social penalties incurred by divorce. Of course, a brighter possibility is that greater effort may be invested in making married life at least tolerable, and hopefully contented. Cochrane (1984) reports that the largest Moslem group in the UK, those from Pakistan, have a low referral rate for mental illnesses, but a fairly high rate of psychological symptoms (similar to that for native British) in a community survey. Cochrane suggests that Moslem families may have ways of coping with psychological distress, for example by sending depressed women back to Pakistan for a refreshing break and renewal of family ties, so that professional help is less likely to be needed. There are however no data on the relationship between marital status and distress or psychiatric status in the Moslem community. There is no reason to suppose that married Moslems are more likely to suffer from psychological illnesses.

Indian immigrants to Britain are largely Hindus and Sikhs. Their lower level of psychological symptoms in community studies is probably related to their higher degree of educational and academic success (Cochrane, 1984). Close-knit families are valued; in Hinduism women appear to have very little economic or other power in marriage, but many second-generation Hindus, who often have high levels of education, adopt many Western middle-class marriage norms. The effects of all this on mental health have yet to be discovered, though Firth (in preparation) suggests that there may be some sadness and guilt for both women and men in compromising traditional religious observances with Western conditions.

In the major traditional religions, marriage is generally encouraged and children are highly valued. The limited evidence suggests that, although there are some specific risks, mental health is generally associated – in both men and women – with the fulfilment of religiously valued roles in family life.

Childcare and mental illness

Childcaring roles are very highly esteemed in most traditional religions, but are they good for mental health?

Loewenthal (1988a) reported on Hasidic-Jewish women who said they felt positive fulfilment and purpose in running a Jewish home. A recent letter in a newspaper published for strictly observant Jews echoes this point forcefully: '. . . after spending a day like a true woman of valour, by simply dressing her children, feeding her family and seeing to their needs, she need not have any empty feelings whatsoever, and if she does then there is definitely something seriously wrong' (Pinter, 1990). Although this letter suggests that 'empty feelings' would not be socially acceptable, it highlights the point that homemaking is something that women in some communities may congratulate themselves on doing.

By contrast, Brown and Harris (1978), quoted above, suggested that women in Camberwell, South London, were more vulnerable to depression if they had no work outside the home and had several young children to care for.

However, other work has failed to confirm these particular findings of Brown and Harris, though they could be applicable to the particular group of urban women studied. Brown and Harris (1986) suggested that the kind of woman in Camberwell, in the 1970s, who finished up with several young children to care for might be suffering from low self-esteem, and it is this psychological factor, rather than childcare as such, that might make women vulnerable to depression under particular types of stress.

Loewenthal and Goldblatt (1993) reviewed work on the relations between family size and depression in women, concluding that since the Brown and Harris (1978) work, several studies had failed to replicate the effects of family size upon the onset of depression. Some studies show an association in the opposite direction. Childlessness, when it is unwanted (involuntary infertility) may be associated with depression (Callan and Hennesey 1988). One Italian study (Calzeroni *et al.*, 1990) concluded that suicide attempts (often associated with severe depression) were less likely in those with larger families. Greene (1989) found that hopelessness was associated with the lack of young children; hopelessness is often said to be an important component of depressive illness, but Greene suggested that this might not always be true.

Loewenthal and Goldblatt looked at some of the different depression symptoms associated with family size in Jewish women. Not having dependent children was associated with hopelessness, as Greene also reported. There were also associations between some family size indices and the absence of other symptoms of depression (early waking, loss of concentration and brooding). In this group of women, however, family size was strongly associated with religiosity, and it is possible that the effects were not due to family size as such, but to some aspect of religiosity. Further analysis however showed that religiosity was associated with the absence of a quite different set of symptoms: depressed mood, loss of interest, suicide plans, early waking and retardation were all less likely in the more religious. The lives of the more religious were just as stressful as the lives of the less religious, and the indices of family size went along with higher levels of stress – so the relations between family size and religion on the one hand, and lower levels of some depression symptoms, could not be explained in terms of lower levels of stress in the more religious or in those with larger families.

I have discussed the question of childcare in relation to depression in women at some length because childcare is often suggested in some feminist (and other) literature to be quite stressful – this may be true. It is also suggested to be depressing. This may not always be true. If and when it is true, it is only true for some women in some societies.

There have been suggestions that childcare may be the explanation for the greater likelihood of women becoming depressed, than men. One suggestion is that childcare may explain gender differences in depression, at least in part.

I have already said that we cannot be sure that women really are more likely to be depressed than men. It also seems likely that, whether or not women are more likely to be depressed than men, childcare has usually not been found to be associated or causally related to depression. In some societies, where childcare is culturally or religiously valued, childcare may be associated with the absence of depression, or at least some of its symptoms.

There is little evidence on the relations between fatherhood and depression in men. Calzeroni *et al.* (1990) found suicide attempts less likely in those with larger families and this was true for men as well as women. Loewenthal *et al.* (1993) found no effect of family size on depressed mood in men. This question cannot be pursued any further, because there is almost no relevant evidence or theory connecting fatherhood, mental health and religion. It is to be hoped that some attention will be given to filling this gap.

As I have said, there are thought to be connections between motherhood, mental health and religion, and this section has described some of the arguments and some of the evidence.

In looking at the different effects of religion on mental health in women and men, we clearly have to bear in mind the religious–cultural context, and we now discuss variations in mental health in different religious groups. Chapter 3 also discussed some examples.

Religions and mental illness

There are variations in rates of reported mental disorder in different religious groups. As discussed in chapter 3, it is difficult to assess the value of the data.

Argyle and Beit-Hallahmi (1975) believe that group differences in reported mental disorder may reflect – at least partly – different degrees of willingness in different religious groups to seek treatment. The Hutterites described in Chapter 3 are an example of a community where willingness to seek treatment is low. In the USA, Jews are over-represented and Roman Catholics under-represented among Americans seeking psychiatric help. Again this may be due to different degrees of willingness to seek help. Strictly orthodox Jews, however, may be unwilling to seek professional psychiatric help (e.g. Witztum, Dasberg and Greenberg, 1990). Minority groups and women may feel that health professionals are making unhelpful assumptions about their values and lifestyles. Sayal (1990) describes similar feelings among black and Asian women in their dealings with the British health service. Loewenthal (1989b) describes orthodox Jewish women's perception of professional helpers. Professional helpers are seen as antagonistic to the client's lifestyle, condescending, lacking in understanding and often insisting on courses of action that are in conflict with the client's values and beliefs.

Cochrane (1984) points out that, in Moslem families, values are such that seeking professional help for psychological problems could discredit the family. At the same time, family support may be so good in some cases that problems are less likely to need professional help. For example Grant (1992) describes a type of 'support' service in the Moslem community: a man whose profession is to seek girls and women who have left home, perhaps because of overbearing or abusive behaviour by father or husband, perhaps to test out alternative lifestyles. The professional's role is to track down the missing person, to gain her confidence and to negotiate satisfactory conditions for the return home.

It can be seen that there are real difficulties arriving at good estimates of the incidence of mental illnesses in different religious groups, because of reluctance to seek help.

A further difficulty is that community surveys of wellbeing in different religious groups are bedevilled by the confounded factors of social class, ethnic origin, as well as lots of other factors like recent migration. For example Hollingshead and Redlich (1958) reported an often-confirmed finding that the psychoses are over-represented in the lowest social class, while neuroses are more likely in the higher socio-economic groups. However, in this (North American) study, social class, religion and ethnic origin were unevenly distributed. Protestantism and Northern European origin were characteristic of the higher socioeconomic groups, for example: these are the groups known sometimes as WASPS (White Anglo-Saxon Protestants).

Another example comes from the difficulties sparked off by Durkheim's well-known suggestion that suicide is more likely in Protestant than in Roman Catholic societies because of differences in social integration and beliefs about the self. Stack's review (1992), however, questions Durkheim's data and conclusions. Stack suggests that suicide is not linked to Protestantism as such, but to low belief in the meaning of suffering and to other aspects of low religiosity.

This excursion into the demography of mental illness highlights the difficulties of trying to look at the 'pure' effects of gender in relation to mental illness and religion. The conclusions drawn in this chapter therefore need to be treated with caution.

SUMMARY

Gender differences in mental health are likely to be affected by the religious and cultural context, but the evidence is patchy and sometimes hard to interpret. Different religions have differing values regarding marriage, celibacy and roles in marriage. The effects of marriage *per se* are difficult to assess because each of the different nonmarried states have particular mental health risks, and these vary with religious and cultural context.

Marriage carries specific risks for men and women, but the general tendency seems to be that lower levels of stress and of distress and disorder in both men and women may go along with the fulfilment of religiously valued roles. This however may in itself involve stress.

The relations between gender and mental illness may be modified by religious–cultural context. For example, the greater incidence and prevalence of depression among women than among men may be a feature of nontraditional societies.

Childcare also has varied relationships with mental illness, again depending on the religious–cultural – and economic – context.

6

Religion and poor mental health: some processes

I now want to try and highlight some processes that are at work in relating religion and mental health. I want to separate – where possible – those processes whereby religion in its various forms is associated with poor mental health and those where religion is associated with good mental health. This chapter deals with some ways in which religion may be associated with poor mental health.

I have tried to avoid recapitulating the evidence and ideas dwelt on in other chapters, though some of the issues that were raised before will make brief appearances here.

The topic will be approached by looking at some of the mental health outcomes, effects or states that are said to be associated with religion. These fall, roughly, into two groups.

The first group of states might be called **extrapunitive**: literally, this means the tendency to direct punishment and blame outside the self and against others. I have included self-importance, prejudice, cruelty, and self-righteousness. What all these have in common is that the 'sufferer' is in a position of relative power, sees himself (or herself) as right, and someone else, who is less powerful, as wrong, and may inflict or wish to inflict physical or psychological damage to the other. This damage is seen as quite justified by the damager.

The second group of states could be called **intropunitive**: literally, this means the tendency to direct punishment and blame inwards, on to the self. I have focused on guilt and scrupulousness, with some mention of related conditions where the sufferer is tied to the repetition of certain actions or thoughts which must be compulsively repeated in order to avoid some dreaded consequence.

SELF-RIGHTEOUSNESS AS ILL-HEALTH

It may seem odd that self-righteousness doesn't get huge coverage in textbooks on psychopathology. This is because those who see themselves as righteous – unlike the anxious, the depressed and the mad, don't normally seek help and often can't be persuaded to seek help. The common psychopathologies stem from unpleasant emotions which in turn relate to the person's social niche(s). Depression is the result of failure, loss of status, not managing to control outcomes – it is the emotion and psychopathology of the powerless. By virtue of their state of mind, a depressed person can easily believe or be brought to believe that they need help. After all, they couldn't manage on their own, could they? So a lot has been written about how to help depressed people.

The anxious are in a limbo, uncertain whether they will manage or not. They are autonomically energized to deal with things, fearful of bad outcomes, but still daring to hope for good . . . they too can believe that they may need help.

But the self-righteous, who may also be the perpetrators of abuse, are the ones who can afford anger. Anger is the emotion of the powerful, those who control the resources to make others experience loss, fear, pain. Berke (1990), drawing on the work of Klein (1932) and others in the psychoanalytic tradition, has shown how cruelty as well as other evil and psychopathological behaviour and feeling stems from early feelings of need, greed, envy and jealousy. Little is generally written on the treatment and management of cruelty. We concede fast enough that cruelty is the product of a sick mind, but a sick mind whose owner never needs to seek help or treatment (unless they get on to the wrong side of the law).

Lerner (1980, 1991) has shown that the belief that the weak and suffering deserve their fate is endemic to all of us, in spite of our dazzling but hypocritical ability to be shocked by such sentiments.

The work of Zimbardo (1969), Milgram (1974) and Williams (1992) has shown that cruelty is at least as much a matter of situation and training as it is of character. Zimbardo, for instance, got student volunteers to take part in a 'mock prison' study. The volunteers were randomly assigned to the roles of prisoners and guards. The guards were simply told to keep order. The level of brutality reached such shocking proportions that the study had to be stopped prematurely, after a very few days. The 'guards' were nice, educated, young people from a liberal democracy (the USA). So were the 'prisoners'. The 'guards' complained that their behaviour was entirely justified and provoked by the prisoners; it was claimed that the prisoners would have got completely out of hand if strong measures had not been taken. Zimbardo's findings would suggest that cruelty is a result of being in a particular position, rather than being a particular kind of person. Milgram's (1974) findings also echo this view. In Milgram's widely quoted study, most participants agreed to obey the scientific authority-figure in charge of the experiment. The orders were to administer electric shocks to the co-volunteer whenever he made a mistake. In Milgram's study, the 'trainers' administering the electric shocks were quite uncomfortable about doing what they had to do, but most felt sufficiently authorized. Williams showed that professional torturers do not appear to differ in any notable respect (except gender?) from other people; they have to be well-trained and the features of training programmes for torturers are described.

We now turn to review the conditions associated both with religion and with the tendency to self-righteousness, prejudice, cruelty and related states.

SELF-IMPORTANCE AND PREJUDICE

I have some nasty stereotypes. For example – s/he is well-dressed, well-covered, complacent, pompous . . . a pillar of religion . . . a figure to inspire fun, fear in those less powerful, pity perhaps, very respectable but never respected, liked or loved. Not a real person, but the ghost of a thousand literary images.

But quite like some real people we may have known? The question is whether religion and religious institutions cause this bastion of respectability to flourish.

Psychologists have had so many words for the attributes of our self-important bastion of respectability that at first the plethora may seem confusing. Authoritarian, dogmatic, prejudiced, conservative, ethnocentric, subservient to those more powerful, condescending or bullying to those less powerful, incapable of real warmth and love, firmly disowns any personal failings . . . most of this catalogue is part of a much longer catalogue eloquently described and researched by a group of social scientists (Adorno *et al.*, 1950), refugees from Nazi Europe, who wanted to show a complacent world that it could happen anywhere. Like Jung a few decades before, they thought that if we hauled it out from under the carpet and showed it to everyone and took a good look ourselves, we might think of something wise or at least sensible to do about it.

Adorno *et al.* described the 'authoritarian personality'; looked at family interactions and social conditions that engendered the tendency to think you were justified in doing whatever necessary to 'them' (foreigners, blacks, Jews, women, children – anyone 'other' with no power). They found that the whole miserable cluster of characteristics listed above tended to co-occur.

The 'authoritarian personality' excited a flurry of interest from social psychologists, who now seem to have forgotten about it, and are now terribly busy with attributions, social representations and other important issues which hopefully will lead them back to the forgotten question of the human potential for evil. At the moment, for instance, many social psychologists concerned with prejudice are busy with Social Identity Theory (Turner, 1975) which deals with the way in which we, as members of group X, tend to see ourselves as better and more right than members of groups Y, Z, A, B and so on.

The psychology of religion, however, never quite let go of prejudice as a characteristic of individuals (rather than a product of social situations). There has a been a long-standing interest in the fact the individuals do (for whatever reason) differ in levels of prejudice. The psychology of religion was particularly concerned with the issue of individual differences in prejudice because of the repeated finding that religious affiliation and attendance tended to go hand in hand with higher scores on measures of authoritarianism, prejudice and the like (Argyle and Beit-Hallahmi, 1975). This finding was annoying or puzzling to the religious, because religion is supposed to be encouraging brotherly (and sisterly) love, respect for all other human beings, in fact respect for all of God's creation, human or otherwise. I guess the nonreligious weren't annoyed or puzzled, perhaps because many had been put off by the self-righteous, bigoted face of religion. A tempting conclusion was that religion was somehow causing prejudice.

In the same year (1950) that *'The authoritarian personality'* was published, a distinguished personality theorist, Gordon Allport, published a book called *The Individual and his Religion*. This was the outcome of autobiographical interviews with people on Ivy League campuses, many of them veterans of the Second World War, about their lives, beliefs and perceived need for religion. Allport suggested that the forms of individual religion and personal philosophy were tightly tied up with character. Allport suggested that some people have 'immature' religions or philosophies; the person is egocentric, and expects or believes that God will look after him or her. As for the problems of others, that's their problem, and – by a process of amazing logic described so eloquently by Lerner (1980) – somehow they deserve it by virtue of their inferiority. So immature religiosity goes along with heartlessness and prejudice. Mature religiosity is the result of dealing with suffering, and its hallmarks are tolerance and sympathy for others, compassion without sentimentality. In the 1960s Allport extended these ideas to predict that prejudiced individuals would be those with a self-serving style of religiosity. Allport (1966) called this style of religiosity **extrinsic**. Those who took the teachings of religion seriously, the genuinely devout, Allport labelled **intrinsic**. He suggested that religious intrinsics would be low on prejudice. To account for the positive correlation between religion and prejudice, Allport suggested that organized religion was swamped with extrinsics. Religion provides status, self-esteem and other gratifications, so the extrinsic individual may turn to God, but does not turn away from the self.

Allport and Ross (1967) did find that extrinsically religious people were more prejudiced than intrinsically religious people. They also identified a group of people who said that they were both extrinsically and intrinsically religious. Allport called these people 'religious muddleheads' and suggested that they might agree with more or less anything. This group of people were the most prejudiced of all.

Table 6.1 shows the sorts of thing that intrinsically and extrinsically oriented people might agree with.

Table 6.1   Items to measure extrinsic and intrinsic religious orientation (from Batson, Schoenrade and Ventis, 1993)

Extrinsic (External):

1. My religion serves to satisfy needs for fellowship and security
2. Certain people have served as 'models' for my religious development

Intrinsic (Internal):

3. It is necessary for me to have a religious belief
4. When it comes to religious questions I feel driven to know the truth

If you are not at least minimally involved in Christianity, you would find that some items are not relevant to you. There has been no effort so far to find out if these dimensions mean anything outside the context of Christian culture.

Table 6.2 shows the first and best-known of the scales associated with serious attempts to measure prejudice.

Table 6.2   Items from the California F scale (adapted from Adorno *et al.*, 1950)

1. Obedience and respect for authority are the most important virtues children should learn
2. If people would talk less and work more, everybody would be better off
3. No weakness or difficulty can hold us back if we have enough will power
4. An insult to our honour should always be punished

Like the religious orientation items just described, the scale is culturally and historically limited and it may not make sense to use it outside the sort of context in which it was developed. The scale has been criticized on other grounds, too. It is one of a group of measures developed by Adorno *et al.* (1950). Other measures included direct questions about ethnocentrism – the tendency to derogate groups other than ones own – and anti-Semitism. The statements in Table 6.2 are from the famous California F scale. 'California' because the researchers – refugees from Nazi Germany – had found a haven in the University of California, and 'F' is a very short abbreviation for 'potentiality for Fascism'. The researchers didn't believe 'it could never happen here', and set out to assess the extent to which decent, even kindly, upright citizens had the potentiality for Fascism. The scale is sometimes said to assess 'authoritarian personality', and it has been criticized on several grounds. But the scale, and the research with which it is associated, represents one of the most important scientific attempts to understand the human potential for bad.

A high score on this scale is said to indicate a high degree of authoritarianism and/or traditionality. A low score is said to indicate a democratic or liberal personality, or set of attitudes. The scale has been heavily criticized. Authorities on the construction of psychological tests (psychometricians) are very hard on this test. One big problem with it is that you get a high score if you agree with every item; a well-constructed test should have some statements that are 'negatively' worded, so that if you are the kind of person that tends to agree with most things whatever they are, you wouldn't automatically get a high score on authoritarianism. Lots of the statements are 'double-barrelled' – they say two or more things in one sentence (items 1–3 are all examples) – and you may agree with one part and disagree with another. There are other problems too. What would Stalin and his men have scored on the F scale? Perhaps not a high score . . . but does that mean they are not authoritarian? There have been more recent attempts to measure attitudes and traits similar to those assessed by the F scale, but it remains an interesting classic, in spite of its faults.

The F scale is supposed to measure a variety of personality characteristics, including:

- anti-intraception, which is a dislike of looking inwards at the self and at one's feelings;
- punitiveness, which is a tendency to direct hostile feelings on to other people and to justify the use of physical force and punishment;
- concern with power and sex rather than intimacy;
- authoritarian submissiveness (grovelling!) to those more powerful, and contempt for those less powerful (bossiness, arrogance).

Two-and-a-half decades later, Allport's suggestions about religion and its relation to prejudice and related behaviours are still being taken very seriously. Chapter 7 returns to this area of discussion.

What of mental health? I pointed out in chapter 2 that several psychoanalytic theorists had distinguished between 'healthy' and 'unhealthy' styles of religiosity, and I said there that Allport's extrinsic religiosity bore a resemblance to 'unhealthy' or neurotic styles of religiosity. So – you might ask – what was Allport's great innovation? One is that Allport has brought to life the relation between religion and everyday nastiness. He has stepped away from conventional understanding of neurosis, in its recognizable forms of depression, anxiety and related illnesses. Allport showed how, in spite of the best intentions of religious leaders and teachers, human nastiness may not be improved within the fold. And all too often, it may flourish.

Allport's other innovation is related to the same point. Genuine sympathy and practical compassion are the faces of intrinsic religiosity, he suggested. This second innovation of Allport's didn't stand up too well to empirical testing. Batson and his colleagues (e.g. Batson, 1976) found that high intrinsics weren't actually any more helpful than low intrinsics. Batson (see, for example, Batson and Ventis, 1982) suggested, reasonably, that if we are asked in a questionnaire whether we take the teachings of our religion seriously, and try to carry them out in everyday life, reasons for saying 'yes' could be impure! It could be that we really are so pious, but it could be that we want to come over as pious and good. This last effect – 'social desirability' – is a well-known bugbear in self-report measures of personality. We say what we wish we were, not what we wish we weren't. Batson showed that measures of social desirability did correlate with measures of intrinsic religiosity. Intrinsic religiosity is thus not a pure measure of sincerity, selflessness and piety. Batson developed a scale to assess the form of religiosity which might relate to practical compassion. Batson called this the **quest** orientation – an open-minded, searching approach to personal religious beliefs, for example ' It might be said that I value my religious doubts and uncertainties'. Quest does correlate with helping behaviour, and does not correlate with measures of social desirability (Batson, Schoenrade and Ventis, 1993).

An interesting study by Talbo and Shepperd (1986) studied the relations between intrinsic, quest and extrinsic religious orientation in 291 American undergraduates, and self-righteousness. Talbo and Shepperd developed a typology of self-righteousness by grouping all the subjects (who all had at least a moderate degree of religiosity) into four groups, according to their level of self-righteousness and self-esteem. The four groups were:

- **the broad-minded**: these were low in self-righteousness and high in self-esteem;
- **the insecure**: these were high in self-righteousness and low in self-esteem;
- **the arrogant**: these were high in both self-righteousness and in self-esteem;
- **the meek**: these were low in both self-righteousness and self-esteem.

The insecure and the arrogant had higher scores on extrinsic religiosity than the other subjects. In other words, self-righteousness went along with extrinsic religiosity. The broad-minded and the meek were higher than other subjects on both intrinsic religiosity and quest religiosity. So low self-righteousness went along with intrinsic and quest religiosity. This study therefore offers good support for both Allport's and Batson's suggestions about religion and personality.

To complete the picture, Batson and Ventis (1982) and Batson, Schoenrade and Ventis (1993) review a large number of studies of religious orientation (extrinsic–intrinsic–quest) in relation to various measures of mental health, distress and psychiatric symptomatology. Extrinsic orientation tends to go along with poorer mental health and adjustment, with the reverse effect for quest.

So ideas about religious orientation have been helpful in disentangling relations between religion, prejudice and mental health. However results are not always as clear-cut as Allport hoped they might be. Wearing and Brown (1972) administered batteries of tests of religious belief, orientation and practice, as well as several personality tests including neuroticism and authoritarianism. The subjects in this study were Australian students. It was found that neuroticism and authoritarianism went (factored out) together, independently of the various measures of religiosity. The religiosity measures also tended to go together. This finding contrasts with other studies: religious orientation did not relate to authoritarianism (nor did other measures of religiosity). Another important lack in research on religious orientation and prejudice has been the failure to incorporate developments in social psychologists' thinking about social identity and social cognition – as will be discussed further.

A tentative conclusion is that we may not be able to implicate religion directly in the underlying character structure, which is moulded in large part by temperament, family and other experiences, affected in turn by general social conditions. However, regrettably, it is clear that religious institutions can give licence and scope to the expression of prejudice and the other unpleasant manifestations of the authoritarian personality syndrome.

Religious guidance could and should encourage the scrutiny and improvement of thoughts and behaviour. But it is, as it were, a sheep that can be skinned alive. The skin and wool are used to clothe the wolf that has been created from attempts to protect a damaged self. And the wolf in sheep's clothing may be more likely to get away with murder.

CRUELTY

Fanaticism, persecution and indifference to suffering all have a common feature – cruelty. They may also have similar psychological roots. They are also held up, rightly, as a shameful and all too frequent feature of organized religion. Holy wars, martyrs, inquisition, crusade, pogrom . . . the worst atrocities in human history are carried out in the name of religion, supposedly justified by religion.

Religious advice on the use of physical force and punishment

This section will show that religious support for the use of physical force and punishment has been very limited, generally confined to places and times which were (even!) more violent than ours, and to the treatment of legally convicted criminals. I will concentrate on examples from Jewish and Christian writings.

In the Jewish legal system, torture and imprisonment occupy no place. Limited beating was applied only to certain adult offenders, after very stringent criteria had been applied to obtain conviction (there had to be two adult witnesses to the offence, and the offender had to have been warned not to carry out the offence). The requirements to secure conviction for capital punishment were similar and so stringent that execution was seldom (according to some sources never) carried out. The 'eye-for-an-eye' principle is agreed by all rabbinic legal codifiers to refer to monetary compensation for injury.

In child-rearing, there was and is some support for light smacking of young children. Loewenthal (1991) quotes an eminent early 19th-century rabbinic authority (Rabbi Shneur Zalman of Liadi) who prohibits the use by teachers of harsh beatings. 'If the pupil refuses to study he should not be harshly beaten but lightly smacked. After this – if he reads, then he reads, but if he does not read [the text under study], then let him just sit with his friends so as to be a member of their group and eventually perhaps he will pay attention.'

Favoured emphasis in child-rearing is on reward, rather than punishment. The 17th-century *Lev Tov* (Good Heart) (quoted by Hundert, 1989) sets out appropriate rewards for different developmental stages:

- sugar and honey cake;
- fine clothes;
- a large dowry;
- a rabbinical career;
- (intrinsic, self-reward).

In the 20th century, even threats and verbal abuse are discouraged by rabbinic authors. Thus Shapira (1991) from the Warsaw ghetto in the 1930s: 'Talk of punishment should be avoided, for it is the surest way to alienate the student.' And Schneersohn (1990) in the climate of the early days of communism in Russia: 'those who attack their pupils with extremely harsh and angry words, insulting and berating them . . . this type of education or guidance yields no lasting benefit whatsoever . . . true education and guidance can be attained only by . . . a self-critique of teaching, [to ensure that it is carried out with] composure, politeness and pleasant speech.'

In a review of Christian views on physical punishment, Oosterhuis (1993) traces the decline in the severity of advocated punishment to changing views of the child. Both Oosterhuis and Larzelere (1993) maintain support for the use of light smacking on younger children. The use of rods and implements is considered cruel and undesirable.

These views suggest that religious support for physical force and punishment is hardly overwhelming. There is some qualified support for limited use of physical punishment, but some authors – especially in contemporary times – appear to be against it altogether.

Cruelty in practice

In theory, religious sanctions for cruelty are limited or nonexistent. In practice, our history books and newspapers and experiences may belie that theory. The following is a dramatized account by Gold (1988) of a torture session of a person accused of heretical behaviour and ideas; the account is based on the official records of the interrogation of Elvira del Campo in 1567 by the Inquisition of Toledo. The victim (V.) has been placed upon the rack after several months of interrogation interspersed with solitary confinement. Apart from V., present at the session are T. (the director of the torture session), a priest and two torturers. V. is asked if he will repent.

> V. remained silent. 'Good', said T. 'I have always felt that repentance at this time does not have much value. His repentance later will be more worthwhile. Let us get on with it'.
>
> T. signalled to one of the hooded men who reached out and twisted the cord. V. grimaced but said nothing. T. signalled again, and the hooded man twisted the cord two more times. V.'s body arched as if he had been struck by a bolt of lightning, and he screamed. 'One more time,' said T.
>
> The hooded man twisted the cords again and V. fainted. T. motioned to the physician who came over and held a bottle of smelling salts to the unconscious man's nose. He stirred and began to moan.
>
> 'V., do you have anything to say?' asked T.
>
> 'I have done all that is said of me', he moaned. 'I bear false witness against myself, because I do not want to be in such trouble. But heaven knows I have done nothing.'
>
> 'You must not bear false witness against yourself. Just tell the truth.'
>
> 'I have told the truth', said V. 'What can I say?'
>
> 'Tell the truth.'
>
> 'I have told the truth. I am innocent.'
>
> T. signalled and the cord was twisted again.
>
> 'I have done all that they say,' screamed V.
>
> 'Tell us in detail what you have done,' said T.

'Please release me,' pleaded V. 'I have already told the truth. What more do you want? Tell me what you want, because I don't know what to say.'

'Tell it to us in detail.'

Another signal and another twist of the cord.

'Oh Lord have mercy on a poor sinner,' V. cried out. 'I did it. I did it. Loosen me! Loosen me a little that I may remember what I have to tell. [V. makes a partial confession]. Loosen me and I will tell the truth.'

Again, a twist of the cord.

'They are hurting me!' he screamed. 'Oh, my arms, my arms! Please release me and I will tell it. Loosen me and I will tell it when I am taken away from here. Oh wretched me!'

'Tell the truth. What have you done contrary to our holy faith?'

'I don't remember! Tell me what I have to say, and I will say it. They are breaking my arms. I did everything. Loosen me, for I don't remember what I have to tell. Don't you see how weak I am? Oh! My arms are breaking!'

Another signal and another twist of the cord. 'Sirs, have you no pity on a poor sinner?' he whimpered.

'Yes, we do. But only if you tell the truth.'

'Oh, please, sirs. I beg of you to have mercy on me. Don't you see they are killing me? They are tearing me to pieces. They are tearing out my soul! Please stop them. I will say anything you want me to say. Just tell me what I should say, and I will say it. For the sake of heaven, release me!'

'Just tell the truth and you will be released.' [V. makes a further partial confession, adding] 'I have taken leave of my senses and I don't remember . . .'

T. held up three fingers to the hooded man. He nodded and twisted the cord three times in succession. V. screamed from the very depths of his soul, and the last remnant of his defences was swept away.

'Are you prepared to tell the truth?' asked T.

'Yes'.

[V. confesses to more, but T. is still not satisfied.]

'I think we can loosen his tongue'.

V.'s eyes were bulging with terror, and his breath came in short gasps. T. raised his hand to signal to the hooded man, but V. screamed even before the signal was given.

'Have mercy on me, sirs!' he cried. 'I will tell you what you want to know.'

T. gave the signal anyway . . .

The session continued.

Note that, from the point of view of the torturer, the victim is withholding essential information and is constantly trying to negotiate a release without having given the information required. The torturer, we must suppose, is doing his duty and feels justified.

This is not an isolated example. As I write, I recall that yesterday's newspaper told readers that women in Iran were being severely punished for violations of religious law regarding modesty and sexual behaviour by vigilantes who were taking the law into their own hands. The report stated that one woman was so badly beaten for the sin of sunbathing in a scanty costume that she had to go abroad to receive treatment for her injuries. Singh (1986) reported that violence against wives in India is widespread, the roots being social and religious. Wife-abuse is widespread, and it may often appear to be sanctioned by religion. Alsdurf (1985) found that 86% of nearly 6000 American and Canadian Protestant pastors surveyed had counselled women who had been battered. Alsdurf quietly comments that the pastors' own personal experiences and attitudes to patriarchy determined their responses to wife-abuse, and suggests that some educational intervention is needed to improve pastoral activity in this area. Brinkerhoff, Grandin and Lupri (1992) studied spousal violence in Canada and found a curvilinear relationship with church attendance. That is, occasional-to-moderate attenders were the worst offenders. Brinkerhoff, Grandin and Lupri suggest that this provides some support for Allport's suggestion that it is the extrinsically religious – extrinsic religiosity normally goes with moderate church attendance, rather than high or none – who are likely to be the abusers. Religious respectability, rather than piety, may provide a license for abuse.

There is a growing body of evidence suggesting that physical violence is sanctioned, even encouraged, for actual or supposed violations of religious law. Victims are likely to be powerless: children, women and minorities.

Both physical and sexual abuse in the context of religious ritual have been reported. Cozolino (1990) reports psychological, physical and sexual maltreatment of children in the context of a 'religious' ceremony. Capps (1992) describes Day's (1989) study of the worship of Molech, a form of idolatry opposed by the prophets of Israel: 'The children, as they expired, screamed from the intensity of the fire. The pagan priests sounded [their trumpets] to confuse the parents and other listeners and to prevent the screams of the children from being heard.' Capps notes: 'So children were abused in the name of religion, but the abuse of children was also decried in the name of religion.'

Beating children is still a widespread practice, and Greven (1991) claims that the religions have legitimated and supported this form of child abuse, both by parents and by other adults. 'Breaking the child's will' and biblical quotations (taken out of context) have been taken as justification for inflicting painful, degrading and often traumatic beatings, spankings or floggings. Capps (1992) quotes widely from Greven's examples. One is from Frady's (1979) biography of Billy Graham:

> His father would beat him with a leather belt, once when he was discovered chewing tobacco, another time dragging him from church where he had been restless, shoving him on out into the vestibule and there strapping him thoroughly. What Billy remembers most about his father is the feel of his hands against him: 'They were like rawhide, bony, rough. He had such hard hands'.

The recollections continue with an account which must have given some satisfaction not only to Billy but to all children who have suffered similarly: 'Once, as his father stood over him flailing away with the belt as Billy was lying on his back, Billy "broke two of his ribs, kicking with my legs".'

Greven points out that a central part of parents' infliction of physical punishment on children is the belief that they are not reacting out of anger as a personal response to the child's misbehaviour, but believe that they are doing it for the child's own good.

Fugate (1980) in *What the Bible Says About . . . Child Training* advises: 'Chastizement . . . should never be administered by an angry or emotional parent. If a parent cannot control himself, he should send the child to his room to wait for his whipping. This action provides the parent with time to "cool down" and it allows the child time to ponder the coming consequences of his actions.' One child's response to a regime of this kind is recorded by McPherson (1979):

> Like all other restless youngsters I was constantly getting into dilemmas and difficulties. After similar outrages to the dignity of my household, I would be banished to my room and told that in exactly one half hour I would be spanked. I was thoroughly familiar with those whippings. They were not gentle love pats, and my parents never stopped until I was a thoroughly chastized girl. The time of waiting for the footsteps on the stair, the opening of the door, and descending palm was the worst of all. On one such occasion I stood wildly looking about for a way out of the dilemma. No earthly recourse was nigh. Taught as I was about heavenly intervention, I thought of prayer. Dropping to my knees on the side of my bed, I began to pray loudly, earnestly. 'Oh, God, don't let mama whip me! Oh God, dear, kind, sweet, God, don't let mama spank me!

Another view is expressed in *Dare to Discipline* by Dobson (1970):

> Nothing brings a parent and child closer together than for the mother or father to win decisively after being defiantly challenged. This is particularly true if the child was 'asking for it', knowing full well that he deserved what he got. The parent's demonstration of his authority builds respect like no other process, and the child will often reveal his affection when the emotion has passed. For this reason the parent should not dread or shrink back from these confrontations with the child. These occasions should be anticipated as important events, because they provide the occasion to say something to the child that cannot be said at other times. It is not necessary to beat the child into submission: a little bit of pain goes a long way for a young child. However the spanking should be of sufficient magnitude to cause the child to cry genuinely. After the emotional ventilation the child will often crumple to the breast of his parent, and he should be welcomed with open, warm, loving arms. At that moment you can talk heart to heart. You can tell him how much you love him, and how important he is to you. You can explain why he was punished and how he can avoid the difficulty next time. This kind of communication is not made possible by other disciplinary

measures, including standing the child in the corner or taking away his [toy].

Although there is growing evidence of the negative conse-quences of the use of physical punishment (e.g. Shaffer, 1985; Leach, 1993), the macabre advice of Dobson is unfortunately characterized by a tragic form of effectiveness. As Bettelheim (1960) noted in *The Informed Heart*, many concentration camp inmates developed an abject, literally slavish 'worship' and desire to be like their tormentors.

Religious defence of physical punishment still continues; for example the *Journal of Psychology and Theology* recently published several (albeit) qualified defences of physical punishment. Titles include 'Empirically justified uses of spanking' (Larzelere, 1993) which mentions studies involving spanking of children as young as two years old, and autistic children, and advocates the 'controlled' use of slapping and spanking with young children, after reasoning and other measures have failed. Larzelere does, however, warn that there is a danger that spanking may be used in place of positive parenting practices, and wishes to distinguish between the controlled use of slapping and the like and physical abuse. He cites an interesting study (Larzelere *et al.*, 1989) of college students' recollections of parent-oriented motives for spanking. The presence of such motives was judged by the attri-bution of the following to the parent:

- anger;
- coldness;
- vengeance;
- frustration;
- enjoyment of power;
- to show who is boss;
- enjoyed inflicting pain.

Where parent-oriented motives for spanking were considered to be present, the students were significantly more likely to say that a biblical justification for spanking had been invoked. There was also a significant relationship with frequency of spanking, and lowered self-esteem. Greven (1991) comments that: 'Love and pain, rebellion and submission, disobedience, punishment and forgiveness thus were intertwined in a powerful mixture of opposing feelings and experiences'.

The children, however, are not as appreciative or submissive as Dobson would wish adults to suppose: 'After punishment the children would be subjected to the even greater "humbling" of being expected to put their arms around their father's neck and to say: "I love you Daddy. Forgive me for disobeying." Then Daddy would respond, "I love you too, but now we must ask God to help you overcome your stubbornness"' (quoted by Capps).

Both Greven and Capps suggest repression or amnesia for childhood experiences with traumatizing religious ideas. Capps writes: 'All had partially or totally forgotten about these experiences. However as more and more details emerged, my companions discovered that they had powerful feelings about the torment they had suffered, feelings of deep sorrow and pity for the child each one was, and rage at the person or persons who had promulgated the religious idea in question.'

But very often, repression or amnesia is not the end of the story. Here is one example of an all-too-common outcome of physical abuse, the setting up of a continuing cycle of abuse: 'In the course of psychotherapy, Mr X. reported that he often punished his children by spanking them. "Why do you do that?" asked the therapists. Mr X. looked taken aback. After a few moments' thought, he replied: "That's the way to do it. That's what was always done to us."'

Each generation of abusers has its own history of abuse. Elizabeth Gaskell (1976: Appendix) writing of rural England nearly two centuries ago records: 'a set of young men, ready for mischief and brutality . . . They would stop ladies . . . who were only attended by a maidservant bearing a lantern, and whip them: literally whip them as you would whip a little child.'

Another common consequence is escape from the environment that fostered, witnessed and allowed the abuse.

Biale (1983) suggests that many Jews turned against religious orthodoxy as a result of the physical abuse they suffered in religious schools. Biale also suggests that there is evidence that, where early marriage was normative and couples were supported by the young wife's parents, some boys were beaten by their mothers-in-law. Complaints of parental abuse were not reported, and so Biale concludes that rebellion against orthodox religion was prompted by physical abuse outside the parental home.

Running away from religion after religiously sanctioned physical abuse has been reported in other religious contexts. For example Grant (1992) suggests this among Moslems in Britain. And here is Elizabeth Gaskell's famous literary example of the rector's son, a teenage boy, who dressed himself in his older sister's clothes.

> – and made the little pillow . . . into a little baby, with long white clothes. It was only . . . to make something to talk about in the town . . . And he went and walked up and down in the Filbert walk – just half hidden by the rails, and half seen; and he cuddled his pillow, just like a baby; and talked to it all the nonsense people do. Oh dear! and my father came stepping stately up the street, as he always did; and what should he see but a little black crowd of people . . . he looked through the rails himself and saw . . . bade them all stop where they were – not one of them to go, not one to stir a step; and swift as light, he was in at the garden door, and down the Filbert walk, and seized hold of poor Peter, and tore his clothes off his back – bonnet, shawl, gown and all – and threw the pillow among the people over the railings: and then he was very, very angry indeed; and before all the people he lifted up his cane and flogged Peter!

Peter disappeared after this. His terrified parents had the ponds dragged, and searched for his hanged body; this testifies to some adult appreciation of the likely effects of physical abuse upon children. Peter had escaped abroad, and did not return in his parents' lifetime.

Lerner (1980) has claimed that the belief in a 'just world' makes us all mini-persecutors and accomplices in persecution. A suffering person is actually seen as inferior, bad and somehow deserving of their fate, simply because they are suffering. When I describe one of Lerner's early experiments in lectures, there are looks of incredulity and disbelief – and then the protests: of course **we** wouldn't think like that! Lerner's experiment was on a class of psychology students. They were all going to get credits for taking part in an experiment, in which one of the class would learn something – getting electric shocks for making mistakes. The rest of the class would fill in ratings of the learner and her performance. A nice girl volunteered to be the learner, and was seen to suffer quite considerably. Were the others grateful? If so, they had a funny way of showing it, because their ratings of the girl showed they didn't think much of her.

Lerner and his colleagues have carried out versions of this experiment with all kinds of controls and comparisons, and the effect is a pretty robust one. Lerner said that no-one would believe it, though basically all show evidence of this type of thinking. The suffering are generally seen as inferior to the comfortable rest of the world, for reasons outlined above. It is suggested that this belief is fostered and/or exacerbated by religious views on sin and punishment. A suffering person must be bad, otherwise they wouldn't be suffering. Maimonides (1967) pointed out that it is forbidden to say or think of another person who is suffering that they must have done something bad, and it is this kind of value that most of us would like to say we really believe. Remember the shock and horror that greeted that awful suggestion about the 'wrath of God' in the early days when the AIDS epidemic first became a matter of public concern? The main victims of AIDS were homosexuals, and there was general public horror when it was suggested that the illness was a punishment from heaven for the sinful behaviour of homosexuality.

How is it that we are so horrified by the idea that suffering people deserve their suffering – and regard as totally horrible and judgmental the people who make public pronouncements to that effect, while in a totally paradoxical way, we actually make judgments like this over and over again, as the work of Lerner and his collaborators have shown. We may even pass judgment on ourselves: there is the appearance of 'self-blaming responses among obviously innocent victims' (Lerner, 1991). Lerner suggests that we are able to carry out a 'charade', whereby we operate at two levels of consciousness:

> 'intellectually sophisticated people can actually plan their lives as if they lived in a world where people ultimately got what they deserved while stating openly that they have no faith in such "fairy tales"'. (Lerner, 1991)

The Social Identity theorists offer a related perspective on these unpleasant aspects of religiosity. They start with the familiar idea that we are proud of the group we belong to. And this pride relates to an aspect of our identity – our social identity. By belonging to group X, we are an X member – and we work quite hard to be proud of it. One corollary of this is that nonmembers of group X may be looked down upon. A fascinating aspect of this is what happens to our explanations of people's behaviour. It turns out that we understand behaviour very differently when 'we' and members of our groups do it, than when 'they' do it – especially if 'they' are threatening to us.

Consider the rhetoric of liberation and terrorism. We, and our group, and those we sympathize with, are fighting for basic human rights, for an end to suffering. We are ready to sacrifice ourselves (and others) to achieve this noble end. We wish to throw off the yoke of the oppressor, and we are justified in using any means to do this. They, and their group, and those who threaten us, are a bunch of inhuman, heartless monsters, without a spark of human feeling and decency. They are ready to torture and murder innocent and helpless victims . . .

For many years, social psychologists have been interested in the 'fundamental attribution error – the tendency to justify one's own behaviour and to condemn others. This is done by producing 'external' attributions for socially undesirable behaviour by ourselves (they are oppressing us and not allowing us to live in our country in freedom), and 'internal' attributions for undesirable behaviour by others (they are a bunch of inhuman, heartless monsters, without a spark of human feeling and decency). This bias applies to people-in-groups, as we can see from the liberation/terrorist rhetoric. Pettigrew (1979) called it the 'ultimate attribution error', and showed that it applied at least as much to people in religious groups as to people in other kinds of groups.

More recently, Hunter, Stringer and Watson (1991) carried out a similar demonstration to Pettigrew's. They studied Catholics and Protestants in Northern Ireland, where both groups are in a state of conflict, perceiving each other as threatening to their own group's wellbeing and security. The subjects watched several clips of newsreel footage, showing various significant events in the Northern Ireland conflict. Also included was one clip of Protestants attacking mourners at a funeral using hand grenades and an automatic pistol, and another clip showing a group of Catholics attacking a car containing two soldiers (British, symbolically and politically aligned with the Protestant cause), using a variety of improvised weapons. Hunter, Stringer and Watson's analyses of Protestant and Catholic subjects' explanations of these behaviours were in line with Pettigrew's predictions about the 'ultimate attribution error'. Violence by one's own group is defensible, more likely to be seen as externally than internally caused: it is provoked. Violence by the other group is indefensible, more likely to be seen as internally than externally caused: it is unprovoked by the innocent victims.

Cognitive processes of the kind described by Lerner, Pettigrew and others play an important part – not just in maintaining conflict, but in making the situation worse. So many conflicts involve confrontations across the lines of religious affiliation, and the cognitive biases involved in justification may be the devils responsible for much of the cruelty in the world. Maybe all of it?

Allport and Ross (1967) illuminated another facet of cruelty: fanaticism. This may be no more than naive over-enthusiasm, but it can lead to very unpleasant excesses. Allport and Ross found that those who were highest on both intrinsic and extrinsic religiosity were the most prejudiced. Remember that high scores on intrinsic religiosity can be obtained by the person wanting to sound like a good person? Allport called these high scorers 'religious muddleheads'. A more sinister view is that these are the fanatics, the ones who think religion is great and whatever it tells them is great and they must go along with it and they'll be great. Unfortunately, religious leadership is not always in the best possible hands, so fanaticism is a potentially dangerous quality in leaders and followers.

Batson (1976 and elsewhere) found that indifference to suffering was related to extrinsic religiosity. High-intrinsics are no more helpful than low-intrinsics. Helping was related to quest religiosity.

This section has discussed many examples of the way religion has been used and abused to justify cruelty, often for self-centred ends. We have focused on some of the causes of cruelty, as related to religiosity, and noted that in the mind of the perpetrator, there is complete justification – often cruelty may be apparently 'sanctified' by religion.

GUILT AND SCRUPULOUSNESS

There are other ways in which religion may be implicated in poor mental health. There is a large group of disturbed behaviours apparently caused by religiously-associated guilt feelings. Or, to be more accurate, the guilt feelings are more probably the result of the ways in which religiously-approved behaviours and ideas were inculcated. Guilt feelings, obsessions, compulsions and quasi- or frankly psychotic delusions and other disturbances can be the unhappy results.

Here is an example from David MacIsaac (1993):

Mrs B. had passed the menopause, and was admitted for psychiatric care, suffering from delusions that the devil was damaging her womb. When she had first gone to her GP to complain about the symptoms that were troubling her, major tranquillizers were prescribed, but this did not help. Finally, a prolapsed womb was diagnosed. Mrs B had never had children. She was a devout Roman Catholic, and had convinced herself that her main religious duty and purpose in life as a woman was to have children. As she grew older and then menopausal, she became very concerned about her failure. When the prolapsed womb was diagnosed she decided that her failure to have children was not simply the result of physical factors. There was an underlying spiritual cause. This resolved into a belief that the devil was doing the damage.

There are details that one might want to be filled in here, particularly to do with Mrs B.'s socialization experiences, patterns of relationships and style of thinking, but the general sad scenario is echoed and re-echoed, with variations, all too many times.

Another example from David MacIsaac:

A young Jewish girl was brought in for psychiatric help. She was diagnosed as suffering from bulimia which included the feature of self-induced vomiting. From a traditional religious background, in the course of mixing with friends she had started to eat whatever they did, which included nonkosher food, including bacon. Then her boyfriend had broken up with her. At that point in time she had begun to feel sick and nauseous. The two sets of events had convinced her that her sinful excursions had brought upon her the wrath of God, and that if she could cleanse her body of the offending food, she would be all right.

Sometimes, it looks as if guilt is relieved by scrupulous attention to religious rituals and actions. Freud (1907) went so far as to suggest that all religious rituals were like obsessional–neurotic actions in many respects. He pointed out many similarities between religious rituals and obsessional actions; both relieve guilt, and their nonperformance arouses more guilt, setting up a self-perpetuating cycle. The 'true' significance of the ritual and the obsessional act is not apparent to the doer.

There are differences as well. Religious rituals are collective and (though Freud avoided this point) may be done not to relieve guilt, but for positive, beautiful and mystical reasons. The items of ritual are charged with symbolic meaning (Freud didn't avoid this point):

> It is easy to see where the resemblances lie between neurotic ceremonials and the sacred acts of religious ritual: in the qualms of conscience brought on by their neglect, in their complete isolation from all other actions (shown in the prohibition against interruption) and in the conscientiousness with which they are carried out in every detail. But the differences are equally obvious, and a few of them are so glaring that they make the comparison a sacrilege: the greater individual variability of neurotic ceremonial actions in contrast to the stereotyped character of rituals (prayer, turning to the East, etc.), their private nature as opposed to the public and communal character of religious observances, above all, however, the fact that, while the minutiae of religious ceremonial are full of significance and have a symbolic meaning, those of neurotics seem foolish and senseless. In this respect, an obsessional neurosis presents a travesty, half comic and half tragic, of a private religion. But it is precisely this sharpest difference between neurotic and religious ceremonial which disappears when, with the help of the psychoanalytic technique of investigation, one penetrates to the true meaning of obsessive actions . . . it is found that the obsessive actions are perfectly significant in every detail.

A girl whom I was able to observe was under a compulsion to rinse around her wash-basin several times after washing. The significance of this ceremonial action lay in the proverbial saying: 'Don't throw away dirty water until you have clean'. Her action was intended to give a warning to her sister, of whom she was very fond, and to restrain her from getting divorced from her unsatisfactory husband until she had established a relationship with a better man.

A woman who was living apart from her husband was under a compulsion, whenever she ate anything, to leave what was best of it behind: for example, she would take only the outside of a piece of roast meat. This renunciation was explained by the date of its origin. It appeared on the day after she had refused marital relations with her husband – that is to say, after she had given up what was the best.

It is quite easy to think of explanations for the neurotic behaviours described other than those suggested by Freud, but it isn't the purpose of this book to be occupied with Freud-bashing! Notice that Freud called these classic examples of obsessive actions 'private religions', and elsewhere, religion was described as the 'universal obsessional neurosis'.

But **is** religion an obsessional neurosis? We have seen that Freud stuck his neck out, and said he thought so. But most commentators would disagree: the distinction between healthy and unhealthy religiosity is a popular one, even though there is not very good consensus about the exact definitions of healthy and unhealthy.

Levin and Zegans (1974), Greenberg, Witztum and Pisante (1987) and Littlewood and Lipsedge (1989) describe cases of scrupulousness. In these papers, people are described whose concern for the minutiae of religious observance had reached clinical proportions (and they had clearly gone beyond and outside the demands of religion). They were unable to function adequately – and were driving their families, friends and religious mentors crazy, because of their fussiness over supposedly religiously required details. This is an example quoted by Greenberg, Witztum and Pisante.

Martin Luther is famous for his revolt against the Catholic Church in 1517 and as a reformer and founder of Protestant Christianity. Many forget that for years he was devout Catholic monk (in fact he dropped his law studies after fearing he would die in a frightening thunderstorm, when he vowed he would become a monk). There is much evidence that, as a monk, he struggled with scruples concerning his failure to achieve justification [freedom from the penalty of sin], and that he used excessive confession and severe penance to atone for his doubtful sins. Luther would repeat a confession and, to be sure of including everything, would review his entire life until the confessor grew weary and exclaimed: 'Man, God is not angry with you, you are angry with God; don't you know that God commands you to hope?' (Bainton, 1950). For Luther, the question was not whether his sins were great or small, but whether they had been thoroughly confessed. The difficulty that he encountered was to be sure that everything has been recalled. From experience he knew the tricks of memory and was frightened when, after six hours of confession, he could still go out and think of another detail he had omitted.

Does religion play a role in exacerbating an underlying character disorder? The question arises here, as it arose with authoritarian personality syndrome. In a sad way, it can do so, precisely because the sufferer can claim that his behaviour is religiously sanctioned. So it becomes harder to argue with him. If he had a idiosyncratic set of neurotic behaviours, these would be out of synch with social norms, and the sufferer would concede that his or her behaviour is not normal. But when the ill person can claim religious injunctions guiding his behaviour, his friends and family and religious mentors may plead in vain. Littlewood and Lipsedge (1989) discuss the dilemmas that confront the mental health professional; their treatment of this issue is described in Chapter 8.

Empirical attempts to examine correlations between measures of religion and measures of guilt and the like have not produced clear results (Gartner, 1983). Hood (1992) has pointed out the importance of distinguishing shame from guilt, and of distinguishing both from self-esteem. Following H. B. Lewis's (1971) psychoanalytic–phenomenological approach, it is suggested that shame and guilt have different sources.

- Shame is an effect of the ego ideal, the internalized idealized parent.
- Guilt is an effect of the superego, internalized threat.

Hood points out that different faith traditions and different individual and collective God concepts are associated with varying emphases on shame and guilt. Hood shows that in examining religion–guilt relationships, the form of religious commitment (extrinsic–intrinsic, God concept, faith tradition, etc.) needs to be specified, as do the distinctions between guilt, shame, sin, self-esteem and related factors. Hood's conclusions include the following.

- Studies in the USA suggest that those who are diagnosed as mentally ill do not appear to differ from others on indices on sin and shame.
- Extrinsic religiosity correlates negatively with sin and guilt measures (among students in the USA).

There is thus no evidence that higher levels of guilt, obsessionality and the like go along directly with religiosity.

As with the authoritarian personality syndrome, it appears doubtful that religion made the person obsessional or over-scrupulous. But we see that the religious context may give licence and new scope for the expression of this type of disorder.

SUMMARY

This chapter deals with some ideas about the effects of religion on unpleasant character traits, thoughts and behaviours. Two broad classes of behaviour and thinking are dealt with: self-righteousness, self-importance, prejudice, authoritarianism and cruelty; guilt, scrupulousness and shame.

It is suggested that religion may be abused to sanction behaviours, traits and attitudes that are cruel. Another route by which religion may contribute to poor mental health is by encouraging guilt and over-scrupulousness.

In both cases there is no evidence to suggest direct associations between cruelty – or guilt – and overall religiosity. Allport's suggestions about intrinsic ('sincere') and extrinsic (selfish) religiosity have been found to be helpful, with some modifications. There are some associations with style of religiosity and the behaviours and thoughts discussed.

7

Religion and good mental health: some processes

Here I shall try to describe the principal ways in which it has been suggested that religion may play a role in improving mental health. Much was foreshadowed by Durkheim (1966) who suggested that social integration and subordination of the individual to group life makes life more meaningful and purposeful. This was by virtue of devotion to others, and beliefs in divine planning.

SOCIAL SUPPORT

Social support has several aspects, including one or more people to talk over problems with, one or more people to give practical (including financial) help when needed, and the absence of troublemakers (so that one can get on with life's tasks without impediment). Some researchers have claimed that it is perceived social support, rather than actual, which is important.

Power, Champion and Aris (1988) distinguish between emotional and practical support, and suggest that it is important to distinguish between ideal and actual support. Table 7.1 illustrates Power and colleagues's social support measure. The client or subject repeats the ratings for the main significant figures in his or her life (spouse, mother, father, best friend and so on).

Table 7.1 Sample items from the Significant Others Scale (short questionnaire version) from Power, Champion and Aris, 1988, 1992)

Answer each question by writing a number from 1 (definitely no) to 7 (definitely yes)

Person_____

1. a) Can you trust, talk to frankly and share your feelings with him/her?
    b) What rating would your ideal be?
2. a) Can you lean on and turn to him/her in times of difficulty?
    b) What rating would your ideal be?
3. a) Does he or she give you practical help?
    b) What rating would your ideal be?

There are several suggested ways of scoring the scale illustrated in Table 7.1, of which the following are the two most important.

- Separate scores can be calculated for emotional and practical support.
- One can look at the discrepancy between the (perceived) support that is being given and the support that the person would like.

Why is social support important? The short answer is that having social support means being respected as a person, feeling that one matters and feeling that what one does is valued. In other words, social support is closely tied to self-esteem and identity. For practical purposes, an important feature of social support is that one has people who help, or who can be called on for help when needed. Here is a description by a woman in her sixties, with an invalid husband, of the support that materialized when she had to be hospitalized with a fractured femur (Shain, 1992).

> In the meantime, Aunt B. called the L.s, and H. and C. arrived a short while later, visibly worried about me. Aunt B. and her husband were able to leave, as H. stayed until after the surgery, and C. remained by my side the entire night.
>
> Be assured that Papa is being cared for lovingly and capably by many 'children'. Let me share the details with you. Y. (a grandson) comes from the college every night. He helps Papa get to bed and spends the night in our house. He takes care of

Papa's needs in the morning and returns to the college after breakfast. Thank Heaven that we have a grandson here.

M. has practically moved into our house with her new infant. She is in charge of seeing that Papa receives all his medication throughout the day, and she serves Papa and Y. breakfast.

P. prepares and serves Papa lunch, and relieves M. for a few hours.

Papa eats his main evening meal by Aunt B.

A woman was hired to do the housecleaning, and another takes care of washing Papa's clothes. I am not sure who does the shopping, but most probably it is my next-door neighbour.

So you should be assured, children, that our relatives and friends have rallied to my side, and I am thankful for their physical and moral support, especially the care they are giving Papa. Don't worry – everything is under control.

Notice the classic features of the support network: it's particularly useful when problems arise – that is to say, when one's own resources are inadequate. It involves relatives, friends, neighbours, even acquaintances, and – quite important – paid help to fill in the gaps. Note, too, the classic emotional reactions associated with social support, especially the issues of worry, that things should be in control, and thankfulness to the supporters.

Brown and Harris (1978) highlighted the importance of social support when they showed that having a confidant acted as a protective factor against the onset of depression. In their Hebridean studies, they suggested that religion may act as a protective factor in its own right, partly because of the sense of belonging that accrues from religious affiliation. Marcia (1966) has suggested that religious or ideological commitment is a major part of identity formation, and Cox (1977), Bragan (1977), Olson (1989) and others have shown how social involvement in religious organizations and the formation of friendships are essential to the intertwined development of commitment, identity, sense of belonging and social support.

By definition, social support in its various aspects militates against various forms of distress, by the provision of practical help, advice, sympathy and so forth. In a positive sense, social support is good for the sense of self. Religious organizations and social networks have – as a very important function – the provision of social support of all kinds, and we could say that the foundation of religious obligations that pertain between people is the provision of social support.

There is some evidence that religiosity goes along with perceived social support (McIntosh, Silver and Wortman, 1993). We would expect that involvement with any kind of religious group increases the availability of actual or potential social support. And of course, most religious groups advocate the practice of the behaviours that are socially supportive, such as respecting others, visiting the sick and providing for their needs, listening sympathetically and nonjudgmentally, and helping all who need help.

Indirect evidence linking religion with social support includes Cox's report that new members of new religious movements said that friendship was the primary attraction – though after a few weeks they tended to offer a more theologically 'proper' answer.

Based on Durkheim, there have been a number of reports suggesting a protective effect of religion against suicide. This effect has been linked with social support in the 'networks' approach of Pescosolido and Georgianna (1989). They elaborate Durkheim's approach and present evidence that where religious groups are organized with a good infrastructure and strong primary group ties, the greater protective effects of religion against suicide are enhanced.

More direct evidence of the effects of social support comes from a study of American parents coping with the loss of a child from SIDS (sudden infant death syndrome). Religious participation and importance of religion were assessed three weeks after the death of the baby. McIntosh, Silver and Wortman (1993) suggest that religious participation would be related to perceived social support, which it was. Both religious participation and importance of religion related to greater wellbeing and lower distress 18 months after the death.

In a different religious–cultural context, Shams and Jackson (1993) studied Moslem men of Asian origin living in Britain. This study showed that the distressing effects of unemployment were mitigated by religiosity. They suggest:

> One benefit of high levels of religious commitment which is likely to be particularly important in the Moslem community is the level of social contact implicated in its practice. Thus,

shared religious activities increase the feeling of group solidarity and strengthen family ties (Lovinger, 1984; Spero, 1985). There are strong group-based pressures to conform to shared norms and practices within the British-Asian community, and the personal costs of nonconformity can be very high, including potential loss of group acceptance and loss of family support. Conversely the benefits of frequent contact with other Moslems around the mosque, and engagement in both structured and informal social contact is likely to foster the affirmation of identity threatened by unemployment. For British Asians therefore, the study suggests that unemployment does not isolate individuals in the way which is often found for white unemployed people.

Thus, stress-buffering effects of religiosity are suggested – and found – to be partly the result of social support, both emotional and practical. Social support is said to enhance wellbeing via feelings of acceptance, identity and shared purpose, self-esteem, and feelings of coping. Theory and evidence suggest that social support may be particularly featured in close-knit religious groups.

SPIRITUAL SUPPORT

Harris (unpublished) presented material collected in the course of study of social causes of depression in women in the Hebrides. Many of the women described feelings of closeness to God, especially important in times of deep distress. In my ongoing work on orthodox Jews, similar material is emerging: faith or trust in God, feeling that everything is really for the best, are regarded as very important especially by people who have undergone or are undergoing severe difficulties.

Maton (1989) described three aspects to spiritual support:

- **emotional**: experience of divine care;
- **intimacy**: experience of a close personal relationship;
- **faith**: feeling that trust is essential to coping.

Maton looked at relations between perceived spiritual support and measures of mental health (wellbeing, self-esteem and lack of depression) in American adults. Some were undergoing or had undergone severe stress, and in this group, spiritual support was related to measures of mental health. Subjects not under stress showed no such relationship: this finding is not surprising since people not under stress don't show tremendous differences in levels of wellbeing and distress. They're all pretty laid-back. So there's not much variation in wellbeing for spiritual support to be related to.

Another aspect of Maton's findings relates to the claim that there are no atheists in foxholes. It is possible that stress induces turning to God. Remarkable data summarized by Argyle and Beit-Hallahmi (1975) suggest this. They summarize several surveys of the effects of battle and other war experiences on US army veterans of the Second World War. Prayer was most commonly mentioned of all cognitive strategies as being helpful 'when the going was tough' (Stouffer *et al.*, 1949) (other cognitive strategies included thinking about not letting the others down). The more severe the stress, the more prayer was found to be helpful. The long-term effect of war was to slightly decrease confidence in organized religion, but to heighten interest in problems of religion (Allport *et al.*, 1948). Stouffer *et al.* found that increased belief in God was much more likely than decreased belief among army veterans, and this effect was much more pronounced in men with combat experience compared to men without.

So there is some evidence that people turn to God and start praying particularly when there seems to be no way out and things are desperate. Prayer potentially involves all aspects of spiritual support. Parker and Brown (1982) grouped prayer with problem-solving behaviours as a coping strategy. This grouping was made on the basis of factor analysis. In this study, the perceived effectiveness of prayer was related to the extent to which it was actually used in coping with crises – this relationship was stronger than for any of the other coping behaviours examined.

In a later study, Parker and Brown (1986) grouped prayer among help-seeking coping behaviours. Here they found no relationship between the use of prayer and improvement, in a group of depressed patients. (In this study, the only coping behaviour that related to improvement was not using self-consolatory behaviour such as food bingeing).

A study which did show some positive effects of prayer was reported by Finney and Maloney (1985). Prayer was used as an adjunct to psychotherapy, with helpful effects in the clients studied. In ongoing work on orthodox-Jewish women, I have found some evidence that women who engage in the traditional coping strategy of saying Psalms are the less depressed. Several interpretations are possible, but the observation is compatible with the view that this type of prayer activity is an effective antidepressant.

This material suggests that spiritual support may be perceived as effective and valuable, especially in times of stress. There is some evidence of actual as well as perceived effectiveness.

Spiritual support is therefore something that deserves closer analysis and investigation.

BELIEFS AND VALUES

Different societies and different religious groups value different states of mind. For example, Huizinga (1960) suggested that melancholy was regarded as an essential aspect of the serious religious person in mediaeval Christian Europe. Loewenthal (1992) concluded that spiritual joy (*simcha*) has always been a highly valued state in Jewish ethical and mystical teachings. Eaton and Weil (1955), as we have seen, suggested that the emphasis on viewing the self as sinful and guilty may have been the cause of the greater prevalence of depressive disorders among the Hutterite communities, compared to the general American population. Buddhism emphasizes detachment from worldly and individualistic concerns.

It is possible that leaders of religious groups may advocate particular states of mind in response to social conditions likely to foster the opposite. For instance Loewenthal (1990) suggested that dedication to the observance of Judaism was urged by religious leadership at a time when Czarist Russian legislation was creating conditions to facilitate assimilation.

However specific beliefs and emotions are advocated, and for whatever reason, we should ask whether this religiously based advocacy has a detectable effect on (a) individual beliefs and emotions, and (b) mental health in general.

Strommen (1972) studied 5000 adult Lutherans in the USA. His main conclusion was that the most important predictors of behaviour were values and beliefs. The most communally active were the people that worshipped frequently, had a strong orientation to the transcendental meaning of life, were willing to serve and believed themselves to be at least as religious as their parents. Strommen's findings suggest that values and beliefs are more important in predicting Lutherans' attitudes and behaviour than are occupation, age, level of education, gender or financial status.

It is difficult to design research in this area, and some cross-sectional studies have produced conflicting results (Pressman *et al.*, 1992). In such studies, the most promising line seems to involve taking into account the style of belief and religious commitment. Bergin, Masters and Richards (1987) for example found an association between low anxiety and intrinsic religiosity ('a style valuing religion for interpersonal enhancement'). They also found an association between low anxiety and low extrinsic religiosity ('a style valuing religion for interpersonal benefits such as social status and acceptance').

The effects of religiously-advocated beliefs depend on whether they are internalized. Pressman and colleagues quote from the diary of Thomsen (1965), a farmer and a peace corps volunteer in South America:

> The statistics, of course, I knew – that in the country areas three out of five babies die before their third year. And I was aware of the Catholic philosophy which made these deaths bearable to the country people. They hold the profound belief that when a baby dies, it dies in a state of grace and (the soul) flies directly to heaven. Within this framework, then, the death of a child is something to celebrate; he has been released from a life of suffering and poverty to become one of God's angels. But, knowing all this, I still could not accept it . . . what was I going to do in that unrewarding spot for 18 more months . . . sent me reeling into a depression.

In studying the mental health effects of beliefs and values, the most useful type of research is longitudinal. McIntosh, Silver and Wortman (1993) found that importance of religion predicted better adjustment (lower distress and higher wellbeing) in American parents coping with the loss of a child. Pressman *et al.* (1990) found that religious beliefs and practices were significantly associated with lower depression and better walking after leaving hospital among elderly American women recovering from broken hips.

Although there is some evidence that religious beliefs and values can affect mental outcomes, it is far from clear **which** beliefs and values are effective. There are suggestions that the perception of purpose and meaning in life (and death) may be important, but how do the effects come about? Chapter 9 returns to take a closer look at these issues.

RELIGIOUS EXPERIENCES

A variety of religious experiences have been described and there is more about them in Chapter 9. Here I want to describe a few types of experience, briefly mention some of the controversies surrounding them, and then turn to the all-important question of their effects on mental health. These effects are claimed to be positive, though you will see that the evidence could be improved.

Many books have been written on religious experience, including some of the most famous works on the psychology of religion. The most often cited are William James's *Varieties of Religious Experience* (1902) and Stace's *Mysticism and Philosophy* (1960). Stace's work became very popular with psychologists such as Ralph Hood (1970) and David Hay (1979), among others, who were working in the 1970s and 1980s on religious experience. Most work has concentrated on describing the different types of experience, and looking at the physiological and psychological differences between 'normal' and religious states of mind. There has also been a lot of interest in the question of whether certain types of people are more likely to have religious experiences and whether certain conditions foster the occurrence of religious experiences. There has been very little work on the mental health effects of these experiences although there are claims that these effects are positive. The main types of experience are the following.

- **Mystical and contemplative**: these involve a quiet person, a comparatively still body and a feeling of communion with the divine.
- **Ecstatic**: here the person is usually not quiet and the body is very active, and the dominant feelings are excitement and of being moved by the divine. Ecstasies included possessions and trances, glossolalia and feelings of being moved by the spirit. Demographic and anthropological evidence suggests that ecstasies are more commonly experienced by deprived,

disadvantaged or oppressed groups (Holm, 1983). I. M. Lewis (1971) concluded that in 'peripheral' cults it was almost exclusively women who were possessed. E., described in Chapter 8, experienced ecstatic possession.

- **Other**: these include near-death and out-of-body experiences, states such as spirit possession and strong feelings of religious mission or purpose. They may occur suddenly without prior preparation by the person, and involve an intense awareness of spirituality, for example that the soul has left the body and is meeting the souls of other people who have died or that the body has been taken over by the soul of someone who has died.

Psychiatrists may have problems distinguishing these states from psychopathological conditions, and some psychopathological conditions may show some features of some of these conditions, such as a belief that one is being persecuted by devils, or a belief that one is some important religious figure such as Jesus or the Messiah. People who have had experiences may say they are afraid of talking about them in case they are diagnosed as mad.

There are a number of states which appear to involve awareness of spirituality, where there is no evidence of psychopathology other than the distress, excitement or concern caused by the condition.

We will concentrate here on mystical states, on which most psychological research has focused.

In Stace's (1960) book, mystical states are seen as having the following qualities.

- **Noetic**: the experience is seen as a source of valid knowledge, not just a pleasant or inspiring experience.
- **Ineffable**: it cannot be described in words.
- **Holiness**: this does not necessarily carry any theological connotations; it means that the experience is seen as special and sacrosanct by the individual.
- **Positive affect**: though the experience is profound, it is not generally seen as frightening – rather, it is positive.
- **Paradoxical**: defies logic, natural-science explanations.

Stace also distinguish extrovertive and introvertive mysticism, the former involving a sense of the 'life' in all things and their unity, and the latter involving timeless and spaceless qualities and a dissolution of the sense of self.

Mystical states may appear to come out of the blue. A major research effort by the Hardy-founded Religious Experience Research Unit in Oxford was to describe these states and some of the conditions in which they occurred (e.g. Hay, 1982). Mystical states may be deliberately fostered and encouraged. Various religious disciplines (prayer, contemplation, fasting and others) may be used to induce greater religious awareness. Although mystical experience is said to be both 'normal and normative' (Spilka, Hood and Gorsuch, 1985), just in case you missed out on it, or didn't recognize it when it hit you, here are some of its qualities as assessed by Hood and his collaborators (you will recognize what such measures owe to Stace): 'Have you ever had an experience . . .

- in which time, place and distance are meaningless?
- in which you recognized oneness with all things?
- of holiness?
- of deep and profound peace?
- which could not be put adequately into words?
- in which a new view of reality was revealed to you?'

None of the above may mean anything to you. But more likely than not, you have had one or more experiences with some of the above features, even though – more likely than not – you may have kept quiet about it.

Here is a description from Hood's Religious Experiences Episodes Measure (1970), based mainly on James's collection.

> I remember the night and almost the very spot on the hilltop where my soul opened out and the inner and outer worlds rushed together. My own deep struggle was being answered by the unfathomable deep without, reaching beyond the stars. I stood alone with him who had made me, and all the beauty, love and sorrow of the world. I felt the union of my spirit with his. The ordinary sense of things around me faded, and for the moment nothing remained but indescribable joy.

How do these experiences affect wellbeing and mental health?

Spilka, Hood and Gorsuch (1985) stress that mystical experiences are more likely to be reported by intrinsically religious people because they value them and have an attributional framework which enables them to interpret them as meaningful. The indiscriminately antireligious have no such legitimating meaning system and so may be less likely to identify and/or report such experiences. This attributional approach suggests that even if mystical experiences are visited upon all equally, they will not have similar effects, because of the way the person evaluates and understands them.

Mystical experiences are more likely to be reported by (and perhaps to occur to) some people rather than others (e.g. Hood, 1970; Fenwick, 1987; Hay, 1982). They may often be deliberately sought, perhaps as a means of relieving distress.

This makes research design and interpretation very difficult, if we wish to examine the positive effects of mystical or other religious experiences on psychological wellbeing.

Pahnke's (1966) subjects reported long-term beneficial effects of a Good Friday religious experience, regardless of whether or not it had been preceded by administration of a 'psychedelic' drug. Pahnke's subjects took part in a moving Good Friday service, after a period of supportive psychological and religious preparation. They generally felt that their views of life and of other people had been improved. Hood (1977) reported that mystical experiences were more likely to be reported by those scoring high on a Maslow-based measure of self-actualization. Spilka, Hood and Gorsuch (1985) conclude that 'using indices of psychological strength, uncontaminated by religious biases, reported mystical experience has been shown to correlate positively with measures of health and psychological strength'.

Without making a meal of the methodological issues, the data are really not very good. Cause-and-effect issues can't be resolved. But there are plenty of suggestions for further research, and enough suggestions that this research should be directed to looking at the perceived and measured effects of religious experience on such aspects of mental health as:

- spiritual wellbeing;
- psychological wellbeing (including absence of distress as well as positive states such as peace and goodwill);
- quality of relationships;
- aspects of cognition (including and perhaps especially attributional style).

MATURITY

Allport (1950) described a mature style of religious or personal philosophy, by which the person was seen as caring for others, nonjudgmental, committed to his or her principles which had been evolved after a prolonged and difficult period of suffering and spiritual and/or psychological searching.

Kohlberg (1969) has described a developmental sequence in the growth of personal moral philosophies, and Fowler (1981) has described stages in the growth of faith. Both Kohlberg and Fowler describe early stages – resembling in some ways Allport's 'immature', egocentric style (of religiosity) – in which the person is basically wrapped up in his own needs and demands and is unable to relate to or even see those of others. At later stages, the needs and demands of others and the laws regulating the welfare of the wider community begin to be taken into consideration. At still later stages, a person may come to perceive that the norms of his or her social group are not necessarily the ultimate moral imperative, and that it may be necessary to change these. For some, higher principles may require working outside the framework of peaceful and legal change and negotiation. Dangerous stuff? What **is** the difference between a terrorist and a freedom fighter, a loony fanatic and a holy martyr?

Nevertheless, the idea that difficulties and problems and crises precipitate psychological growth – or stagnation, regression and illness – has been a perennial theme of every developmental theorist working on every front: for example Freud on emotional development (1933), Erikson on psychosocial development (1963) and Piaget on cognitive growth (1967).

Jung (1958), James (1902) and many others have argued that the process of crisis negotiation could be – and perhaps essentially is – a religious process. So the idea of maturity in relation to religious growth remains a popular one. Batson, Schoenrade and Ventis (1993) relate Allport's early formulations of mature religiosity – involving complex, critical reflection on religious issues – to cognitive structure models of personality change and to their own analyses of religious experience. They suggest that mature religion involves: 'a highly complex cognitive organization for dealing with existential questions . . . which has emerged from repeated creative changes in response to existential conflicts'.

It was Allport's formulation of maturity that gave rise to more readily measurable formulations of extrinsic, intrinsic and quest religiosity, which have been shown to relate in fairly consistent ways to measures of mental health and wellbeing. Batson, Schoenrade and Ventis's (1993) magnificent review (of mainly American studies, often with student samples) suggests the following.

- The extrinsic (means) orientation to religion – indicating a self-centred, instrumental use of religion – is generally associated with lower levels of mental health, wellbeing, responsible social behaviour, personal competence and control, self-actualization and purpose, and with higher levels of depression, guilt and worry.
- The intrinsic (end) orientation – reported religious sincerity – is generally associated with higher levels of mental health and wellbeing, responsible social behaviour, personal competence and control, and purpose, and with lower levels of depression, guilt, worry and dogmatism. Note that the picture is not the mirror-image of the picture *vis-à-vis* extrinsic (means) religiosity, since the majority of studies reviewed showed no relation with self-actualization, and there were some reports of a positive relationship with dogmatism.
- The quest dimension is supposed to indicate an open-minded, questing approach to religion, and (unlike intrinsic religiosity) its measurement is free of social desirability bias. Quest is associated mainly with measures of open-mindedness and flexibility, with little evidence of association with other measures of mental health.
- As discussed in Chapter 6, with regard to social attitudes, extrinsic religiosity tends to be associated with prejudice, intrinsic religiosity with low prejudice.
- Quest is generally a good predictor of behavioural measures of helping; intrinsic religiosity has no relationship with helping behaviour.

The statistical evidence, then, is that taking religion seriously goes along with the sort of qualities that are associated with good, even saintly people.

There are examples of people who have aspired to the saintly ideal with unfortunate results:

Mr D. had very minimal contact with religion as a child. His childhood seems to have been a rather sombre one, with no apparent traumas or highlights. His parents always had to work very hard to struggle for a living to support their two children, and Mr D.'s grandfather who lived with them. Mr D. went to college, found a reasonable job and married. He tried to live up to his humanistic/religious ideals which he felt strongly about: to be a very kind and caring person. As a young adult, he began to suffer from bouts of 'depression'. As time went by, he became convinced that he was seriously ill, that this was caused by rays from the media, who were seeking him out and hunting him down because he was the Messiah.

His marriage broke down and he lost his job. He spends his time hiding in his flat, with occasional contact with his doctor, his family and a few concerned friends.

Such sad examples abound in the psychiatric literature. They may be the exceptions. Examples of psychological success stories are not found in the psychological and psychiatric journals. Hagiography can give us some clues, but biographies of saints and great people are often all too obviously one-dimensional, painting-over-the-cracks exercises. We learn about the wonderful person's good deeds, charitable attitudes, wise sayings and life achievements, without any glimpses into the interior. However, such stories may serve as useful and inspiring role-models, as suggested by Sunden (see Wikstrom, 1987). Batson, Schoenrade and Ventis (1993) quote the words of Burtt (1957):

A conviction of moral obligation toward all men, simply because they are men, is born. The wall that circumscribed sympathetic feeling and kept it within the tribe is broken down, and the sense of community is encouraged to open out beyond that limit; the idea takes root that we are essentially members of a society embracing all human beings on the same terms and in which therefore all men are brothers. This involves a radical and decisive transcendence of customary morality and of the attitudes which pervade it.

And William James's (1902) view of saintliness: 'A shifting of the emotional centre towards loving and harmonious affections, towards "yes, yes" and away from "no" where the claims of non-ego are concerned . . . increase of charity, tenderness for fellow-creatures'.

And a description by Branover (1982) of a meeting with a Jewish leader (the Lubavitcher Rebbe), who

> had already held about 50 such private meetings that night. Yet his face showed no signs of fatigue . . . [we] felt as if we had known him for years and were continuing a conversation begun long ago. I was astonished at how well-informed the Rebbe was in politics, about various natural sciences, literature, economics . . . his greatness in Torah is well-known . . . most incredible was how much he knew and remembered about our family affairs and circumstances. I have never met anyone who can listen . . . who can cut off all disturbances and distracting interests . . . he understands immediately . . . and speaks the truth . . . and you always feel that his advice is made only for the good . . . both in the spiritual and in the simple, worldly sense. It is impossible to imagine him having personal interests.

Maton and Pargament (1987) describe a number of examples of practical programmes illustrating the roles of religion in prevention of personal and social problems, and in promoting the welfare of both individual and society. They suggest a number of routes by which these effects may be achieved, including spiritual and personal growth, personal quest, personal defence and stress buffering. They describe a 'personal quest pathway' operationalized by a congregation oriented to social action:

> Church of the Saviour is an ecumenical church of 125 members in an east-coast city, with an energetic, talented and charismatic leader. Members are organized into small groups with a great deal of autonomy.
>
> Their personal and spiritual growth is encouraged by daily diary-writing, prayer and study. There is less emphasis on a personal and intimate relationship with God than in some Christian groups. There is emphasis on practical mission work, such as assisting abandoned or abused children, renovating deteriorated housing for the elderly and helping them

to maintain it, and educating the affluent about their financial obligations towards the less well-off.

It is suggested that self-searching, contemplation and prayer, study, good deeds and the emulation of role models are all aspects of religiously recommended paths to personal and spiritual growth. On the whole, the outcomes seem to be desirable, but the processes described are worth closer study.

SUMMARY

This chapter reviews several routes via which it has been suggested that religion may have positive effects on mental health.

One route is social support (notably confidants, practical help, absence of conflict), which is often high in religious groups. A second route is spiritual support, while other routes involve religiously encouraged states of mind – beliefs, emotions and mystical and other religious experiences. A final route is following one of many recommended paths to development.

In each case, there is some evidence that there are overall positive effects on mental health, but more investigation is often required.

8

Clients and therapists: bridging the gap?

This chapter deals with a set of much-discussed problems:

- the alleged insensitivity of psychotherapists to the religious needs of their clients;
- the lack of theory and technique in many psychotherapies to deal with spirituality;
- the feeling of some clients that manifestations of religious practices and needs are automatically regarded as symptoms of psychopathology by the professionals.

The doyen of psychoanalysis, Freud, is generally viewed as having dismissed religion as an 'illusion' and an 'obsessional neurosis' (e.g. Freud, 1927). This is a bit of an over-simplification – Freud could be sensitive and thoughtful on issues to do with religion, not simply negative and dismissive. But it is probably true to say that Freud thought that anything religion could do, psychoanalysis could do better, and that there was no real space in psychoanalytic theory and technique for religion. Many psychotherapeutic systems may not have the conceptual apparatus to deal with the profound existential–religious questions clients may be struggling with. Of course there are exceptions to this rule. Jung (1933), Frankl (1965), Spero (1992) and others have developed ways of doing psychotherapy that attend to the patient's spiritual needs and spiritual growth as part and parcel of the whole process. These notwithstanding, clients may perceive psychotherapy and psychotherapists as a totally godless crew.

RELIGIOSITY AND PSYCHOTHERAPY: RELIGIOUS CLIENTS AND
GODLESS THERAPISTS

One of the interesting effects of the tide of reform and assimilation sweeping through European Jewry in the 19th century was
that a number of Jews turned to generating secular ideologies.
Marx and Freud are the two best-known, and what concerns us
here is Freud's well-known attempts to create, in psychoanalysis,
an alternative to religion. In many ways, psychoanalysis was to
be superior, enabling man to gain insight into what had previously been bamboozling him and causing him to make a
neurotic mess of the affairs of humanity (1927, 1930). Sometimes
psychoanalysis is given the force of a new religion, with Freud as
its prophet. Freudian psychoanalytic therapy is the grandfather
or uncle of so many psychological therapies that are in use today
that it is not surprising that attention to the patient's or client's
spiritual needs may not figure very largely in the training of
psychotherapists. When religious and spiritual issues crop up,
they may be regarded as nuisances.

What is psychotherapy? Psychotherapy is a general term for a
huge variety of psychological therapies for unhappiness – which
bothers the person suffering from it – and for difficult behaviour
– which bothers other people, and which may be associated with
unhappiness in the person who is behaving badly. Sometimes a
psychological illness (one of the neuroses or psychoses) may be
present; sometimes therapy is undertaken for distress or disordered behaviour without there being any psychiatric illness. A
related discipline of counselling deals with people who are
usually not psychiatrically ill, but who feel they could use some
help in dealing with problems that are causing distress.

A summary of an individual case history is offered by Brown
and Pedder (1979). This offers a nice insight into the way in
which psychotherapeutic approaches may help with emotional
and behaviour problems that don't respond well to pharma-
cological intervention:

Mrs A. went to her family doctor, suffering from bouts of
tearfulness and from acute panic and anxiety attacks. Her
doctor thought that she was suffering from a depressive

illness and prescribed antidepressant medication. This was not helpful, and Mrs A. feared that she was going mad.

When Mrs A. looked for another view on her problems, she was asked to recall when her attacks had begun. She said they seemed to originate when she and her husband had started to talk about sending their six-year-old daughter away to boarding school. The A.'s lived in the country and it was very difficult to transport their daughter to school each day. Further recollection produced the memory that when Mrs A. herself was six years old, her parents' marriage had broken down, and she was sent to live with an aunt. She had not been at all happy, and it now seemed to her that the possibility of separation from her little daughter was not only depressing in itself, but awakened painful feelings from Mrs A.'s childhood.

Mrs A. found that now she had reviewed her recent feelings in relation to her past, her panic and depression began to resolve.

Some psychotherapies are psychoanalytic, which means they may use theories and techniques that owe something to the work of Freud. Others use theories and methods that owe so little to Freud that they cannot really be called psychoanalytic. Examples would be client-centred therapy (Rogers, 1959), rational–emotive therapy (Ellis, 1962), therapy based on the personal construct theory of Bannister (Bannister and Mair, 1968), and cognitive–behavioural therapies (Beck *et al.*, 1979). Many of the difficulties to be discussed in this chapter have arisen in connection with psychoanalytic therapies, although some of the criticisms and fears of the religious towards psychotherapy might equally well apply to the non-psychoanalytic therapies. This chapter will focus on psychoanalytic therapies. Many such therapies do not use a Freudian framework, but some other psychoanalytic framework, and many psychoanalytic therapists would call themselves eclectic – using any theories and techniques which seem helpful.

In *The Question of Lay Analysis* (1926), Freud saw psychoanalysis as a procedure for improving or curing nervous disorders. Brown and Pedder (1979) see psychoanalysis as a form of conversation, involving both listening and talking to those in trouble, with the aim of first understanding and then assisting to a resolution of the predicament. Put like this, one might wonder why all the fuss. We can all listen to our friends' problems and suggest solutions, so who needs to spend all that time training as a psychotherapist, and who needs to spend all that money paying the therapist to listen to their problems?

There are several important differences between an ordinary sympathetic conversation and psychotherapy. First, the therapeutic relationship is professional and often a paying one. This means the therapist has a different role and different obligations from a friend. Second, most therapists must cultivate the trust of their patients and develop a realistic working relationship. Third, most therapists will not divulge much information about themselves. They are not trying to be secretive or superior, but they are trying to form a context in which a 'transference' will develop. Transference is the appearance of strong feelings in the patient which have been experienced towards key figures in the past and which are now directed towards the therapist. Many therapists see the appearance and analysis of transference as crucial to psychoanalytic therapy. Fourth, most therapists try to monitor their own reactions and feelings to the patient, in order to get clues about the patient's relationships with other people, and generally to deepen their therapeutic understanding of the patient. There are a number of other special features of psychoanalytic therapy (Sandler, Dare and Holder, 1992), but I hope I have said enough to show that psychoanalytic therapy is quite different from a sympathetic conversation between friends. Psychotherapy is definitely not to be attempted by amateurs, who may cause great damage with ill-judged 'interpretations' based on ill-judged speculations about early relationships.

Psychotherapy, as I have described it, does seem a fairly unspiritual venture, in which religious issues may appear but are unlikely to be central.

Purpura (1985) and Fenchel (1986) subscribe to this view. They see an almost unbridgable chasm between Catholicism and psychoanalysis. Psychotherapists are reported to be ignorant of Catholic practices and values. Intertwined with ignorance is prejudice: therapists have negative attitudes to religion and religious people, and fail to see that religion has a positive and adaptive function in the lives of many people.

Quackenbos, Privette and Klenz (1986) however show that among psychotherapies there are wide ranges of accommodation to religious values. They give a range of examples, suggesting for instance that Mowrer (1961) had an orthodox religious position: in his view mental problems are the result of guilt, caused by sin, destroying personal integrity and the relatedness of the community. Ellis (1975) is atheistic, and Rogers (1951, 1980) is seen as 'neutralistic' *vis-à-vis* religion. Oden (1967) however has a theistic, existential viewpoint. Quackenbos, Privette and Klenz are among many who would like to see more professional psychotherapeutic techniques brought into pastoral work and more sensitivity to religious issues among mental health professionals.

Spilka (1986) suggested a number of ways in which religion needed to be taken account of by psychotherapists. In Spilka's view, religion relates to mental disorder as an expression of abnormality, as a socializing and suppressing force, as a haven, as a therapy, and as a hazard. Religion may provide meaning, self-esteem, and a sense of control. Both therapists and their clients need to be aware of all these possible effects of religion in their work.

So there is a keen perception of a chasm between some forms of psychotherapy and religion. Ministers of religion will cope with large numbers of self-referrals for problems similar to those seen by mental health professionals (Lowe, 1986). And mental health professionals will cope with large numbers of problems similar to those seen by ministers of religion: the sequelae of bereavement and other losses, family conflicts, and the 'common colds' of psychiatry – depression and anxiety – all these are equally likely to refer first to a medical practitioner or a minister of religion as to a mental health professional. But there is very little cross-referral between psychotherapists and ministers of religion.

Some professionals may wear both hats at once. People may train both as ministers of religion and as psychotherapists. The advantage of this is that religious clients may trust the therapist not to misunderstand their religious beliefs and practices. But – maybe this is a game where there are no winning moves: according to Cunin, Cunin, and Cunin (1993) a whole crop of new problems can arise.

- Religious patients may over-idealize the religious therapist.
- Patients may expect a 'magical' cure.
- The therapist may be placed in the role of a priest, rabbi or religious mentor and be expected to dispense advice and counsel not appropriate to psychotherapy.
- The therapist may have his or her own difficulties with religion ('unresolved conflicts'); for instance, this could add to the difficulties of distinguishing between 'healthy' and 'unhealthy' religiosity.

In spite of well-meaning noises about psychotherapy and religion learning from each other, pastoral counselling and psychotherapy are seen as different ball-games by their customers – and very often by their practitioners.

PERCEPTIONS OF PSYCHOTHERAPISTS BY CLIENTS

The general situation is one of mistrust by potential clients who are religious. This is endorsed by some religiously oriented psychological professionals, such as Amsel (1976) and Purpura (1985) who see very little evidence of accommodation by psychotherapy or psychotherapists to religious needs.

In my local orthodox-Jewish community there is a splendid mythology of perceived misunderstandings of religious clients by irreligious professionals, who may be ignorant of the religious norms of the community. The following are examples.

One claim concerns a woman who was accused of neglecting her children and spending too much time and money on her personal appearance. The basis of the accusation was said to be that a visiting social worker had seen a wig on the dressing-table in the client's bedroom. Wigs are worn by orthodox Jewish women for reasons of modesty, and in many strictly orthodox circles the possession of at least one wig is considered a religious essential for every married woman. The woman was having difficulties managing to feed and clothe her children adequately. The social worker had viewed the wig as a sign that the woman was a poor manager, had got her priorities wrong and had really got an adequate income which she was selfishly spending on frivolous self-adornment (the wig) rather than on essentials for her children.

> At a recent well-attended meeting in memory of a promi-
> nent, recently-deceased woman, a leading rabbi was
> reported to have warned his audience against the dangers
> of psychology, psychologists and psychiatrists.

> As described in Chapter 3, religiously orthodox Jews
> claimed that a psychologist diagnosed a boy as 'disturbed'
> because he swayed backwards and forwards while praying
> and studying – as is encouraged among many religious
> Jews.

Littlewood and Lipsedge (1989), quoting material from their
experience with West Indian and orthodox-Jewish patients in
London, claim that it is indeed very hard for psychiatrists to
judge when a client's behaviour is disturbed and when it is
socially sanctioned or encouraged. The position is complicated
when the client or patient is using religious sanctions to justify
behaviour that is unacceptable to his or her family or co-religion-
ists. This can easily lead to a situation where the professional is
uncertain where to draw the line between religiously sanctioned
behaviour and psychological disturbance.

To distinguish zealousness from pathological scrupulosity is
often impossible when religious ritual and observance are so
highly valued and intensely integrated into all aspects of everyday life.

M. was born into a displaced person's camp in Germany in
1946. In a situation where children were extremely uncom-
mon, his parents devoted a considerable proportion of their
rations to their son. The only child among the remnants of the
Hungarian Hasidim in the camp, his birth seemed a portent
for the future. His parents came to Britain and joined the
Hasidic community in London in 1949. All their relatives had
perished.

M.'s education followed the traditional pattern of the *cheder*
and the *yeshiva*, where he learnt to analyse the Talmud and its
commentaries and how to reconcile apparent contradictions

in the sacred texts. A quiet and conscientious student, he was not particularly successful and failed to live up to his father's hopes that he would become an outstanding scholar. Eventually his parents arranged a marriage in Antwerp with a girl from the same Hasidic community. He left to join her and, at the age of 26, began work for the first time, helping in the family workshop. Although M. met [his father-in-law's] criteria of lineage, Talmudic learning and orthodox practice, the marriage failed because M. was impotent, and he was divorced. On returning to London he appeared to his worried parents preoccupied and quiet, was unable to concentrate on his studies and failed in his attempt to earn a living in a small factory owned by a friend of his father.

M. was brought to our hospital two years after his divorce by his understandably anxious mother after his weight had fallen to six stone as a result of extreme dieting. He was fasting for long periods, spending up to 20 hours daily in the study house and standing for hours immersed in the *mikveh* (ritual bath) in order to 'disperse unholiness'. Family meals were a battle, as M. politely but firmly refused to eat, his mother alternately cajoled and wept, while his father appeared strangely unconcerned. Communication with M. was difficult – his knowledge of English was limited since he had never moved out of his Yiddish-speaking environment. He quietly told us that his mother was mistaken in her belief that he was *meshugge* (insane). When asked why he was fasting and what the religious sanction for it was, he remained silent and slightly supercilious. Did M. believe that he had been specially chosen by God? He answered evasively. He refused to talk about his marriage, gazing past us into the distance.

His father, a figure out of a Chagall painting in black caftan and broad-brimmed hat, was less dogmatic than the mother about M.'s behaviour and suggested that perhaps he was just 'very religious'.

It was difficult to accept that M.'s excessive religiosity and fasting were symptoms of a serious mental illness, despite his mother's insistent demands that he be admitted to hospital for 'treatment'. Lack of information about the marriage and exactly what was passing at home (an attempt to join a family meal proved unsuccessful) meant that we had little to go on apart from M.'s fasting and bathing. Both had religious sanction. We talked to members of his community who tended (especially the women) to share his mother's view, but a minority dissented. We tried to reassure [M.'s mother], who blamed her son's 'illness' on her own failure to fulfil scrupulously the requirement to separate and burn a small portion of dough when baking.

Psychiatric colleagues offered a variety of opinions and diagnostic labels. The refusal to eat and M.'s assertion that his weight was adequate were suggested by one doctor to be anorexia nervosa, with its characteristic distortion of body-image: M. denied being thin even when severely emaciated.

A social worker interpreted his religiosity as M.'s understandable attempt to increase his status within the community. He had failed in his role as husband and scholar, and was perhaps striving to gain recognition by his ascetic piety. For another, the ritual significance of food in Jewish family life, especially a family who had survived near-starvation in concentration camps, was thought to offer M. a powerful tool in some family dispute of which we were still unaware.

A nurse described as 'schizophrenic' M.'s explanation that he was simply carrying out God's command to fast and purify himself. He had heard these divine instructions during his long hours of prayer. M.'s feeling that he was being 'made' to carry out God's will appeared to resemble the schizophrenic experience of passivity.

Another psychiatrist suggested that M. was depressed even though he did not look dejected or miserable and denied feeling unhappy. He pointed out that M. was unlikely to admit to depressive feelings and ideas since a melancholy attitude is anathema to devout Hasidim: 'At times the evil inclination misleads man into supposing that he has committed a serious sin when it was actually no more than a mere peccadillo or no sin at all, the intention being to bring men into a state of melancholy. But melancholy is a great hindrance to God's service. Even if a man has stumbled and sinned he should not become too sad because this will prevent him from worshipping God.'

The diversity of medical opinion mirrored the conflicting attitudes to M.'s behaviour shown by his family and community. How acceptable were his ideas and ascetic practices by the standards of his own congregation? In a community in which all activity is guided by precedent and authority it appeared logical to do the same and look at the traditional teachers . . . according to Jacobs (1973) there has never been rabbinic advocacy of ascetic exercises which may endanger health. He quotes Rabbi Moses Hayim Luzzatto: 'You may accept as a true principle that men should abstain from things in this world which are not absolutely necessary. But if, for any reason, a thing is physically indispensable, he who abstains from it is a sinner. To this there is no exception.' On the other hand, M. himself appealed to the life of Rabbi Nachman of Brazlav. Nachman, great-grandson of the Besht (Rabbi Israel Baal Shem Tov, founder of Hasidism), indulged in prolonged fasts, followed by immersions in an icy cold *mikveh*. 'The world imagines', he said, 'that because I am a descendant of the Besht, I have attained a high status. It is not so. I have succeeded because I have afflicted my body . . .' (quoted by Rabinowicz, 1960).

Given the historic precedent for self-mortification we have refrained from diagnostic labels. Meanwhile M. remains perilously underweight and we are far from certain that we have understood his predicament.

Another example from Littlewood and Lipsedge:

In our hospital, as in many others, the majority of the nurses and domestic staff were West Indian immigrants. One Sunday morning when on duty at the hospital, one of us was asked by the matron to see a nursing auxiliary who, after attending her church, had started work on the ward. She had 'become peculiar, singing hymns loudly, neglecting her patients but then, after telling them to have faith in her, had suddenly burst into tears'.

Forty-five-year-old E. was born in Jamaica and had come to Britain when she was 30, after having worked in the capital, Kingston, as a typist. She had difficulty finding work in London and, disappointed in her wish to become a secretary, worked successively as a packer in a factory, a domestic and a laundress, before eventually finding a permanent niche in the local hospital. She was well liked by her colleagues, black and white, whose only complaint was of her excessive religious zeal, which made them feel rather uncomfortable, particularly when it was directed towards the patients.

Nine years after arriving in London, E. had joined her local Pentecostal church, which has a predominantly West Indian congregation. She remains unmarried and her social life is centred exclusively around religious activities. The highlights of her week are the five meetings of her church, a small independent sect of about 30 members, which meets in a rented school hall. Soon after joining she began to 'speak in tongues', one of the 'gifts of the Spirit' encouraged in her sect. She continued working in the hospital, apparently happy, although her only close friends were fellow members of her congregation. E. lives alone in a rented room, leaving it only for church or work. In spite of her enthusiasm she never takes any part in running the church or organizing activities but can always be relied on as a volunteer for street-corner testimony and evangelization. She believes that her coming to Britain was part of God's purpose to spread the gospel to a people who had forgotten it and to bring them back to Christ. Although deeply religious, she is certainly not sanctimonious and can laugh at herself and others. A travel poster in our waiting room has been embellished by her with the words 'England is not so bad after all' and she has added 'You need the Lord Jesus' to another which advertizes a psychotherapy group.

When we first met I did not know she had seen a psychiatrist previously. E. had in fact been admitted briefly to another hospital some months before 'in a state of ecstasy'. She saw me quite happily, immediately grabbing my arm and making me sit down, but then started sobbing against my shoulder. Before I could ask what the trouble was she suddenly gave a scream and rolled over on the floor, crying out something I could not grasp. It was difficult to understand exactly what she was saying, but her speech had a coherent rhythm, something like that of an evangelical preacher or a racing commentator. Suddenly she jumped up, sat down next to me again and explained rather breathlessly and at great length that she was being unfairly treated in the hospital for spreading the word of God and that she was being martyred. Then she quizzed me on my knowledge of the Book of Revelation.

She started singing gospel hymns and, pushing me into a corner of the room, began an ecstatic dance on her own, punctuated by rousing cries of 'Praise the Lord'. She would not answer any questions and I sat by helpless, laughing when she laughed and consoling her when she cried: she was able to make me feel I was sharing her enthusiasm even if I did not really understand it. It then occurred to me that as she was a Pentecostalist she had just been 'speaking tongues'. She had probably been carried away during the service and the fervour generated by the 'tongues' had somehow been continuing since. With relief I suggested this to the nurses and asked them to telephone the members of her church, who would know what to do. They did not seem very convinced. I sat down and waited next to E., who continued as before. About 10 of her friends arrived. To my astonishment they told me this was nothing like speaking in tongues, that E. was 'sick in the head' and I had better give her an injection immediately. With this advice I decided that perhaps she could be psychiatrically ill after all. I offered her some medicine and she fell asleep. She has attended my clinic since then, takes daily prophylactic medicine cheerfully, agrees with her church that she has had a 'break-down', continues to attend her church and during the service **still speaks in tongues**.

This episode gave rise to a number of problems.

i) The diagnosis was made by a religious sect, not the psychiatrist.

ii) The way I interpreted E.'s behaviour varied with whichever model I had in my head. Her rapid staccato speech with repetition, religious content and occasional unintelligibility could be perceived both as religious fervour and 'hypomanic' speech. Even after I attended services at her church with her, I was still not convinced I could always tell the difference if it were not for the **context** in which the behaviour occurred.

iii) It was difficult to separate E.'s experience into the two types of experience – religion and mental illness. Could the two be the same phenomenon? Had being a member of the church stopped her from becoming ill before, or on the contrary had over-zealous participation in activities like speaking in tongues driven her to a position where even her sect saw her as ill?

iv) It occurred to me that possibly another more 'extreme' sect might have said that E.'s behaviour was not pathological. Maybe she was just too enthusiastic for this particular group. To protect themselves from being seen by society as deranged, her group had perhaps labelled her as ill. If this was the case, the medical profession was being used to delineate ritualistic differences between churches!

v) What was glossolalia (speaking in tongues) anyway? To what extent was it a 'normal' phenomenon? Were charismatics mentally unbalanced?

Littlewood and Lipsedge's question about glossolalia (widely practised and advocated in Pentecostal and charismatic Christianity) is answered by their conclusion that it is a highly stylized ritual behaviour, which does not appear to be associated with mental illness. Indeed Kiev (1964) is quoted as concluding that Pentecostal church members who speak in tongues may be better adjusted than those who do not. Szasz (1993) however argues that there are similarities between glossolalia and 'crazy talk' (schizophrenese). Littlewood and Lipsedge seem to suggest that in E.'s case, the difference is largely one of context, while Bentall and Pilgrim (1993) tacitly support the view that glossolalia is 'a form of crazy talk'. However, in a reply to Szasz, Leff (1993) claims that the two are distinct. Leff's claim is clearly stated, and though Littlewood and Lipsedge reported difficulties in distinguishing which was being uttered by E., Leff's criteria might be usefully applied to E.'s case. Leff states that in his experience, glossolalic utterances consist of a string of phonemes which do not constitute recognizable words in any human tongue. Glossolalia lasts for only a few minutes. Glossolalia always occurs in the context of a religious ceremony and although the sounds are incomprehensible, the symbolic meaning is clear to all participants. In schizophrenic speech disorder, the individual words in the discourse are recognizable, but the links between them cannot be followed. The speech disorder of schizophrenia continues for days, weeks or longer. Unlike glossolalia, although the individual words are comprehensible, the overall meaning is obscure. Leff quotes an example of disordered schizophrenic speech which will sound sadly familiar to many readers:

> In my mind is a gist of something that's coming you see and to get them prepared unto on and then when the Lord is ready that gist that's back in my head when the Lord says so my Lord there's then supplied the people who who's ready to who have been applied to come in and coincide their in on the thing the Lord bringeth forth to for me to say that on that

day on how and how and there and when to coincide their in unto with me.

Although Littlewood and Lipsedge's account of E.'s speech in her interview with the psychiatrist is insufficiently detailed for all Leff's criteria to be applied, we were told enough about E.'s speech both to understand why it was hard to distinguish from glossolalia ('something I could not grasp' . . . 'difficult to understand exactly what she was saying' . . . 'her speech had a coherent rhythm'). We could also infer that it seems to have had at least some of the features of schizophrenese ('she was being unfairly treated for spreading the word . . . she was being martyred . . . she then quizzed me on my knowledge of the Book of Revelation . . . an ecstatic dance . . . punctuated by rousing cries of "Praise the Lord"'). We might wonder, quite reasonably, if E.'s 'crazy talk' actually included some speaking in tongues, along with all the rest about her martyrdom and her religious excitement.

It is quite a common scenario, in cases like M.'s and E.'s, for clients and patients to perceive that the mental health professionals do not understand them and their religious needs. In spite of the modest reservations of Littlewood and Lipsedge, it is often possible to make the well-worn distinction between healthy and unhealthy religiosity. Leff, for example, makes the distinction particularly clearly in the case of glossolalia and disordered speech. M. clearly felt that he was being wrongly judged, and that his behaviour had clear religious sanction. E. was more compliant, but note that the psychiatrist was not labelling her glossolalia as disturbed: he was just wondering whether her speech in the psychiatric interview was glossolalia (and therefore not disturbed). We might be fairly safe in assuming that if E.'s psychiatrist had behaved analogously with M.'s case and wondered whether E.'s **glossolalia** was in itself disturbed, then E. might have felt as wrongly judged as M.

We have seen examples of how mistrust of psychotherapists and other professionals dealing with religious issues might arise. Many may not go for treatment because of their mistrust, fearing that their religious behaviour and feelings may be misjudged. There is evidence of such mistrust of mental health professionals. For instance Grossberg (1979) in a study of American Jews found reluctance to use professional social service helpers, unless they were Jewish. This reluctance was greater among the more religious. Some clients prefer that helpers should be not only Jewish, but of a similar degree and style of religiosity – so that the assumptive world can be shared (Wikler, 1979). Generally, in Wikler's view, perceived similarity of religiosity between client and therapist can help the therapeutic process, for example by enabling the therapeutic alliance to be formed. But it can be counter-productive, by increasing resistance.

Normally there is less stigma involved in seeking pastoral counselling or therapy from a member of one's own religious group (Wikler, 1986) than in going to an irreligious psychotherapist. Going to an irreligious professional may be seen as a last resort, certainly by some orthodox Jews, and possibly by members of other religious groups – whether minority or majority!

An interesting study by McMinn (1991) looked at the perceptions by American students of psychotherapists who valued sensitivity to religious issues. Such therapists were perceived to be more likeable, approachable and trustworthy than therapists who placed more value on clinical skills. However, people with low religious commitment preferred the emphasis on clinical skills. In other words, the subjects of this study, who came from the majority religious culture, preferred a therapist who was sensitive to religious issues.

However, few mental health professionals advertise their own religiosity, or the ways in which they may be able and willing to explore religious issues in counselling or psychotherapy.

So the result is that religious patients with problems to resolve may seek help from religious counsellors, usually going to priests, ministers or rabbis as appropriate and only turning to mental health professionals when there is no perceived improvement with religious guidance. Professionals with similar religious views to the patient will normally be preferred.

Psychotherapy has had a bad press in many religious circles. Perhaps this is justified. But are the psychotherapists themselves such a godless crew?

THERAPISTS' ATTITUDES TO RELIGION

Some commentators think that psychotherapists as a breed have negative attitudes to religion, and may feel anxious about confronting religious issues raised by their clients (Lannert, 1991). Bergin (1980) concludes that mental health professionals are not as religious-minded as the general population, and that mental health professionals' attitudes are somewhat more liberal than the norm in the population at large. A great many misunderstandings genuinely occur in medicine, psychiatry, psychotherapy, social work and so on. But it may be too simple a view to conclude that they are the result of the professionals' negative attitudes to religion.

Littlewood and Lipsedge (1989) describe a prototypical example:

> One psychiatrist we know, an intelligent and compassionate doctor, offered her hand in greeting to an orthodox Jew, brought to her clinic by his family. His bland refusal to shake hands with her was however interpreted as 'catatonic negativism.' The psychiatrist was unaware that orthodox Jews do not shake hands with members of the opposite sex.

Shirley Firth (1991) describes the behaviour of Hindu patients, hospitalized in Britain, who realize that they are about to die.

Hindus believe that the soul leaves the body through one of the orifices – the higher in the body, the better. Hindus may therefore find the insertion of intravenous and other needles a matter of serious concern especially if the patient's condition is critical, since the creation of new orifices is undesirable.

(As described in Chapter 3) the Hindu should lie on the ground, to prepare for 'good death'. Unfortunately, the nursing staff perceive the patients who persist in getting out of bed and lying on the ground as deranged, or making a nuisance of themselves, and definitely in need of being replaced where they belong – in bed.

Mental health professionals say that the negative reactions they have and the clinical judgments they reach are the result of inadequate information about the causes of the patients' behaviour. They are not the result of negative attitudes to religion and/or religious–cultural minority groups, just of lack of information about the rules governing other people's behaviour. It is likely that clinical judgments made of religious people might be fairer if professionals had a fuller knowledge of the rules and customs of each religious group, but it is very likely that some misjudgments would still occur.

Thus we have two opposing views, which I will caricature slightly. Put at their most extreme they are:

- the clients say that most mental health professionals are an irreligious lot, who categorize every bit of religious behaviour as a delusion, an obsession or a compulsion, or as some other manifestation of mental illness caused by religion;
- the professionals say that they are a sensitive bunch, who admit to having difficulties in sorting out which behaviours and feelings are pathological and which are related to healthy religiosity; they (the professionals) are sensitive to religious issues and would like more information, so that they can make more informed judgments.

Both these views have some truth in them, but of course neither tells the whole story!

For instance, although it is often concluded that mental health professionals are more irreligious in general than the general population, the difference may not be marked, and it may not apply to all areas of religious feeling and behaviour. Bergin and Jensen (1990) did a survey of the religiosity of 425 mental health professionals in the USA. A religious preference was expressed by 80%, but only 41% regularly attended religious services. This does not appear to be markedly below reported averages, though it is hard to make exact comparisons. Gallup (1972) reported that the percentage of the adult population in the USA reporting weekly church attendance in the 1939–71 period was of the order of 40–45%. The *Yearbook of American Churches*, quoted by Argyle and Beit-Hallahmi (1975) reported that the percentage of the USA population aged 13 and over who were church members in the 1906–72 period ranged from 50.7 to 62.4. By these standards of comparison, the mental health professionals surveyed by Bergin and Jensen do not seem to be generally irreligious, compared to national standards.

Thus the mistrust of psychotherapy by the irreligious may not be the result of the irreligiosity of the psychotherapists as people. As previously suggested, there are at least two possible reasons for the mistrust of psychotherapy: first, the therapists' lack of knowledge of particular religious customs, beliefs and values, especially where patients and clients come from different religious groups from the professionals – as we have seen this may cause confusion about what is really disturbed behaviour; second, the failure of some psychotherapeutic systems to integrate religious values, practices and needs into their frameworks.

A third possible candidate for inclusion in this list is the possibility that some psychotherapists may simply be hostile to religious ideas, but this does not seem to be a very adequate explanation for many of the cases of misunderstanding and misjudgment that we have described.

Nevertheless, information about the religiosity of a client may have a very profound effect on the clinical judgment of the professional, possibly regardless of the professional's own beliefs and attitudes. Here is a striking study by Gartner *et al.* (1990):

A total of 363 clinical psychologists were asked to rate and to diagnose two patients on the basis of case histories. The case material was manipulated, so that one of the sets of case material seen by each psychologist included information about the ideological commitment of the patient. This information indicated that the patient had a strong commitment (for some psychologists this was described as right-wing religiosity, for some left-wing religiosity, for some right-wing political commitment, and for some left-wing political commitment). Regardless of the type of commitment, the psychologists were more likely to judge the committed 'case' more negatively in clinical terms than the uncommitted case. There were qualitative differences, too: the most striking finding was that the committed cases were more likely to be judged as obsessive-compulsive, and less likely to be judged as anxious.

We see then that there are a number of factors affecting the treatment of religion and religious issues in therapy. It is too simple to conclude that mental health professionals are anti-religious. There are many possible relevant factors in therapists, including:

- expressed negative attitudes to religion;
- biases in judgment caused by awareness of the client's religiosity;
- lack of knowledge of the religious bases of behaviours and beliefs;
- lack of personal experience of religion or of handling religious issues in therapy;
- lack of theoretical conviction that religious issues are important, or lack of relevant therapeutic skills.

STUDIES OF CLIENT–THERAPIST RELATIONSHIPS

A number of psychotherapists and other professionals have reflected on their attitudes to religion, the place of religion in their own professional training, conception of therapy and practice. All this reflects on the therapist's view of the client and his/her difficulties, and the nature of the feelings the therapist has about the client (including the counter-transference of the therapist to the client).

I have already mentioned the difficulty described eloquently by Littlewood and Lipsedge (1989) in deciding when a particular behaviour or idea is pathological, when the client is from a different cultural background or religious tradition. Mester and Klein (1981) describe some of the feelings experienced by non-religious Jewish therapists in dealing with religious clients. Envy is one commonly experienced feeling, fear of the unknown, and also boredom.

Spero (1980) speaks of the rescue fantasies entertained by such therapists: they will enlighten their backward and constricted client and help him/her to find freedom. Spero also speaks of the disdain which goes along with these fantasies.

Wikler (1979) gives a poignant account of a process he calls 'fine-tuning' which accompanies therapeutic encounters. Every now and then, the client slips in yet another question about the therapist's beliefs and practices: the client wants to know how far he/she can go in talking about his/her religious and existential dilemmas – how far will they be understood, and how far can he/she trust the therapist not to misjudge him/her in the ways of the kind described in this chapter. Fine-tuning questions include:

- Do you fast on . . . (a particular religious fast day)?
- Where did you attend school?
- Where do you attend services?
- With whom do you discuss religious questions?

Some therapists may indeed be capable of judgments that sound negative and oversimplified. Lovinger (1990), in a generally informative and stimulating exploration of issues to do with religion and counselling, writes of members of one religious group (Seventh Day Adventists): 'I think they would be vulnerable to anxious concern about making errors and falling prey to evil from which they could not extract themselves in time . . . I would look for intense, repressed anger and consider the possibility of a history of abuse in childhood, or early severe neglect.'

Rayburn (1992) writes an otherwise approving review of Lovinger's book, but attacks him bitterly for the remarks just quoted. She does not find these remarks 'especially fitting' Seventh Day Adventists on the basis of her clinical experience with members of that group. She accuses Lovinger of not having worked with even one client from the group.

Much useful progress may be made by therapists using and exploring religious values, feelings and practices in psychotherapy. Bergin (1991) and others have done much to help psychotherapists understand the clinical relevance of religious issues and values, and to alert mental health professionals to healthy and unhealthy styles of religiosity.

Margolin and Witztum (1989) provide a fascinating account of what can be achieved in this direction, although in the case they describe the patient's improvement was 'spontaneous', and the therapeutic achievement lay largely in gaining an understanding of the religious–cultural values underlying the illness and its cure, and thereby enabling the patient to feel that, finally, he was understood. Margolin and Witztum's patient was:

> 28 years old, a technician, married and father of three children. He came to our mental health clinic in a state of anxiety and restlessness, and complained of a sudden appearance of impo-

tence. His past history revealed that he was born in Iran, coming to Israel with his family when he was 14 years old. He was the second of five children. His father was described as a difficult man to get on with, who used to drink alcohol from time to time and beat his children. It seemed that the mother was passionate but a weak person. Because of the difficult financial situation, the patient left his home when he was young and started working and learning in the evening at a technical school. He was drafted into the army, and after finishing his service he was married to a woman who was also of Iranian origin. During this time the couple had three children. The patient denied any psychiatric problems or difficulties in sexual relations with his wife, and argued that he did not understand what had happened to him. During the intake interview he was very tense, and the examiner had the impression that the patient was hiding something. It turned out that the impotence had appeared several days after the death of the patient's father. The patient refused psychotherapy and asked for a medicine that would bring back his potency. A trial of anxiolytic drugs was unsuccessful, and behavioural–marital therapy was also tried without any success. Three months after his first appointment, the patient left treatment because he didn't 'believe anything could help him'. Nine months after the patient stopped his treatment, he contacted his therapist and told him about a dream in which his deceased father appeared. The patient claimed he didn't remember the content of his dream, but three days later he suddenly became potent again. The therapist felt there was a story behind the patient's story and he thought it may have a connection with the patient's cultural background.

Witztum consulted with an Iranian-born therapist who was aware of customs of the patient's culture, and developed a hypothesis to account for the patient's symptoms and recovery. Part of the hypothesis involves a phenomenon called 'binding', which is reported to be practised among Christians, Moslems and Jews, though it is not regarded with approval by religious authorities in any of these religions. The practice involves making a man impotent, for instance unable to have relations with any woman other than his wife, or unable to impregnate, or unable to achieve penetration at all. In the Christian world it is generally caused by witchcraft: the supernatural powers of the witch, often in league with the devil, cause the impotence by direct supernatural means. Among Moslems and Jews, sorcery is required, often the magical practice of making knots: 'binding'. This practice is carried out for reasons of revenge and hatred. Margolin and Witztum review Jewish, Christian and anthropological sources on this topic.

Margolin and Witztum's complete hypothesis regarding the patient is described as follows:

> The background of the patient's story lies in his difficult and traumatic relationship with his father, to whom he probably related very ambivalently. The patient, who was not a religious man but who had a traditional religious background, had likely had sexual relations with his wife during the seven days of mourning after his father's death, which is strongly forbidden according to the Jewish law. That event had caused the patient's impotence through his feelings of guilt. It can also be dynamically explained as a binding castration of the patient by his hated and tyrannical father. The patient felt ashamed of what had happened. He didn't discuss it and didn't believe that he could get any help, because he was 'tied' as punishment by his father. A year later, after the end of the mourning period, the father appeared in the patient's dream and untied him, and three days after the dream, the patient's potency came back.

The therapist wished to discuss this possibility with the patient. However the therapist felt that a direct confrontation would be seen as threatening and insulting. Therefore the patient was consulted as a possible expert, and told a version of the story and its explanation as if it happened to another person. The patient was asked if it made sense, and whether it was possible. The patient said it was possible, and then began to discuss the details in the first person, as they had been experienced by him. The therapist did not however confront the patient. Eventually, the patient left the therapist in some excitement, saying that this time he felt the therapist understood him.

Moyers (1990) also emphasizes the importance of resolving religious conflicts in psychotherapy. His experience is with fundamentalist Christians, and he stresses the need for the therapist to have an understanding of religious tenets and practices.

Tan (1991) goes further. In discussing training for lay Christian counsellors, he advocates a biblical approach to counselling, the use of specifically Christian interventions, such as the use of prayer and Scripture, and reliance upon spiritual gifts and the power of the Holy Spirit.

Others have also argued that counsellors and therapists should make more use of religiously based practices in counselling and therapy. DiBlasio and Benda (1991) look at the uses of forgiveness in psychotherapy. Therapists may be able to help clients use forgiveness, and to explore forgiveness as a means of dealing with anger and depression. Another approach is described by Scarnati *et al.* (1991), who attempted a residential treatment programme for violent psychiatric patients. The programme emphasized religion as part of an overall holistic biopsychosocial–spiritual approach. The patients felt that religion was an important part of their treatment, and they showed decreased amounts of violent behaviour and angry feelings.

In a somewhat similar vein, Prasinos (1992) discusses the adoption by therapists of a spiritually oriented healing stance, in which feature the unitive and spiritual values of peace, eternity, forgiveness, faith, hope, love, truth, mystery and God, and a sense of fallibility and gratitude: 'There has always been a covert spiritual foundation to psychotherapy. It is, after all, a loving, caring ritual based on interpersonal communication. To acknowledge this foundation puts the morass of theories and techniques into perspective. Furthermore, we can be more effective helpers if we consciously recognize what is essentially helpful within the enterprise of psychotherapy.'

Another approach to dealing with self-reproach, guilt and the like has been suggested by Rotenberg (1986). He suggests that the turning-over-a-new-leaf rehabilitation model might be replaced by a process in which past 'failings' – though regrettable and not to be repeated – could be viewed in a positive light. Rotenberg suggests that this was frequently done by rabbinic authorities who were able to view the sins of biblical role models in a positive way. A famous biblical example is Joseph, whose envious brothers hurled him into a pit and then sold him into slavery. After several ups and downs, Joseph achieves a position of great prominence in Egypt, and is able to save his brothers and the rest of the extended family from starvation in famine-stricken Canaan. Joseph tells his brothers not to feel bad about what they did to him. It's true that you meant it to be bad at the time, he says, but God meant it for good, and because of it the whole family has been saved. Rotenberg calls this process biographic rehabilitation. It clearly involves forgiveness, and also a deliberate cognitive search and reinterpretation – to explicitly state the desirable outcomes of actions that in themselves may have been less than desirable.

There are few empirical studies of therapeutic outcomes following religiously founded therapeutic techniques, apart from a spate of work on transcendental and other meditation techniques. One study is reported by Finney and Maloney (1985). They were particularly interested in the use of contemplative prayer in association with psychotherapy. Participants in this study were nine adults in therapy. The use of prayer enhanced spirituality and appeared to reduce distress.

There is growing interest in the psychological profession in the issues raised by the closer linking of religion and psychotherapy, and a number of journals concerned with discussing them, and the issues arising regarding the role of religious feelings and ideas that occur in the course of counselling and psychotherapy: examples include the *Journal of Pastoral Psychology*, the *Journal of Psychology and Judaism*, the *Journal of Religion and Health* and the *Journal of Psychology and Theology*.

As well as the attempts I have described to encourage psychotherapists to gain an understanding of religious issues, and perhaps to import religiously based techniques into their therapy, there are a number of psychotherapeutic systems which accommodate religious needs within the theoretical frameworks of psychotherapy. Some aspects of this were explored in Chapter 2. Jung (1933), Frankl (1965), Oden (1967), Lovinger (1984) and Spero (1992) are among the prominent practitioners who have pursued these problems successfully. By way of illustration, I conclude this chapter with a detailed case history from Spero (1992) of: '. . . the intensive, four-year treatment of a highly intelligent, combative and jealousy-prone Roman Catholic nun with a narcissistic character disorder. We shall enter the therapy at a relatively advanced point during the late half of the third year of treatment.'

At this specific stage of psychoanalysis, the patient began to focus on her repressed envy of the older men in her present and past life. She particularly admired the gait of tall, muscular men and began to ridicule the 'neutered' way of walking she had to force herself to adopt during religious training. In a remarkable association, she added that she found the therapist's body type and gait effeminate, yet at the same time provocative, mysterious and dangerous, qualities she readily associated with the lure of the therapist's orthodox Jewish faith. She had always viewed Judaism, and Jewish men, as 'dark', shadowy, and had come to realize through therapy that this connoted the projection of a specific qualitative aspect of her repressed sexuality. The patient, at first, preferred to intellectualize that the 'shadow' had to do with the Bible and Mosaic law and the Christian doctrine of their foreshadowing the Gospel. However she moved stepwise toward acknowledging that the 'law' she feared was the 'Jewish' psychoanalyst's uncanny ability to read her thoughts – which challenged her Catholic supremacy and her omnipotence, and frightened her. Soon, she began to consider the possibility that the 'shadow' concept alluded to a screening function over an early childhood trauma.

Until this point in therapy, she considered all such thoughts sinful, and therefore inadmissible, and had kept such thoughts secret, not only in therapy, but even in formal Confession, which she also managed to rationalize. The parallel idea of keeping thoughts from the therapist by appeal to religious doctrine (that is, their sinfulness) was, in one sense, a rather simple level of 'religious' or 'catechistic' resistance (Kehoe and Gutheil, 1984), not different in kind or quality from her overall narcissistic suspiciousness, and not particularly significant for its religious trappings. The deeper structure of the resistance had to do with the phallic significance of the 'sinful' thoughts about men and the conflictual sexual or gender implications of her fear of her shadow.

The resistance, in other words, defended against the fuller articulation of latent homosexual wishes and other unresolved oedipal conflicts. She not only idealized the male body from the heterosexual vantage point, but wished to inhabit the male body in the fantasy that it would be a stronghold against the intrusiveness of a sexually cruel mother. Even so, she devoutly believed that her closeness with God depended upon somehow offering herself to him in a way that was vaguely sexually exciting; a way which 'required', as she expressed it, that she be satisfied with a feminine identity. Thus the complex religious structures that had been built upon her God representation, and which for years had remained relatively autonomous or 'adaptive', slowly became irradiated with conflict by association to the core conflicts.

It became increasingly evident that religious themes and resistances were inextricably tied to basic aspects of sexual identity and the emergent transference relationship. God, on one hand, was to be approached as an idealized masculine image by the patient's feminine identity, whereas the therapist was to be approached by masculine aspects of the patient's identity as a split-off and projected representation of her femininity. From the standpoint of technique, much of this material emerged rather nicely by encouraging the patient to talk about 'sinfulness' and the types of experience this concept included, which led obliquely to a natural abandonment of the ideological rationalizations behind her resistance.

Further levels of conflictual identification came to light as the patient began to report dreams in which she experienced envy towards the therapist, featuring transference-laden descriptions of him as a gaunt yet omniscient Jesus-like teacher. She noted that in her fantasies, Jesus's head was always covered, which she recognized from certain works of religious art, but more specifically identified with priests' skullcaps and then with the therapist's skullcap. Her earthly father most probably was the first object behind this representation, conspicuous in his suffering passivity, which she refurbished and projected onto the image of the nonprotesting Jesus and the neutral (she termed it 'absorbing') therapist. She associated the headcovering with the worn-out, dirty fedora her father wore constantly. She detested her father's ignorance, whereas an omniscient being could be passive yet powerful in his foreknowledge. Partly, she had realized this idealized state in her own life through scholarly achievements, transforming herself into an object of envy. This, in turn, evoked a certain amount of shame and guilt, characteristically expressed initially in religious terms, such as doubting the piety and purity of her motives, and only subsequently in a manner thematically closer to the core experience of dynamic conflict.

In reflecting upon the Jewishness of Jesus, both in historical fact as well as in the transference-laden images in her dreams and fantasies during prayer, the patient began to belabour intellectually the odd relationship between Judaism and Christianity, the Father and the Son, the 'older brother' and the 'younger brother'. This we often viewed in terms of the relationship between the therapist and patient. Occasionally, there was a hint of her appreciation that these dichotomies expressed indirectly her objective relationship with God. It eventually surfaced that she had fixated on the possibility of converting to Judaism, or at least embarking on a career in Judaic scholarship, even as her sexual fantasies about the therapist were redolent with latently anti-Semitic conceptions, while other of her idealizations seemed blatantly counterphobic.

At this juncture, I interpreted her sudden interest in Judaism in the light of the available psychodynamic picture, underscoring the concurrent ambivalence towards the Jewish faith and the therapist. Yet, despite the high level of functioning of her judgment and reality testing, the patient began experimenting secretly with a few Jewish rituals, especially those which her scholarship had revealed were forerunners of current Catholic rituals, and attempted not to practise certain Catholic rituals. She felt she had become a 'Marrano in reverse' ('Marrano' is the derogatory Spanish term applied to Jews forcibly converted to Christianity. Many Marranos continued to maintain Jewish practice in secret). [She] was somehow sure that the therapist's family name suggested Marrano ancestry. However the history of the Marranos disturbed her as she was sure she would have chosen death over forced conversion. Yet, during one such discussion, she remarked in an absent-minded way, and all the more chillingly, that as a good Catholic she doubted whether she would have resisted much of the orders of the Inquisition. There was an implication in her subsequent associations that even when she had earlier supposed she would face death rather than convert, she was essentially directing murderous impulses towards herself as Jewess. These doubts and wonderings suggested the emergence of unconscious resentment toward the introjected idealized representation of the therapist. Further work made clear that this idealization secondarily masked emergent feelings of rage toward her impassive father and toward a God who so relentlessly tested and tried.

Subsequently, the patient began to explore the sexual element conspicuously absent in all her idealized male representations. In her own mind, the therapist's and her own mutual commitments to what she termed 'professional and religious celibacy' rendered both parties mutants, 'neutered', capable of a relationship that was at once platonic in a relieving way and, given that she often experienced herself as masculine, also distortedly homosexual. She wondered intellectually about the special satisfactions of the Jewish woman, whom she viewed as enjoying a fully equal relationship with the Jewish male. Her thought expressed apparent ignorance of how idealized this view was. She remained unconscious of the strength of her envy and combativeness and of the equally powerful wish to eliminate any difference – sexual, cultural, religious – that might symbolize her preoedipal and later oedipal crises. For example she was especially attracted to the Orthodox Jewish menstrual laws and fantasized about the great power in being able effectively to keep the lustful male at bay for close to two weeks. Her interest in these particular laws again suggested the continued need to hide behind asexuality. While this clarified another aspect of her attraction to celibacy, it actually caused her to experience a weakening in identification with the therapist since for a moment it seemed as if 'Judaism offered not much more than Catholicism'.

The resulting dent in her identification with me led to a depressive period. She harangued church leaders and even Jesus for all manners of antifeminine attitudes and policies, but the bulk of her critique, if in some way valid, was laden with oedipal anger and disenchantment. Indeed she experienced my interventions against her identification with Judaism as an assault, an authoritarian blow, a deprivation and a castration. Given the feminine maternal identity she projected upon me during this stage of the analysis, my intervention was also experienced as a continuation of her mother's abuses. If the patient venerated Judaism on the phallic level, motivating an intense though ambivalent identification with the therapist, she venalized on the level of the oral and anal significances its traditions and customs bore for her. Similarly, associations about these themes in her own Catholic devotions and doctrines brought up great emotional turmoil on the dynamic level and disturbingly primitive introjections on the object-relational level.

The eventually successful analytic journey revealed a religious woman who, for the first time in her life, felt an especially close relationship with God, one no longer mediated by theological understandings which happened to cater to her narcissistic, concretistic view of reality and her constricted sexual identity. She became much more devoted to thinking about Jesus, whereas for her whole life she had primarily read or learned about Jesus. If until now she felt she recognized God, it was only because he was an extension of familiar object experiences from home. She now began imagining what started as a healthy, girlish relationship with his image and gradually grew into a trusting investment in his newly identified capacity for caring and activity.

Spero goes on to describe the patient's imagery in her 'deeply moving' representations of God, and also to describe her changed and improved relationships with her fellow nuns and other significant persons.

There is clearly a need for closer specification of religiously and spiritually based interventions in psychological therapies, with a view to specifying and studying outcomes. At the moment, there are many published descriptions of different types of religiously based interventions, but these are often rather vague and hard to replicate. Until replicable, outcome and efficacy cannot be established.

SUMMARY

This chapter dealt with psychotherapy and psychotherapists and how they deal with religion. Both therapy and therapists may lack the equipment to deal with religion and religious issues – and patients may mistrust them because they suspect this. The chapter describes some cases of misunderstandings in dealing with religious issues in psychotherapy.

However, many therapists and therapeutic systems do try to deal with religious issues in psychotherapy, with some reported success, but little systematic study of outcome; some examples are given.

9

Thinking beautiful thoughts: cognitive processes

The thoughts we think may be at least as important in determining our mental health and wellbeing as the feelings we feel. There used to be a widespread view that our thoughts and ideas followed from our moods and motivational states, and that the reverse effect was unlikely or impossible.

The last few years, with the rise of the cognitive–behavioural therapies, have seen a departure from the view that put feelings as primary and viewed the thoughts as a floating accompaniment to the feelings – so-called 'epiphenomena' – mildly interesting but not very helpful when it comes to understanding the causes of distress, and not very helpful when it comes to finding remedies. Now the tables are turning and clinical psychologists and others are getting some mileage from the view that the head may be able to rule the heart.

This chapter looks at some cognitive theories of mental illness, and then explores some ways in which aspects of religion may be important in affecting the cognitions (thoughts!) that go along with mental illnesses, distress and wellbeing. Obviously, the main points of interest are:

- whether religious messages actually affect mental health;
- whether other aspects of religious involvement affect cognitive processes, which in turn may affect mental health.

In practice, the first point is the salient one.

COGNITIVE THEORIES OF MENTAL ILLNESS

Cognitive theories of mental illness gave rise to a wide range of cognitive–behavioural therapeutic techniques and got their impetus from a group of seminal publications in the 1970s.

Seligman (1975) suggested in his book *Learned Helplessness* that the depressed state may be analogous to the condition suffered by dogs in a cruel electric-shock experiment. This experiment involved two phases. Dogs were put into an enclosed box and strong – unpleasant but not actually lethal – electric shocks were applied through the floor. The poor dogs ran and jumped around but there was no way they could escape the electric current. After several of these horrible experiences, the conditions in the enclosed boxes were changed so that it became possible for the dogs to escape the electric shocks by leaping over a partition. On previous occasions this had not helped, but under the new regime, this was a way of escaping. The poor dogs, however, had by this time apparently given up hope. Cowering, lethargic and apathetic, they endured their suffering without taking the escape action that would have been an effective relief. This, Seligman suggests, is analogous to the condition of many depressed people. They have ceased looking for solutions; they endure in silent misery, hopeless and helpless. Seligman called this condition 'learned helplessness', suggesting that depressed people have a strong, generalized expectancy of failure.

By 1978, learned helplessness theory had been reformulated: Abramson, Seligman and Teasdale (1978) suggested that it wasn't the (lack of perceived control over the bad) situation that mattered so much, but the explanations made for the bad events.

A strong influence on cognitive theories of depression and other psychological illnesses has been Kelley's attribution theory (1967). Kelley suggested that in everyday life, a great deal of conversation carries many implications about people's analyses of the causes of events and actions. The causes of social action are worked out by inductive principles, which are normally implicit. Supposing for instance you learn that you have done very well in a particular exam. Kelley would suggest that you would do a causal analysis of this, involving three kinds of information:

- **consensus**: how well most people performed in this exam;
- **distinctiveness**: how well you are performing in exams in general at this point in your life;
- **consistency**: how well you normally do in this type of exam.

As a result of this, you emerge by placing your performance on several dimensions of causality, of which the three to which psychologists have paid most attention are:

- **internal/external**: 'I did well because I worked hard' (internal); 'I did well because I am pretty good at this sort of thing' (internal); 'I did well because it was a pretty easy exam' (external);
- **stable/unstable**: 'I did well because I worked hard – for this exam' (internal, unstable); 'I did well because I am pretty good at this sort of thing (internal, stable); 'I did well because it was a pretty easy exam, unlike the others this year' (external, unstable);
- **global/specific**: 'I did well because I'm pretty good at pretty well everything' (internal, stable, global); 'I did well because it was much easier than exams in this subject usually are' (external, specific).

For instance, the last attribution would be made when there was high consensus (most people did well in the exam) and low consistency (you don't usually do well in this type of exam).

Of course, when we say or think these kinds of things, we do it on auto-pilot. We take a 'natural' interest in how other people did in the exam, and recall 'naturally' how we did in the past, how we felt about the exam paper and so on. We don't have to tell ourselves to look for consensus, distinctiveness and consistency information, or how to compute the internality, stability and globality of our attributions.

Those interested in cognitive theories of psychological illnesses would probably say that it's a great shame that we don't or can't tell ourselves to look more carefully for consensus, distinctiveness and consistency information, and that we don't control the way we compute this information. They suggest that we get locked into particular attributional habits or styles, and these can have a counterproductive effect on the way we see ourselves, and on the way we relate to other people. In other words, our attributional styles can make us ill (Peterson and Seligman, 1980).

Initially, most attention was focused on depression though, more recently, some attention has been given to attributional processes in other psychological illnesses, especially paranoia (Kaney and Bentall, 1989; Hingley, 1992; Kinderman *et al.*, 1992).

The best-known suggestion is Peterson and Seligman's, that depressed people differ in their attributional styles from the nondepressed. The nondepressed are said to show a 'self-serving' attributional bias, by which successes are attributed to internal, stable, global causes ('I'm pretty good at everything'), and failures to external, unstable, specific causes ('It was a beastly exam paper this time'). This attributional tendency is sometimes termed the **self-serving bias**. The depressed suffer from the opposite tendency. Successes are attributed to external, unstable, specific causes ('It was just a fluke'), while failures are attributed to internal, stable, global causes ('I'm no good at anything'). There is some evidence that depressives' attributional analyses are more accurate than those of nondepressives, so these attributional tendencies are sometimes labelled **depressive realism** (Alloy and Abramson, 1979). In paranoia, there is said to be an exaggerated self-serving bias, which is generally consistent with the paranoid view that 'I am the greatest' and 'they are no good and they are out to destroy me'). There is much discussion of the causal role played by attributions in the aetiology, maintenance and offset of illness episodes.

Rather strangely, there is another important set of theories about explanations of events that seemed to get lost in this activity of applying social–cognitive approaches to the understanding of psychological illnesses. These theories derive from the work of Rotter (1966), appearing on the scene at almost exactly the same time as attribution theories and concerned with very similar issues. Rotter was concerned with the perception of the locus of control of events, and the way in which this could become generalized and lead to expectancies about the person's degree of control over future events. Rotter distinguished between perceived internal and external control. A person with an internal locus of control is said to feel that they have more personal control over events that might happen to them than the person whose locus of control is perceived to be external. This person feels doomed to be the victim of chance, luck, fate and those who have power.

Notice that Rotter and Kelley were concerned with very similar issues: our understanding and analysis of the causes of everyday events. But Rotter's perspective emphasizes feelings of perceived control, and expectancies of control over future events. Kelley's perspective looks at explanations (attributions) for past events, and the way that systematic tendencies in attribution may affect social interaction. If you think they come to nearly the same thing, you may be forgiven! You are not the only one. For example, think back to the poor tortured dogs who could not get away from the electric shocks. Their expectations of escaping to better places were zeroed by the experience of zero control over escape. Learned helplessness theory appeared originally to owe more to Rotter than to Kelley, and attributional (Kelley-type) explanations only came to be adopted when the learned helplessness approach to depression did not hold up to the blast of empirical and theoretical attention lavished upon it in the late 1970s (Brown, 1986).

This is not to suggest that locus-of-control theory has been abandoned. It remains very influential and has been very well developed, particularly in the understanding of classroom behaviour (Weiner, 1979), health behaviour (Suls and Mullen, 1981; Bradley *et al.*, 1990) and – perhaps to a lesser extent – in the study of religious thinking (Proudfoot and Shaver, 1975; Spilka, Shaver and Kirkpatrick, 1985; Pargament and Hahn, 1986; Furnham and Brown, 1992; Loewenthal and Cornwall, 1993).

So far, I have described work on attributional processes in mental illnesses, and have said that there is little work on perceived locus of control in mental illnesses. This by no means exhausts the catalogue of ways at looking at cognitive processes in mental illness. Other approaches include:

- the study of memory processes: for instance there is controversy about whether depressed people selectively remember, or selectively forget, bad experiences. Two questions of interest are whether bad or sad past events have helped to make the person depressed, or whether sad people are more likely to remember sad events out of a total pool of memories which are no sadder, on the whole, than the memories of other people. However it is by no means certain that depressed people are more likely to recover miserable (negatively-toned) memories than other people;
- looking at alterations of attention in distressed states and in distressed or psychologically-ill people; for instance looking at the question whether anxiety states increase vigilance, and particularly attention directed towards likely sources of threat. This means that anxious people might take more notice of disturbing words or objects than nonanxious people (Eysenck 1992). Other work has looked at schizophrenia and the attentional disturbances that may occur in this condition;

- looking at alterations of consciousness and attention in meditative and other religious states of mind, and examining the effects of meditative and related practices on mental health (Valentine, 1989; Batson, Schoenrade and Ventis, 1993);
- examining the ways in which plans for the future and views of the world are affected in different conditions of distress and psychological illness, as for instance in MacLeod, Williams and Bekerian (1991);
- at least one attempt to relate changes and disturbances in social relationships, with stage-developmental theories, including developmental theories which deal with changes in cognitions. Spero (1992), in making such an attempt, also deals with changes and disturbances in the relationship with God. This will be described in the next part of this chapter.

To date, it looks as if the study of causal explanation of everyday events is one of the most likely to relate to existing work on the study of religious thinking. However, there are other ways in which psychologists have looked at religious thinking, and we now turn to look at some of these.

FAITH AND TRUST: THE DEVELOPMENT OF RELIGIOUS
THINKING

Writings on the psychology of religion emphasize the developmental aspects of religious thinking. Religious faith and belief are not generally seen as something you have or you don't have. Rather, religious ideas escort and/or help the developmental process, and co-vary with the stage of development. Most authors distinguish between mature and immature styles of thinking, as has been described in earlier chapters: Allport's (1950) is the best example of this approach. However a number of authors have developed more elaborate schemes, typically involving six stages (e.g. Fowler, 1981; Spero, 1992).

We could start by describing some fundamental tenets of belief, common to at least the major religions:

- that there is an underlying unity in the universe;
- that the appearance of good and bad, pleasure and pain, is only from the material perspective – from a higher

perspective, God (the source of spiritual and material worlds) is in control, and everything is ultimately for the good;
- people have free will, however, to do good – which increases harmony and unity – or the opposite – which increases the appearance of strife and separation.

Religious faith involves a trust that everything that happens is ultimately for the good, plus the apparently paradoxical belief that it is up to the individual to do the right things.

The more childlike type of faith, that God will do what I want for me, is said to be appropriate for children, but in developmental accounts of religious faith and belief (for example, Allport, 1950; Fowler, 1981), this must be outgrown when the individual is confronted with the awful facts of life.

Stage-developmental theories

A great deal of work has been done on the development of faith in relation to other aspects of psychological development. The pioneers of stage-developmental theories are undoubtedly Freud, Piaget and Erikson, with major contributions to the understanding of moral development being made comparatively recently by Kohlberg, religious belief by Rumke, faith development by Fowler and development of religious relationships by Spero.

What all stage-developmental theories have in common is the notion that one stage grows out of its predecessor, and that we cannot 'skip' a stage, though we can always function at the level of earlier stages. Stage-developmental theorists all stress the importance of conflict or paradox as the means of development. When the ideas or modes of functioning that have been serving quite nicely are suddenly challenged, then the individual has to get busy. She/he may just avoid the challenge. This is especially likely if the challenge is overwhelming or catastrophic. In terms of Erikson's (1963) psychosocial scheme, for instance, an individual who does not succeed in negotiating the crises of each stage of life will suffer from basic mistrust, or shame, or guilt, or despair or some other negative-toned posture *vis-à-vis* life and people. As was said in Chapters 6 and 7, immature religiosity – a belief that God should and will do all right by me – is in Allport's (1950) terms the result of similar developmental 'failure'.

Some useful links have been shown between cognitive–developmental theory and the development of faith by Fowler, who based his scheme of faith development on three separate strands in stage-developmental theory: the psychoanalytic, the social and the cognitive, particularly taking into account the work of Erikson (1963), Piaget (e.g. 1967) and Kohlberg (e.g. 1968). The fundamental stage-developmental theory is Piaget's, which is concerned with cognitive development. Piaget is said to have transformed our understanding of the child's thought. The development of thinking was said to have been understood as a series of successively more polished and accurate versions of adult thought. Piaget showed that children's thinking was radically and qualitatively different from that of adults. This is not the place for a detailed exposition and discussion of Piaget's very controversial views, but for the benefit of those readers who have so far escaped lectures on Piaget's view of cognitive development, I will just briefly outline the main stages:

1. **Pre-operational thinking**. In very early development, in early infancy, thinking is concentrated on the infant's sensory impressions and motor movements in the here-and-now. 'Schemata' (which are, roughly, schematized memories, images, plans of action) are built up. In early childhood, the beginnings of symbolic thought appear.

2. **Concrete operational thinking**. From about the age of six the child becomes capable of elementary logical operations and manipulations of things in relation to each other, but not, Piaget claims, at an abstract level. The child's thinking is no longer dominated by immediate sensory impressions. A classic demonstration of the transition from pre-operational to operational thinking is to ask a child in the 5–7 age-range to make two balls of Plasticine of exactly the same size. One ball is then rolled out into a long string and the child is then asked if the two pieces of Plasticine are the same. Younger children will reply: 'No – that one is bigger' (this might be either piece, the longer or the fatter one). Older children will reply without hesitation, as do adults, that they are still the same, the same amount of Plasticine. Children in transition will show some hesitation, and will often announce the mature, conservation-of-quantity response with some excitement: 'No – yes – it's still the same, it looks different but – it isn't!' The declaration is made with the air of one who

has just made an important scientific discovery, which indeed is quite justified – an important scientific discovery **has** been made!

3. **Formal operational thinking**. From around the age of 11 onwards there is increasing ability to undertake abstract logical operations. A simple example: John is taller than Michael. David is taller than John. Who is taller, Michael or David? Formal operational thinking increases in type, sophistication and power with age.

Piaget himself made some attempt to relate stages in the development of operational thinking to religious thought, as did a number of Piagetians, such as Goldman (1964). However there were no serious attempts to relate Piagetian theory to theories of distress and psychopathology until comparatively recently. Fowler's work shows the germs of such an attempt. Table 9.1. shows Fowler's systematization of the parallels between stages of development in different theories.

Table 9.1 Fowler's stages in the development of faith, and parallels with other cognitive–developmental theories (adapted from Fowler, 1981)

Stage	Form of logic (Piaget)	Moral Judgment (Kohlberg)	Bounds of social awareness	Form of world coherence	Symbolic function
I	Preoperational	Punishment–reward	Family, primal others	Episodic	Magical–numinous
II	Concrete operational	Instrumental hedonism	'Those like us'	Narrative–dramatic	One-dimensional literal
III	Early formal operations	Interpersonal expectations and concordance	Consensus of valued groups	Felt meanings symbolically mediated	Evocative power inheres in symbol
IV	Formal operations (dichotomizing)	Societal perspective	Ideoligically compatible communities	Explicit system	Symbols separated from symbolized
V	Formal operations (dialectical)	Principled	Extends beyond class norms and interests	Multisystemic symbolic mediation	Postcritical rejoining of irreducible power and ideational meaning
VI	Formal operations (synthetic)	Loyalty to being	Experienced judgement, non-egoistic, linked to principle of being	Unitive actuality felt	Evocative power of symbols

Table 9.2. shows a part of a faith scale, based on the work of Fowler, developed by Barnes, Doyle and Johnson (1989).

Table 9.2   A shortened form of a scale for assessing level of religious faith of Roman Catholics, based on Fowler (adapted from Barnes, Doyle and Johnson, 1989)

(2) 1a.	Those who do what God wants are given special rewards
(3) 1b.	God grants comfort and strength to those who are loyal and faithful
(2) 2a.	God can do what God wants without any particular reason
(4) 2b.	It is important to try and make sense out of how God acts and why
(2) 3a.	A good way to relate to God is to do what God wants, so that God will help you in return
(5) 3b.	It is best to think of God as utterly and freely giving
(3) 4a.	It is important to follow the leaders to whom God has entrusted His church
(4) 4b.	Religious leaders must respect the need for reasonableness, consistency, and coherence in their interpretation of doctrines
(3) 5a.	It is often hard to understand why people are disloyal to their family and religion
(5) 5b.	People have to make their own best choices about religion, even if it means following new ways
(4) 6a.	God's revealed truth is meant for all people everywhere
(5) 6b.	No set of religious beliefs is the whole and final truth for everyone

The scale is a useful catalogue of ideas said to be characteristic of the middle four (the most common in adults) of Fowler's six stages in faith development. Note that Fowler uses the term faith in a broad sense to encompass the general meaning 'philosophy of life', rather as Allport (1950) did. Explicit religious affiliation and doctrinal acceptance is not necessary, in Fowler's view, to the development of mature faith. If you want to test yourself, you choose which of each pair of statements reflects your views more accurately – but to get a fair score you should cover up the figures in brackets on the left-hand side of the page until you've finished. When you've finished making your choices, you can give a score to each of your choices, which will be the number in brackets next to it. Your final score can be worked out by adding the six scores together and dividing by 6. You should get a number somewhere between 2 and 5. A score like 4.23, for instance, would suggest that you have a rather mature level of faith (in Fowler's scheme). The scale was developed to be relevant to Roman Catholics, and if you are a Christian of a different denomination, or an adherent of a non-Christian religion, remember the scale was not meant to apply to you and your score may not mean much.

Another account of faith development which draws on Fowler's work, and which draws on more psychoanalytic theory and case material than does Fowler, is Spero's (1992). This is a valuable account, because (following Meissner, 1984) it presents a fuller idea of the kinds of cognition characteristic of the different stages of faith, and also gives some ideas on different kinds of psychopathologies and religious styles associated with different levels of development. Spero, like Fowler, looks at stages in psychological development in relation to faith development. He adds a psychoanalytic perspective to an approach which is otherwise like Fowler's in many respects. Spero also attempts to show how relationships with the religious community and relationships with God are linked to phases of self–other differentiation (suggested by Mahler (1971) and others).

If – and it's a big if – we could agree that religious awareness, faith or trust is a primary feature of religiosity, we could see that the sorts of scheme I have just been describing do go some way to linking cognitions, mental health and religion via the notion of stages in psychological growth.

But there is a fundamental type of question left open. Given that there are numerous aspects of development, is a change in any one aspect likely to cause changes in other aspects – and if so, which? And how? For instance, is a step in cognitive development likely to result in a step in religious understanding? And *vice versa*? And how? One theorist who attempted to deal with this type of question was Goldman (1964): he thought that the changes in cognition were primary, and this is often said to be the Piagetian view. But the general question, and its specific forms, are still being hotly debated. In Fowler's accounts, there appears a complex interplay between social experience, religious thinking and personal philosophy. For example:

J. came from a large family and an inner-city, working-class background. His mother was Italian and his father Irish. His father was alcoholic and there were violent marital disputes. J. felt pity and anger towards his father, and afraid on behalf of his mother. He did well in school, J. thought, because he looked neat and came regularly, not because he was particularly able. He was moved to a Catholic parochia school from public schol, where it was harder to do well and where religion was emphasized.As a result, he became more devout, attending Mass regularly, and undergoing a kind of religious conversion in his early teens. He made a bargain with Jesus: he would be one of his special children and a good boy in return for an improvement in his father's drinking.

The bargain was not upheld on either side. The class bullies put a stop to J.'s religious fervour, after he had been publicly praised for it by a well-meaning teacher. J.'s father's drinking got worse.

At 19, J. joined the army. He found that he got on well with others, especially others from inner-city backgrounds like his own. He discovered that the anti-black attitudes he had learned were unfounded. Via his army friendships, he became interested in black music and then in Black Power writings, and then in politics generally. He 'began to think politically' – to realize that poor whites were being pitted against poor blacks.

J. had a brother who was also politically concerned. This brother was very supportive to J., which increased his conviction of the importance of his new-found direction. However, when he left the army, he felt out of place. His old neighbours viewed his political views suspiciously, but he felt uncomfortable with the articulate college graduates whose political views resembled his own.

J. married a girl from a middle-class background, who gave up her career as their children came along. She worked as a waitress part time to supplement his salary. Both J. and his wife are keenly involved in political action. At the time they were interviewed they were active in tenants' rights: 'As long as there are people like these suffering and struggling for their rights, I'll be in the fight,' said J.

Fowler comments that the effects of leaving home and joining the army and discovering new outlooks on life were to enable J. to adopt a new and more mature faith level (individuative–reflective, stage 4, rather than synthetic–conventional, stage 3).

From our point of view, J.'s history shows a number of changes in J.'s relationship with religion. His touching early adolescent ardour was effectively squashed by the hideous experience of bullying, following his labelling as the 'goody-goody'. The compassion he felt for his parents was extended in adulthood, to compassion to many (but not all) of humanity. He went through several periods of psychological distress, in which religion and religio-culturally sanctioned behaviour (such as his Irish Catholic father's drinking) played an important role. Although frequently distressed, J. never became psychologically ill and he emerges as a fine and caring person.

Speech and role-taking

We have seen suggested links between different aspects of development – particularly relevant are the suggested links between cognitive and religious development and forms of psychological distress and social relationships. I would like to suggest that one neglected set of factors is important in establishing causal links between changes in different areas of development. This factor is speech, particularly self-addressed speech. In a sense this factor is not overlooked, because when psychologists talk about cognitions, they are often talking about self-addressed speech. This speech is almost always silent, inner speech in adults, and it is often automatic. The great Russian psychologists Vygotsky (1962) and Luria (1961) were the first to emphasize the importance of self-directed speech in accompanying and directing and organizing behaviour. Inner speech is the internalization of messages we have received from others, and the important work of Mead (1934) showed the importance of this for social development, the development of self-awareness and the capacity to empathize with others. Many contemporary psychotherapists echo these themes, when they talk about the messages we give ourselves and the scripts we are playing our lives by. The theorists I have just mentioned were absolutely overshadowed by the mega-output of Piaget, who was insistent that language is totally secondary to cognitive development – as indeed is everything else! Piaget's view was echoed by Kohlberg, who saw moral development as contingent on cognitive level. Nevertheless, Kohlberg's examples of how to cause change in levels of moral reasoning involve the mediating effect of speech. Kohlberg's recommended method of increasing the maturity of moral reasoning is to involve a group of people in the discussion of a moral dilemma, such as:

> A prisoner was given permission to leave prison for a week-end on parole. One of the parole conditions was that she should not leave the state boundaries. The prisoner however wanted to see her children, and this involved crossing the boundary into another state. When she returned to prison, she confided her parole violation to a prison warden with whom she had become close. What should the warden do?

Some say that the warden should report the breach of parole so as not to get into trouble, others say the warden should maintain the confidence out of loyalty to a friend, others that the breach should be reported to maintain the justice system, while others feel that the justice system should take account of this prisoner's dilemma. The longer-term perspective on this prisoner and her family is seen as the most important feature for many. (These examples are given in the order of maturity of moral reasoning, starting with the least mature).

Kohlberg suggested that change was brought about by listening to other people who are just slightly more advanced in their level of moral reasoning. If the 'role model' is too far advanced, their reasoning will just be over the top of the heads of their listeners, and they will be perceived as talking boring rubbish. But if a slightly more advanced level of reasoning is presented, then the ideas will be seen as exciting and worth adopting.

Of course the mere act of verbalizing or discussing something may be enough to cause changes in ways of thinking (Loewenthal, 1967). Clark (1993) points out that conversation may have benefits for mental health additional to the benefits of feeling supported and attended to. For instance, conversation may diminish the occurrence of intrusive unwanted thoughts and the attentional problems associated with distress.

Sunden (see Holm, 1987; Kallstad, 1987; Wikstrom, 1987) has pointed out that the Bible and other religious texts are full of (verbally depicted) role-models – shining examples of religiously endorsed social skills, cognitions, ways of dealing with life's dilemmas. Sunden suggests that religious modes of experiencing are possible because we have absorbed religious messages about how to do so. Rotenberg (1986) for example, suggested that instead of regretting past actions, the biblical and midrashic models suggest search for good outcomes of the regrettable behaviour (alongside a resolution not to repeat the undesirable action).

This emphasis on the importance of speech is crucial, I think, when it comes to looking at ways in which religion relates to mental health via cognitions. As I hope I have shown, theoretically there are two serious possibilities which are not necessarily exclusive. They are:

1. that type of religion and type and presence of distress both depend on level of development, which in the powerful Piagetian view rests on level of cognitive functioning;
2. that type of religion and type and presence of distress can be affected by verbal messages.

The first possibility has already been discussed; it is inherent in the stage-developmental schemes outlined above. I wish to devote the rest of this chapter to examining the second possibility. Our concern is with the role of speech, initially communicated from others and then internalized and self-generated, in affecting attributional processes and other cognitions and self-addressed messages which are important both in religion and in mental health.

PRAYER, MEDITATION, MYSTICAL EXPERIENCE AND THEIR EFFECTS

One activity fundamental to religion is prayer. This is essentially a verbal activity, in which the person addresses God. Meditation is not quite the same. Verbal means or self-instructions are used, often along with other techniques such as fasting, music, sacrifice or adopting special postures, to focus the mind and to induce special states of awareness, variously called awareness of the divine, spiritual union, mysticism, spiritual ecstasy and so forth.

There is a widespread suggestion that meditative practices may improve wellbeing and reduce psychological distress (though Batson, Schoenrade and Ventis (1993) are cautious about the evidence). There are two likely reasons for any such effects.

1. Meditative practices are an alternative to states of psychological distress. They are among a large gamut of antidepressant or anti-worry ploys that people may use to relieve psychological distress.

2. They may help to change the contents of intrusive, brooding or ruminative thoughts. Our section on cognitive theories of mental illness discussed some of these. They include brooding on dreadful scenarios, either from the past or imagined as the result of anticipated failures, damaging self-directed messages such as 'I'm no good at anything', 'Nobody ever likes me', 'I'm too disorganized/lazy/stupid/clumsy to accomplish anything worthwhile'. Meditation may help to change the expected probabilities of bad and good things happening, or improve the emotions associated with bad outcomes ('God can help me to cope with it'), or other possibilities, for example by distancing the person from intense involvement with the stressful ideas, or by causing them to alter priorities.

These effects may also result from prayer. However there is a great variety of prayer states. Meadows and Kahoe (1984) distinguish at least five types of prayer:

- **petitionary prayer**: the cry for help;
- **intercessory prayer**: pleading for help for another person;
- **thanksgiving**: for help and favours received;
- **adoration**: expressing awe, wonder, praise;
- **confession, dedication, communion**: righting and consolidating the relationship with God.

Meadows and Kahoe add meditation to this list, as well as distinguishing between objective prayer (focused on the object of worship) and subjective prayer (focused on the self). They also distinguish between less mature forms of prayer – expecting God to answer petitionary prayer, for example, and more mature forms of prayer – characterized by dedication and communion. Prayer may follow a set text or be composed spontaneously;

there may be nonverbal elements. But all prayer has the common features of at least some verbal component and the focusing of attention on to the self in relation to the divine.

There have been a number of suggestions about the psychological effects of prayer. Johnson (1956) suggests the following.

- Makes us aware of our needs and of realities, as we face the One who knows all, and as we examine ourselves.
- Allows confession and a sense of forgiveness as we see ourselves, but as inadequate, since self-sufficiency is self-deception.
- Engenders faith and hope that relaxes tensions, worries and fears and brings confidence and peace of mind.
- Puts our lives in perspective as our meditations solve problems and produce practical plans of action.
- Clarifies goals to which we can dedicate ourselves, focus our lives and unleash latent powers to achieve.
- Renews emotional energy, through the euphoria of communication with the divine.
- Makes us responsive to the needs of other persons and channels our social and altruistic motives.
- Affirms our values and prepares us to accept with joy whatever happens.
- Fosters our loyalty to the Ultimate and perseverance in devotion.
- Integrates our personalities through focusing upon a supreme loyalty.

That is a list that sounds like everything one could hope for from psychotherapy – and then some!

There has been some investigation to see whether there is empirical confirmation of the claims just described.

Unfortunately, early work on prayer was thrown off track by Galton's (1883) amusing but sketchily conceived and theologically naive work on the effectiveness of petitionary prayer. Galton suggested that, since monarchs are prayed for more often than other occupational groups, they ought to be longer-lived, but in fact they are shorter-lived. Galton also found no differences in the rate of stillbirths between praying and non-praying parents.

This diverted attention from the study of the conditions of use and psychological effects of prayer.

However there have been a number of studies, less well-known but better-conceived than Galton's. Pargament and Hahn (1986) for example analysed American undergraduates' views of God's role in health difficulties. These undergraduates saw God as a source of support more than as moral guide.

One of my favourite, albeit poignant findings, is that there are indeed (almost) no atheists in foxholes. Argyle and Beit-Hallahmi (1975) review studies of military personnel who report wide-spread use of prayer when in battle conditions. Stouffer (1949) reported that about 75% of US army Second World War veterans reported that 'prayer had helped a lot when the going was tough'. Prayer was reported to be the most helpful of the cognitive strategies employed to keep going under battle conditions, and was reported to be the most helpful by those who reported being the most frightened. Argyle and Beit-Hallahmi conclude from their review of several American studies that war experience can increase interest in religious and spiritual matters, but war veterans were often less involved with organized religion than others and held nonorthodox views. Often, war experiences disillusioned people, so that they reported becoming less religious, but those who reported an increase in religiousness said that it was the result of the help they had experienced from the use of prayer in battle. Argyle and Beit-Hallahmi's review, then, suggests quite good evidence that prayer has at least some of the psychological effects listed by Johnson.

Parker and Brown (1986) in an Australian study included prayer as one of many possible strategies for coping with negative events and feelings. It was associated (statistically) with help-seeking behaviours. A group of clinically depressed subjects were studied on three occasions. Help-seeking was not associated with improvement in a depression scores. The strongest finding of this study was that self-consolatory behaviours (such as eating, drinking alcohol and spending money) were associated with a worsening of depression. This study therefore does not support the idea that prayer may be associated with an improvement in depression, but note that the study does not look at the 'pure' effects of prayer directly. Loewenthal and Goldblatt (in preparation) looked at regular prayer and the saying of psalms in a sample of Anglo-Jewish women, and found that the latter went along with lower depressed mood (though saying psalms went along with status in the religious community, too, which might explain the effect on wellbeing):

> Mrs C. has many troubles. Her husband has severe back problems so that his job is under threat. There are serious money problems and some of the children have difficulties; there are also elderly parents to care for. 'When things get a bit too much, I sit down with a book of *tehilim* (psalms). After a few minutes, I feel better, calmer. Things get into the right perspective. What more important job could I be doing?'

Schatz-Uffenheimer (1993) has linked contemplative prayer in Hasidism with an emphasis on joy and a ban on sadness and regret. The essence of contemplation is focusing on unity; Schatz-Uffenheimer quotes the 18th-century Hasidic master, the Maggid of Mezeritch: 'there is nothing in the entire world but the Holy One, blessed be He, for the whole world is full of His glory . . . that man sees himself as naught and nothing, and that his essence is only the soul that is within him, which is a portion of God above . . . and there is no place empty of Him'. This type of contemplation is recommended as an accompaniment to daily prayer.

A great deal more investigation is needed before the psychological effects of different types of prayer – particularly on immediate and long-term mood – can be clarified and understood. However the suggestion is that prayer is generally felt to be helpful.

During the 1970s and 1980s, some research attention was focused on the use of meditation, very often in the context of new religious movements. The cautious consensus seems to be that regardless of the religious context, meditative techniques may be associated with improvements in feelings of wellbeing, relaxation, lowered stress, increased 'awareness' and some cognitive changes, for instance improved performance on memory tasks (Batson, Schoenrade and Ventis, 1993).

Mystical states may also have beneficial effects, though there are more problems here in distinguishing mystical states from psychopathological conditions. Meadows and Kahoe (1984) discuss some suggestions drawing parallels between some mystical and religious ecstatic states and some psychopathological states, notably schizophrenia. Both types of state involve the rejection of something bad, a feeling of alienation and disappointment in interpersonal relationships, and the construction of a more gratifying reality (Zales, 1978), but the mystical experience is consciously controlled and prepared for. Mysticism involves an expansion of consciousness, rather than an involuntary fleeing from an unbearable reality. There are thus numerous crucial differences between the states. Nevertheless there have been reports of psychotic breakdowns following altered states of consciousness, often drug-induced. A well-known controlled study on this topic, however, is Pahnke's (1966) study of committed Christians who were involved, after careful preparation, in an intense group religious experience on Good Friday. Some of the group had been administered a psychedelic drug, others a placebo. The main outcome measures were based on Stace's criteria for mystical experience (noetic experience, transcending time and space), and the psychedelically drugged subjects scored higher on these shortly after their experience. But in the longer term, several months later, both groups reported changes (improvements) in their outlook, to an equal extent.

Fenwick (1987) has devoted efforts to investigating the neuropsychological correlates of mystical experiences.

A remarkable class of experiences which has received much attention in recent years consists of experiences reported by people who have been at the point of death, and who have returned to life. The experiences involve a feeling of being out of the body, and are variously called near-death experiences (NDEs) or out-of-body experiences (OBEs). The soul is aware of what is happening around the body, hears what people say and sees what they do. Following this, experiences of being drawn towards a light, of being in touch with people who have died and of feeling a great sense of peace are commonly reported. Then the soul is, as it were, informed that their mission in life is not yet completed and that they must return. Subsequently, people who have had this experience commonly report that they are conscious of re-evaluating their priorities in life, are more appreciative of life, more conscious of their spirituality and more concerned to do good and live a spiritually purposeful life (Moody, 1975).

Unlike prayer or mystical experiences, NDEs and OBEs have not been deliberately engaged in or sought after. The cause is severe illness or injury and a state close to or resembling clinical death. Their effect on the person's subsequent inner life is said to be profound. I am not aware of any evidence or suggestion that these states are psychopathological; the suggestion is that these states may have quite salutary effects. Fenwick (1987) has suggested that these states are more likely in those with a history of epilepsy. The strongest evidence that the states are 'genuine' is the verbatim reporting of conversations by people around the body, which an unconscious person would not normally be able to register or recall.

One such experience is described by Rachel Noam (1992), who was a young woman walking down a city street at the time just prior to her experience. The experiences described are characteristic of NDEs, though at the time she had never heard of near-death experience, thought her experience was unusual and did not at first disclose it to anyone except very close confidants, for fear that she should be considered deranged. Noam's description is exceptionally detailed:

> Suddenly I felt a violent blow strike my head. I fell flat on the ground in front of the big woman. A heavy, 18-foot wooden beam, plunging from the scaffold on top of the five-story structure, hit me and sailed into the street as if thrown by a catapult. Given the height of the building, the impact of the force of gravity and the fragility of my skull, it was a miracle I was still alive.
>
> All at once, I felt I was outside my body, floating upward about 12–15 feet above the sidewalk, watching the scene below. I did not know how I left my body, or how I got up there. Everything happened so suddenly that I was caught completely by surprise. I saw the big woman bending over my body, trying to detect a sign of life in my motionless form. Then she started screaming for help. Several passersby stopped and stared at my body. Reacting to the insistent cries of the woman, the people became alarmed and deliberated as to what to do.
>
> The woman, still kneeling beside me, looked up. 'Where's the building contractor?' she yelled. 'Where's the foreman on this job?'

The other people joined in the shouting.

On the roof, a young man emerged.

'What's going on down there?' he shouted. 'What's all the commotion?'

The woman pointed at my body. 'I want to speak to the building contractor this minute!'

The young man disappeared, returning a short while later. 'The contractor is up here,' he said. 'He won't come down, and he won't talk to anyone.'

I could see my body stretched out on the sidewalk.

This is my body, I thought, but I am not inside it. I am looking at it from above. How is this possible? With what eyes am I seeing this, and where are my ears? How could I be hearing all this noise in the street?

It was strange to look at myself from the outside, knowing that this was my body. I was viewing it from a different perspective, since while I was inside my form I could not see it from the outside. Now I was looking at my body the way I used to look at other people. I was baffled. Obviously I existed, I was real, I was conscious, but not inside my frame. I always thought that 'I' and my body were identical. I did not know that I was a being with more than just a physical body.

I was not at all afraid. Quite the contrary, I felt fine. I felt no pain or bruising; I felt relaxed, buoyant, worry-free. I existed independently of my bodily functions. I did not need any physical organs to see, to hear or to think. All the while, my body was lying dead-still on the sidewalk, unable to function without my presence. All its faculties were now with me, outside my body, hence, my flesh-and-bone frame was unable to react or move. I was observing it from my external vantage point. When I was inside my body, I saw with my physical eyes; now I perceived without them, and they – my eyes of flesh – saw nothing.

My sense of vision, thus, existed even without my physical eyes; the ability to reason existed even outside my brain. All my life, I had seen by means of my eyes, heard by means of my ears and reasoned by means of my brain. My consciousness had been fully integrated with my body into one inseparable unit. But now everything was different. Being separated from my body was an amazing, supernatural experience. I was surveying the scene from above, looking not only at other people but at myself, at my own material body.

A gradual change began to my status of 'observer'. The events in the street began to fade away into darkness, and through this darkness, I perceived a glimmer of brightness. As the radiance came closer it grew in intensity, becoming a glorious powerful light, radiating an abundant flow of exalted spirituality.

In harmony with this flow of illumination, the events in my life began to pass before my eyes. The images were three-dimensional, and I saw myself taking part in them. My entire life flashed by, from the day I was born until the very moment I fell to the ground.

The vision I saw was like a wide-screen film in which I had the starring role and was also the audience. The images streaked by very rapidly, yet not a single detail was omitted. It was like a video on which every incident is recorded, every musical note, every shade and colour that enhanced my life, and now everything was being played back at high speed and with astounding sharpness. I do not remember the actual vision I saw. What endures in my memory is my surprise at the amazing vividness of the images, recalling long forgotten events and details. I wondered where this visual memory was coming from. How did I suddenly remember my entire infancy and childhood? These questions cropped up as I was watching the replay of my life. When the vision ended I asked myself whether it had really been my own life. I came to the conclusion that indeed it had been. The entire experience filled me with an indescribable sense of exalted happiness.

Once again, I saw the blinding luminescence, glowing in a soft velvety white, as if an infinite number of brightly flashing magic sparks were uniting in a burst of spectacular brilliance. I tried to compare this brilliant glow to the colours of light from various sources I had seen when I was inside my body, but even sunlight paled in comparison to this awesome super-abundance of immeasurable brightness.

The magnificent stream of light was accompanied by a flow of sublime love, a kind of love I had never before experienced. It was unlike the love of parents towards their children, the love of friends and relatives . . . Any love I had ever felt was nothing but a tiny speck compared to this exalted, powerful love. Even if all the sparks of love that abound in the world were to combine they could not equal the powerful, pure love I sensed. Faced with this overpowering love, I felt incapable of remaining an independent entity; I simply melted away. I was too small to withstand the flow of goodness streaming toward me and into me. I tried to defend myself, to close my eyes, but I had no eyes to close! I had no way of hiding before the radiance. I had no body. I felt completely stripped of the outer shell that had protected me in this world. There was no possibility of evading the current of love that enwrapped me. No words can describe the enchantment, the wonder, the incomparable, infinite goodness. I discerned in it qualities of compassion, spiritual pleasure, strength, happiness and beauty, all in infinite profusion.

I was powerless. I had no way of expressing myself. My body was lying on the sidewalk, totally incapacitated . . . my 'self' dissolved into nothingness . . . I felt a strong pull to become part of this wonderful eternal flow . . .

'I am drawn to following my inclination,' I said, 'but I ask to be returned to my body. I ask to be given another opportunity in this world.'

This description continues. It shows most of the features common to NDEs: out-of-body experience, hearing, seeing and recalling conversations and behaviour of people around one's body, an experience of a great light, a fast replay of life experiences, a sense of love. Other NDE reports include an experience like passing through a tunnel before encountering the light, and meeting people (or their souls) who have passed away. Most NDEs include an experience in which the person becomes aware that they are to return to their bodies since their mission in life is unfinished, and most people report that they have been affected in a positive way by their experiences, feeling a stronger awareness of the spiritual side of their nature, a stronger belief in nonmaterial existence, and a stronger sense of purpose in life. However there is scope for more rigorous work in assessing the effects of this type of experience.

Down to earth again, we turn from mystical states and other spiritual experiences to a less exotic, nonmystical form of prayer: confession and penitential prayer. The individual is supposed to catalogue actual and possible failings, and this is meant to awaken feelings of regret and a resolve to do better in future – but it may be the case that people are left with permanent feelings of guilt and unworthiness. Belgum (1992) writes:

> My earliest childhood memory of guilt as an all-pervasive aspect of life goes back to the confessional prayer . . . 'we are wholly and absolutely deserving of punishment and condemnable' . . . later I saw another dynamic at work. After confession one was totally forgiven . . . one went from a minus ten back up to zero . . . but it was pessimistically assumed that everyone came back the next Sunday with a minus ten again, in big trouble with 'thought, word and deed'.

Begum goes on to say that pride and too high self-esteem were seen as very dangerous, and he associates the prayer-induced guilt and worthlessness with a higher than average suicide rate.

These particular suggested associations between prayer and psychopathology have not been systematically investigated.

This section has looked at prayer and related activities, in which an essential component is religiously based privately spoken verbal messages. There are a number of suggestions about the psychological effects. The consensus is that, with some important reservations, prayer is felt to be supportive and helpful, but there has been remarkably little systematic investigation.

SOME SPECIFIC COGNITIONS IN RELIGION AND THEIR EFFECTS

We have looked at some ways in which mental health has been said to be related to cognitive processes, and we have looked at the two great underpinnings of the religious life: faith and prayer/meditation. Both involve cognitions to a major extent. We have examined the extent to which faith and prayer have been suggested and found to be related to mental health. We now turn to some other religiously based cognitions and look at the extent to which they may be related to mental health.

Structure of beliefs

A number of investigators have looked at the structure and nature of cognitions in religion. O'Connor (1983) used repertory grid techniques to study the 'people, places and things known and thought about, believed in and valued'. O'Connor's work, in Australia, compared nonreligious subjects with committed Roman Catholic priests and sisters. Repertory grid techniques are based on Kelly (1955) (not to be confused with Kelley, who figures fairly prominently in this chapter), and they are used to elicit the individual's **construct system**. Constructs are the key concepts and values used by the individual to construe and organize their world, and regulate their lives and social relationships. Religious subjects were found to include more constructs and elements in their grids than did nonreligious subjects. The religious subjects included fewer elements from their immediate families and more authorities, which one would expect given the required lifestyle of Catholic priests and sisters. Religious subjects included more constructs to do with the feelings and behaviour of others towards the subject. This study does show some important effects of a religious lifestyle upon cognitions; in this case the differences are what might expected from our knowledge that Catholic priests and sisters do not found families of their own. O'Connor has not been concerned with the direct effects of the cognitions studied on mental health.

Brown (in preparation) is using somewhat similar methods, also based on Kelly, to look at beliefs and how these fare in different forms of stress. The work of Allport (1950), and Argyle and Beit-Hallahmi's (1975) review of other work on war veterans would lead us to expect that stress would affect beliefs and cognitions, but Brown's is the first research to look at this in detail. Brown's subjects are asked for a detailed list of beliefs held in various contexts, and a detailed study is being made about how the importance, uses and contents of these beliefs are affected by crises of various kinds, including burglary and chronic illness. This research does not look directly at mental health outcome measures. In both O'Connor's and Brown's work there are tempting speculative links to be made with the cognitions studied, and mental health.

A study which does look at a specific set of beliefs in relation to mental health is Maton's (1989). Maton developed a spiritual support scale asking for the extent to which several statements about spiritual support are felt to be true for the person (see Chapter 7). Maton administered his scale to American adults. Some were under major stress, while others were unstressed. Maton found that, in the unstressed subjects, the reporting of spiritual support was unrelated to levels of depression, which were in any case quite low in this group. In the stressed subjects, the reported presence of spiritual support was associated with lower levels of depression.

Several studies have looked at internalized religiously based messages and their use and effects on mental health.

Loewenthal (1992) has reported the use of antidepressant self-instructions in orthodox-Jewish people. These include the following.

- I stop [feeling bad] and tell myself to start going through everything I have to be thankful for.
- I know I don't have time to be depressed. I keep busy with the things I have to do (looking after my family, doing my work, helping others).
- I know that God has been a tremendous support to me in my past troubles and I keep telling myself he'll get me through this too.

These were more likely to be reported by the more religious subjects. Although there is no systematic evidence related the use of these cognitions to outcome measures of mental health, Loewenthal and Goldblatt (1993) showed that religiosity was significantly related to lower levels of specific depression symptoms in orthodox-Jewish women. These were:

- depressed mood;
- loss of interest;
- suicide plans;
- early waking;
- retardation (slowing down).

The suggestion is that religiosity was associated with a greater zest for life, and less disillusionment. The effects could not be explained in terms of possible confounded factors (stress levels, family size), and it was thought that mediating cognitions might play an important role.

An indirect effect of religiosity in Loewenthal and Goldblatt's study was that family size (which is encouraged in some religious groups) had its own independent association with absence of specific symptoms, as described in Chapter 5.

A study by Gilbert (1992) on white American parents looked at the role of religion as a resource for recently bereaved parents.

Usable qualitative interviews that were collected from 54 people, all of whom had suffered loss of a child, or of a late pregnancy, some time in the period eight years prior to the interview. Of the subjects, 30 reported finding religion helpful. Most of these were church attenders. Religion was found to be unhelpful by 12; 11 of these were church attenders. Religion was found to be irrelevant by 12; only three were church attenders. This study is of interest because it illustrates the kinds of idea that are found to be helpful or otherwise when in a distressing situation. Those who found religious ideas helpful seemed to have produced self-addressed speech, whereas the unhelpful and irrelevant ideas tended to come from others.

Here are some reports from Gilbert's study by those who found religious consolation.

> There's no doubt in my mind . . . if we didn't know that God had it all under control, then things would have been a lot different. I think I would have had a real hard time.

> I accepted that God knew there was something wrong and that's why she had died. And He knew that, whatever was wrong, we couldn't handle it, between ourselves, and that was His will.

> God gave this to me because I could handle it more than other people.

> They say there's reasons for God to do everything, you know. I think that's very true because I love him [the second child, born after the death of the first] a lot more now than I would have, had our first son been here.

> It was at that time that I really got close to Him through prayer and that, and it was that summer after she died that I surrendered to the ministry.

In Gilbert's sample, religion was more often reported helpful than otherwise. As we would expect, stressful experiences may cause anger against God:

> It was just very hard to be close to God, and I just kind of wanted to turn away, to be angry . . . At the time, I felt like I wanted to be as far away from God as I could get. Do things to make him angry, that kind of thing, because I felt He had made me angry.

Attempts to provide religiously based consoling thoughts by others were a source of anger; well-meaning suggestions were seen as irritatingly sanctimonious:

[The priest] told me I should be delighted that I had an angel in heaven . . . He was worse than nothing, the man was a jackass.

I got 'It's God's will' . . . and I finally laid into one person and I said, 'What possible good could come from making my wife so sick and killing my child?' And they said, 'Well, you don't always understand the plan.' And I said, 'I'm sorry, but there is no ultimate plan to justify this,' and I said, 'Hitler had a plan'.

I just remember feeling that frustration . . . Some people, meaning well but doing the typical thing of coming up and telling me that it was God's will and all that stuff and I didn't want to hear it at the time.

I had a preacher come in when my son was dying and, oh, you would've thought! I cursed this guy, you know, because he said, 'We don't always understand but I, you know, maybe with something you appreciate things more' or something. I can't remember what he said. And I, oh, I just went nuts on this guy! And I said, 'Let me take you through there and show you these babies with their arms off and their guts hanging off, and if this is supposed to make me appreciate my arms more, you know, if God sent this baby here, I think He's crummy!'. . . I don't believe that God would send a child here to make you appreciate things more.

[When people told me it was for the best] Really, would you like to tell me why, what's the best about it? It's for the best and someday you'll know what God's plan was for you and there's a reason for all this. Oh really! There's no reason for this stuff. You can't tell me there's a reason.

And others who had found religion helpful felt that they had to re-evaluate their relationship to God:

I realized that I had to change my attitude towards life, that I had to forgive myself, forgive my husband and praise God that we were still all alive . . . And I think I turned to God then too.

> He said, 'Who do you blame?' And I said, 'Well I blame God and He caused it to happen.' And he made me realize that it wasn't God's fault.

Those who found religion irrelevant tended to be people for whom religion was not part of the assumptive world:

> I don't think either one of us considers ourselves terribly religious, so that wasn't something I would fall back on. It wasn't something I would count as something that would help at that time. But then, even before, it wasn't.

Gilbert's study gives a good idea of the kind of thoughts that were offered, and sometimes found consoling (or infuriating), by American Christians. These seemed to be the three most common themes.

- Even seemingly terrible things may be part of a divine plan.
- If this suffering was given to me by God, I must be able to bear it.
- Closeness to God.

A similar list of consoling beliefs is offered by Stack (1992). McIntosh, Silver and Wortman's (1993) major quantitative study of bereaved parents (described in Chapter 7) suggested that such thoughts may play a positive role in adjusting to bereavement, and in reducing the likelihood of long-term distress.

The just world

Another important type of religiously based cognition which may play an important role in mental health is the so-called belief in a just world (Lerner, 1980; 1992). Lerner derived his ideas about the just-world belief from a set of experiments with striking, counter-intuitive findings. One such experiment (described in Chapter 6) involves a class of psychology students who are asked to take part in an experiment to get credit points. The class is told that they will watch a volunteer undergoing a learning task and receiving an electric shock every time a mistake is made. They will then make ratings of the volunteer and his/her performance. A volunteer is then called for, and pleasant-looking girl steps forward. The rest of the class watch through a screen while she struggles with a difficult learning task, makes mistakes, and receives painful electric shocks. Afterwards, some of the class are told that she wasn't a real volunteer; she was a colleague of the investigators and her sufferings were not real – she was just acting, and the electric shocks were phoney. Other members of the class are left to believe that the volunteer's sufferings were genuine, and that she was suffering for their sakes.

Which group of students is going to think better of the 'volunteer'? Maybe you are more worldly-wise than me, but if you are, you are part of a very small and select company. Most people flatly refused to believe Lerner's findings, even when they had been widely replicated in a variety of settings. The unsavoury truth is that the girl whose sufferings are believed to be genuine is seen as less good and able and likeable on a whole range of characteristics. Lerner's suggestion is that – based on religious tradition – we see the unfortunate and the suffering as somehow deserving their fate. They are less worthy than those who are all right. This of course is a double-edged weapon. Suppose that the victim of such complacency (according to Lerner, that includes virtually all of us) does suffer some misfortune. In addition to any other consequences of the misfortune, we may become the victims of the just world logic: we are unworthy, we do somehow deserve this. So on top of our other troubles, our self-esteem takes a nose-dive, which may be enough to plummet us into a clinical depression. Of course there are attributional manoeuvres to get out of this – if you recall the beginning of this chapter, you may remember the suggestion that nondepressed people tend to see bad outcomes and events as due to external ('not my fault') factors. One of Lerner's suggestions however is that religions may encourage fault-finding in the self. In theory, they may do, but the empirical evidence (linking religiosity and depression) does not really seem to show that this always happens in practice. Lerner's suggestions about the links between just-world beliefs, misfortune and depression remain very compelling and well worth closer investigation.

Attributions and expectations

Some investigators have looked at attributions and expectations by religious people.

Snow and Machalek (1984) looked at converts to a new religious movement, while Staples and Mauss (1987) compared Christian converts to lifelong adherents. Both sets of investigators studied biographical accounts, and proposed that one characteristic of religious thinking was a 'master attributional scheme', whereby every event in the person's life is seen as the result of God's grand plan.

This is certainly how events were frequently described in the biographies of the religious people studied. This rhetorical device may be part of a process whereby the religious self is presented as right and perfect. This rather speculative link is a connection between this kind of religiously based cognition and mental health. The idea that everything is part of God's grand plan is supported by Spilka, Shaver and Kirkpatrick's (1985) suggestion that attributional processes are used to understand the conditions under which God might satisfy the person's needs. Further, attributional processes are used, it is suggested, to impose meaning on events in a way that enhances self-esteem and enhances the feeling that the person has some degree of control.

Sometimes, however, God's role as a causal agent may be less obvious than the role played by mundane factors. Ritzema (1979) has compared conditions in which natural and supernatural explanations are used, or some combination of the two. Brown (1966) in a cross-cultural study showed that among the children studied prayer was seen as more appropriate in some situations (e.g. life-threatening or crucial) than others. Some investigators have compared religious believers and others in their causal analyses of events.

Furnham and Brown (1992) looked at subjects' beliefs about the causes of bad events. 'Theological explanations' – stating that God is a cause of events – were most likely to be endorsed by Jews and Moslems, and least likely by agnostics and atheists, with Christians in between. The more severe events were less likely to be seen as caused by God. Natural explanations were generally more popular than theological ones. This study was concerned with theodicy, the question of why bad things happen, and perhaps the most striking finding was that the explanations preferred differed according to the type of attempt, to an apparently similar extent to the way explanation was affected by religious background.

Loewenthal and Cornwall (1993) looked at explanations for different types of event: illnesses and other severe health problems, like miscarriage; economic and job-related difficulties, like unemployment; and interpersonal difficulties, like marital breakdown. As in Furnham and Brown's study, the events were hypothetical ones that the subjects had not necessarily had any personal experience of. The subjects in this study were all British, some Christians, and some agnostic or atheist. As expected, the religious subjects were more likely to see God as a causal agent than the nonreligious subjects. However, there were no other differences between religious and nonreligious subjects in their causal expectations: they were equally likely to see self, powerful others and chance as causal factors. The surprise in this study came when we looked at subjects' causal analyses of different types of event. It turned out that religious and nonreligious subjects did not differ in seeing God as a causal factor in work, economic and interpersonal difficulties. With these types of event, God was unlikely to be seen as a cause. It was only with the life-threatening conditions that God was very likely to be seen as a cause by the religious, but unlikely to be seen as a cause by the nonreligious.

In current work, Andrew MacLeod and I hope to look at the specific thoughts reported by religious and nonreligious people after suffering real-life stressful events. We hope to look systematically at the reported use of different cognitions:

- perception of good things that have happened as a result of the event;
- perception of bad things that have happened;
- perception of bad things that were forestalled by the event;
- perception of good things that were forestalled;
- causal attributions for the event (the extent to which God and other factors were seen as responsible);
- the extent to which, overall, the event was seen as being for the good.

These studies illustrate how the suggested stress-buffering effects of religiosity may be partly understood by the individual's causal analyses of life-events. It still remains to be seen whether the causal analyses can have a direct effect on mental health. The understanding of events is affected by religious messages in at least three distinct ways.

1. Feelings of purpose and meaning may have a measurable consolatory effect.
2. The idea that unpleasant happenings may be a punishment for wrongdoing is unpopular on the conscious level. It is claimed to be pervasive however, and likely to affect judgments of others in misfortune, and may affect self-opinion.
3. God may be seen as causal, particularly for crucial events, and as supportive and helpful.

SUMMARY

This chapter described cognitive theories of mental illness.

Cognitive–developmental analyses of religion were then described, and the importance of the internalization of religious messages in the development of religious thinking was suggested.

Prayer and meditation and their effects were discussed, and finally some specific religiously based cognitions were described and the evidence regarding their effects on mental health reviewed.

10

Conclusions

This book has looked at the ways in which factors that are associated with religion are also associated with variations in mental health.

In this short chapter we take a backward overview and make a few guesses about the future.

We saw that religion itself is too comprehensive a category to look at in relation to mental health – and that mental health is too comprehensive a category to look at in relation to religion! Studies that have tried to look at religion and mental health without being more specific have been inconclusive.

Specific aspects of religion that need to be defined include the religious group and sub-group, the cultural context and personal orientation to religion. All these factors have been shown to be associated with variations in mental health.

Specific aspects of mental health include depression and anxiety, both as clinical and as distress states. Some schizophrenic symptoms have religious overtones. A problem for psychiatrists is deciding when behaviour and feelings are psychopathological and when they are religiously and culturally endorsed.

Aspects of religion that go with poor mental health include (apparently) religiously endorsed cruelty, scrupulosity and self-righteousness. Good mental health may go with religiously encouraged social support, religious ideas, feelings, experiences and orientation.

Positive mental health states have been somewhat neglected. More attention could be given to the internalization of religious ideas and self-instructions and their role in regulating mood and behaviour.

Religious change has been closely linked with personal change. A great deal of attention has been paid to religious conversion: is it a panacea, a placebo or a basic necessity? Methodological problems plague this area of research in particular. More attention could be paid to religious change over the lifespan, to religious movement, including movement 'away' from religion and movements that are less obviously dramatic than conversion and deconversion.

The psychotherapy professions have traditionally had very strong – but ambivalent – relationships with religion. Prototypically, the psychotherapist has a strong disinclination to religion, and psychotherapy has had quite a bad press in religious circles. Nevertheless there has always been a strong current of interest in the analysis of religious feelings, and theory and technique in this area are said to be developing.

THE FUTURE

Where to next?

Looking at the past suggests many areas where growth could occur.

My preferences would be for more attention to be given to defining and assessing positive mental health states – positive mental health is not merely the absence of psychopathology and not even the absence of distress.

Thus, attempts to measure general happiness and wellbeing may be inadequate to deal with phenomena like smiling torturers (they may be happy but are they healthy?) and weeping saints (they are unhappy over other people's distress, but they do something to help – which is healthy).

The cognitive processes involved in mediating between religion and mental health need more specification and study. Particularly important seem to be the verbal messages, the instructions and advice. Which get internalized? How? Under what circumstances? What are their effects? What happens when messages are rejected?

Although sociologists of religion have studied religious groups, these have not received much attention from social psychologists. There have been a few studies of out-group derogation in religious groups, but much more attention could be given to the study of leadership, family life, social relationships and social support in religious groups, as well as more attention to communication and messages and closer study of religious influences on causal analysis.

Many methodological improvements could be made in research. Although prospective research is often too expensive, there is scope for developing economical prospective research designs. Better sampling is also called for. Although research funding bodies have not given large amounts to research on religion and mental health, this may not be because of lack of recognition of the importance of this field. It may be because better research is needed. Given good research designs, more research funding may be forthcoming.

For mental health professionals, there are two obvious needs. One is dealing with the scenario:

- a patient is referred with 'symptoms';
- the patient says this behaviour is religiously encouraged;
- the patient's friends and relatives insist that the behaviour is symptomatic of illness;
- the professional has difficulty in deciding who is right.

This is a common scenario, and happens daily outside the field of professional mental health practice. The common denominator is self-justification of behaviour that causes intolerable distress to others. The world would certainly be a better place if we could work out solutions to this problem. In rabbinic thought, it is known as the **religious evil inclination**: it is picturesquely described as the evil inclination dressing him/herself up in pious clothes and demeanour and encouraging misguided behaviour in the name of religion.

Another need for professionals is the continuation of developments that are occurring in psychotherapeutic theory and techniques for dealing with religious feelings and with spirituality. Even where the feeling to spiritual and moral issues is indifference or hostility, to overlook or ignore this area could be dangerous to the psychic economy.

It would need another book to explore the reasons for the low profile given to religion in psychological and psychiatric circles. The energy and time needed for that enquiry would be better spent in developing understanding of the ways in which the factors that go with religion may be used to help improve mental health.

References

Abramson, L.Y., Seligman, M.E.P. and Teasdale, J.D. (1978) Learned helplessness in humans: critique and reformulation. *Journal of Abnormal Psychology*, **87**, 49–74.

Adorno, T.W., Frenkel-Brunswik, E., Levinson, D.J. and Sanford, R.N. (1950) *The Authoritarian Personality*, Harper, New York.

Allison, J. (1967) Adaptive regression and intense religious experiences. *Journal of Nervous and Mental Disease*, **145**, 452–463.

Alloy, L.B. and Abramson, L.Y. (1979) Judgment of contingency in depressed and non-depressed students. Sadder but wiser? *Journal of Experimental Psychology: General*, **108**, 441–485.

Allport, G.W. (1950) *The Individual and His Religion, a Psychological Interpretation*, MacMillan, New York.

Allport, G.W. (1961) *Pattern and Growth in Personality*, Holt, Rinehart & Winston, New York.

Allport, G.W. (1966) The religious context of prejudice. *Journal for the Scientific Study of Religion*, **5**, 448–451.

Allport, G.W., Gillespie, J.M. and Young, J. (1948) The religion of the post-war college student. *Journal of Psychology*, **25**, 3–33.

Allport, G.W. and Ross, J.M. (1967) Personal religious orientation and prejudice. *Journal of Personality and Social Psychology*, **5**, 432–443.

Alsdurf, J.M. (1985) Wife abuse and the church. *Response to the Victimisation of Women and Children*, **8**, 9–11.

Amsel, A. (1976) *Judaism and Psychology*, Feldheim, New York.

Amsel, A. (1976) *Rational Irrational Man*, Feldheim, New York.

Argyle, M. and Beit-Hallahmi, B. (1975) *The Social Psychology of Religion*, Routledge & Kegan Paul, London.

Atkinson, J.M. (1993) The patient as sufferer. *British Journal of Medical Psychology*, **66**, 113–120.

Bainton, R.H. (1950) *Here I Stand: A Life of Martin Luther*, New American Library, New York.

Ball, R. and Clare, A. (1990) Symptoms and social adjustment in Jewish depressives. *British Journal of Psychiatry*, **156**, 379–383.

Bannister, D. and Mair, J.M.N. (1968) *The Evaluation of Personal Constructs*, Academic Press, London.

Barnes, M., Doyle, D. and Johnson, B. (1989) The formation of a Fowler scale: an empirical assessment among Catholics. *Review of Religious Research*, **30**, 412–420.

Bart, P.B. (1970) Portnoy's mother: depression in middle-aged women, in *The Jewish Woman*, (ed. E. Koltun), Schocken, New York.

Batson, C.D. (1976) Religion as prosocial: agent or double agent. *Journal for the Scientific Study of Religion*, **15**, 29–45.

Batson, C.D., Schoenrade, P.A. and Pych, V. (1985) Brotherly love or self-concern? Behavioural consequences of religion, in *Advances in the Psychology of Religion*, (ed. L.B. Brown), Pergamon Press, Oxford.

Batson, C.D., Schoenrade, P.A. and Ventis, W.L. (1993) *Religion and the Individual: a Social-Psychological Perspective*, Oxford University Press, Oxford.

Batson, C.D. and Ventis, W.L. (1982) *The Religious Experience: a Social–Psychological Perspective*, Oxford University Press, New York.

Bebbington, P. (1987) Marital status and depression: a study of English national admission statistics. *Acta Psychiatrica Scandinavica*, **75**, 640–658.

Bebbington, P., Katz, R., McGuffin, P. and Tennant, C. (1989) The risks of minor depression before age 65: results from a community survey. *Psychological Medicine*, **19**, 393–400.

Beck, A.T., Rush, A.J., Shaw, B.F. and Emery, G. (1979) *Cognitive Therapy of Depression*, Guilford Press, New York.

Beck, A.T. and Steer, R.A. (1987) *The Beck Depression Inventory*, The Psychological Corporation/Harcourt Brace Jovanovitch, San Antonio, CA.

Belgum, D. (1992) Guilt and/or self-esteem as consequences of religion. *Journal of Religion and Health*, **31**, 73–85.

Bentall, R.P. and Pilgrim, D. (1993) Thomas Szasz, crazy talk and the myth of mental illness. *British Journal of Medical Psychology*, **66**, 69–76.

Berger, B.D. and Adesso, V.J. (1991) Gender differences in using alcohol to cope with depression. *Addictive Behaviours*, **16**, 315–327.

Bergin, A. (1980) Psychotherapy and religious values. *Journal of Consulting and Clinical Psychology*, **48**, 95–105.

Bergin, A.E. (1983) Religiosity and mental health: a critical re-evaluation and meta-analysis. *Professional Psychology: Research and Practice*, **14**, 170–184.

Bergin, A.E. (1991) Values and religious issues in psychotherapy and mental health. 98th Annual Convention of the American Psychological Association Distinguished Professional Contributions Award Address, 1990, Boston, MA. *American Psychologist*, **46**, 394–403.

Bergin, A.E. and Jensen, J.P. (1990) Religiosity of psychotherapists: a national survey. Special issue: psychotherapy and religion. *Psychotherapy*, **27**, 3–7.

Bergin, A.E., Masters, K.S. and Richards, P.S. (1987) Religiousness and mental health reconsidered: a study of an intrinsically religious sample. *Journal of Counselling Psychology*, **34**, 197–204.

Berke, J. (1990) *The Tyranny of Malice: Explaining the Dark Side of Character and Culture*, Summit Books, New York.

Bettelheim, B. (1960) *The Informed Heart*, Free Press, New York.

Bettelheim, B. (1983) *Freud and Man's Soul*, Chatto & Windus, London.

Biale, D. (1983) Eros and enlightenment: love against marriage in the Eastern European Jewish enlightenment. *Polin*, **1**, 50–67.

Bowlby, J. (1969) *Attachment and Loss: Vol 1. Attachment*, Basic Books, New York.

Bowlby, J. (1973) *Attachment and Loss: Vol 2. Separation: Anxiety and Anger*, Basic Books, New York.

Bowlby, J. (1980) *Attachment and Loss: Vol 3. Loss*, Basic Books, New York.

Bradley, C., Brewin, C.R. and Duncan S.L.B. (1983) Perceptions of labour: discrepancies between midwives' and patients' ratings. *British Journal of Obstetrics and Gynaecology*, **90**, 1176–1179.

Bradley, C., Lewis, K., Jennings, A. and Ward, J. (1990) Scales to measure perceived control developed specifically for people with tablet-treated diabetes. *Diabetic Medicine*, **7**, 685–694.

Bragan, K. (1977) The psychological gains and losses of religious conversion. *British Journal of Medical Psychology*, **50**, 177–180.

Branover, H. (1982) *Return*. Feldheim, Jerusalem.

Bridges, R.A. and Spilka, B. (1992) Religion and the mental health of women, in *Religion and Mental Health*, (ed. J. Schumaker), Oxford University Press, Oxford.

Brinkerhoff, M.B., Grandin, E. and Lupri, E. (1992) Religious involvement and spousal violence: the Canadian case. *Journal for the Scientific Study of Religion*, **31**, 15–31.

Brown, D. and Pedder, J. (1979) *An Introduction to Psychotherapy. An Outline of Psychodynamic Principles and Practice*, Tavistock, London.

Brown, G.W., Andrews, B., Harris, T.O. *et al.* (1986) Social support, self-esteem and depression. *Psychological Medicine*, **16**, 813–831.

Brown, G.W. and Harris, T.O. (1978) *The Social Origins of Depression*, Tavistock, London.

Brown, G.W. and Harris, T. (1986) Stressor, vulnerability and depression: a question of replication. *Psychological Medicine*, **165**, 739–744.

Brown, G. and Prudo, R. (1981) Psychiatric disorder in an urban and a rural population 1: Aetiology of depression. *Psychological Medicine*, **11**, 581–599.

Brown, J. (In preparation) Beliefs and crises. University of London. PhD thesis.

Brown, L.B. (1962) A study of religious belief. *British Journal of Psychology*, **53**, 259–272.

Brown, L.B. (1966) Egocentric thought in petitionary prayer: a cross-cultural study. *Journal of Social Psychology*, **68**, 197–210.

Brown, L.B. (1987) *The Psychology of Religious Belief*, Academic Press, London.

Brown, R. (1965) *Social Psychology*, MacMillan/Free Press, New York.

Brown, R. (1986) *Social Psychology*, 2nd edn, Free Press, New York.

Buber, M. (1947) *Tales of the Hasidim: the Early Masters*, Schocken, New York.

Buckley, P. and Galanter, M. (1979) Mystical experience, spiritual knowledge and a contemporary ecstatic religion. *British Journal of Medical Psychology*, **52**, 281–289.

Burtt, E.A. (1957) *Man Seeks the Divine: a Study in the History and Comparison of Religions*, Harper, New York.

Callan, V.J. and Hennesey, J.F. (1988) The psychological adjustment of women experiencing infertility. *British Journal of Medical Psychology*, **61**, 137–140.

Calzeroni, A., Conte, G., Pennati, A. *et al.* (1990) Celibacy and fertility rates in patients with major affective disorders: the relevance of delusional symptoms and suicidal behaviour. *Acta Psychiatrica Scandinavica*, **82**, 309–310.

Capps, D. (1992) Religion and child abuse: perfect together. Presidential address of the Society for the Scientific Study of Religion 1991, Pittsburgh, PA. *Journal for the Scientific Study of Religion*, **31**, 1–14.

Carmen, E., Russo, N.F. and Miller, J.B. (1981) Inequality and women's mental health: an overview. *American Journal of Psychiatry*, **138**, 1319–1330.

Carta, M.G., Carpiniello, B., Morosini, P.L. and Rudas, N. (1991) Prevalence of mental disorders in Sardinia: a community study in an island mining district. *Psychological Medicine*, **21**, 1061–1071.

Chang, J. (1991) *Wild Swans: The Daughters of China*, Harper Collins, London.

Clark, J. (1979) Cults. *Journal of the American Medical Association*, **242**, 279–281.

Clark, L.F. (1993) Stress and the cognitive-conversational benefits of social interaction. *Journal of Social and Clinical Psychology*, **12**, 25–55.

Cochrane, R. (1983) *The Social Creation of Mental Illness*, Longman, Harlow.

Cochrane, R. (1993) Women and depression, in *The Health Psychology of Women*, (eds C.A. Niven and D. Carroll), Harwood Press, Switzerland.

Conway, F. and Siegelman, J. (1982) Information disease: Have cults created a new mental illness? *Science Digest*, **Jan**, 86–92.

Cox, H. (1977) *Turning East*, Simon & Schuster, New York.

Cozolino, L.S. (1990) Ritualistic child abuse, psychopathology and evil. *Journal of Psychology and Theology*, **18**, 218–227.

Craissati, J. (1990) Mental health care in India. *Psychologist*, **3**, 19–22.

Crumbaugh, J.C. and Maholick, L.T. (1969) An experimental study in existentialism. *Journal of Clinical Psychology*, **20**, 200–207.

Cunin, B., Cunin, B. and Cunin, S. (1993) Psychotherapy with orthodox Jewish patients: on clarifying distortions and conflicts. *Journal of Psychology and Judaism*, **16**, 123–131.

Cutler, S.E. and Nolen-Hoeksema, S. (1991) Accounting for sex differences in depression through female victimization: childhood sexual abuse. *Sex Roles*, **24**, 425–438.

Day, J. (1989) *Moloch: a God of Sacrifice in the Old Testament*, Cambridge University Press, Cambridge.

DiBlasio, F.A. and Benda, B.B. (1991) Practitioners, religion and the use of forgiveness in the clinical setting. Special issue: religious values in psychotherapy. *Journal of Psychology and Christianity*, **10**, 166–172.

Dittes, J.E. (1969) Psychology of religion, in *The Handbook of Social Psychology*, (eds G. Lindzey and E. Aronson), 2nd edn, vol. 5., Addison-Wesley, Reading, MA.

Dobson, J. (1970) *Dare to Discipline*, Living Books, Wheaton, IL.

Dodge, J., Armitage, J. and Kasch, H. (eds) (1964) *Encyclopaedia Britannica*, William Benton, London.

Dunnigan, T., McNall, M. and Mortimer, J.T. (1993) The problem of metaphorical nonequivalence in cross-cultural survey research: comparing the mental health statuses of Hmong refugee and general population adolescents. *Journal of Cross-Cultural Psychology*, **24**, 344–365.

Durkheim, E. (1966) *Suicide* (original edition 1897), Free Press, New York.

Eaton, J.W. and Weil, R.J. (1955) *Culture and Mental Disorders: a Comparative Study of the Hutterites and Other Populations*, Free Press, New York.

Eliade, M. (1978–85) *A History of Religious Ideas*, (trans. A. Hiltebeitel and D. Apostolos-Cappadona), 3 vols, University of Chicago Press, London.

Elkind, D. (1971) The development of religious understanding in children and adolescents, in *Research on Religious Development: a Comprehensive Handbook. A Project of the Religious Education Association*, (ed. M. Strommen), Hawthorn Books, New York.

Ellis, A. (1962) *Reason and Emotion in Psychotherapy*, Citadel, Secaucus, NJ.

Ellis, A. (1975) The case against religion: a psychotherapist's view, in *Counselling and Psychotherapy* (ed. B. Ard), Science & Behaviour Books, Palo Alto, CA.

Erickson, J.A. (1992) Adolescent religious development and commitment: a structural equation model of the role of family, peer group, and educational influences. *Journal for the Scientific Study of Religion*, **31**, 131–152.

Erikson, E.H. (1963) *Childhood and Society*, Norton, New York.

Eysenck, H.J. (1952) The effects of psychotherapy: an evaluation. *Journal of Consulting Psychology*, **16**, 19–24.

Eysenck, H. (1967) *The Biological Basis of Personality*, Charles C. Thomas, Springfield, IL.

Eysenck, H.J. and Wilson, G.D. (1973) *The Psychological Basis of Ideology*, Medical and Technical Publishers, Lancaster.

Eysenck, M.W. (1992) *Anxiety: the Cognitive Perspective*, Lawrence Erlbaum, London.

Eysenck, S.B.G. and Eysenck, H.J. (1964) *The Eysenck Personality Inventory*, Hodder & Stoughton, London.

Fenchel, G.H. (1986) Similarities and differences between Catholic religious traditions. *Issues in Ego Psychology*, **9**, 61–62.

Fenwick, P. (1987) Meditation and the EEG, in *The Psychology of Meditation*, (ed. M.A. West), Clarendon Press, Oxford.

Fernando, S. (1975) A cross-cultural and familial study of some familial and social factors in depressive illness. *British Journal of Psychiatry*, **127**, 46–53.

Festinger, L., Riecken, H.W. and Schachter, S. (1956) *When Prophecy Fails*, Harper Torchbooks, New York.

Finlay-Jones, R. (1989) Anxiety, in *Life Events and Illness*, (eds G.W. Brown and T.O. Harris), Unwin Hyman, London.

Finney, J.R. and Maloney, H.N. (1985) An empirical study of contemplative prayer as an adjunct to psychotherapy. *Journal of Psychology and Theology*, **13**, 284–290.

Firth, S. (1991) Changing patterns in Hindu death rituals in Britain, in *Hindu Ritual and Society*, (eds D. Killingley, W. Menski and S. Firth), S.Y. Killingley, Newcastle upon Tyne.

Fisch, R.Z. (1992) Psychosis precipitated by marriage: a culture-bound syndrome? *British Journal of Medical Psychology*, **65**, 385–391.

Fowler, J.W. (1981) *Stages of Faith: the Psychology of Human Development and the Quest for Meaning*, Harper & Row, San Francisco, CA.

Frady, M. (1979) *Billy Graham: a Parable of American Righteousness*, Little, Brown & Co., Boston, MA.

Francis, L.J. (1978) Attitude and longitude: a study in measurement. *Character Potential*, **8**, 119–130.

Francis, L.J., Pearson, P.R. and Kay, W.K. (1982) Eysenck's personality quadrants and religiosity. *British Journal of Social Psychology*, **21**, 262–264.

Frankl, V. (1959) *From Death Camps to Existentialism (Man's Search for Meaning)*, Beacon, Boston, MA.

Frankl, V. (1965) *The Doctor and the Soul: from Psychotherapy to Logotherapy*, Knopf, New York.

Freud, S. (1907) Obsessive acts and religious practices, in *Collected Papers, 1907/1924*, Hogarth Press, London.

Freud, S. (1917) *Introductory Lectures on Psycho-Analysis*, Hogarth Press, London.

Freud, S. (1926) *The Question of Lay Analysis*, Hogarth Press, London.

Freud, S. (1927) *The Future of an Illusion*, Hogarth Press, London.

Freud, S. (1928) *Totem and Taboo: Resemblances Between the Psychic Lives of Savages and Neurotics*, Dodd, New York.

Freud, S. (1930) *Civilisation and its Discontents*, Hogarth Press, London.

Freud, S. (1933) *New Introductory Lectures on Psycho-Analysis*, Hogarth Press, London.

Freud, S. (1939) *Moses and Monotheism*, Hogarth Press and the Institute of Psychoanalysis, London.

Fromm, E. (1950) *Psychoanalysis and Religion*, Yale University Press, New Haven, CT.

Fugate, J.R. (1980) *What the Bible Says About ... Child Training*, Aletheia Publishers, Garland, TX.

Furnham, A. and Brown, L.B. (1992) Theodicy: a neglected aspect of the psychology of religion. *International Journal for the Psychology of Religion*, **2**, 37–46.

Galanter, M. (ed.) (1989) *Cults and New Religious Movements*, American Psychiatric Association, Washington, DC.

Galanter, M., Rabkin, R., Rabkin, J. and Deutsch, A. (1979) The 'Moonies' – a psychological study of conversion and membership in a contemporary religious sect. *American Journal of Psychiatry*, **136**, 165–170.

Gallup, G.H. (1972) *The Gallup Poll: Public Opinion 1935–1971*, Random House, New York.

Galton, F. (1883) *Inquiries into Human Faculty and Development*, MacMillan, New York.

Gartner, J. (1983) Self-esteem tests: Assumptions and values, in *Your Better Self: Psychology, Christianity and Self-Esteem*, (ed. C. Ellison), Harper & Row, New York.

Gartner, J., Hermatz, M., Hohmann, A. and Larson, D. (1990) The effect of patient and clinician ideology on clinical judgment: a study of ideological countertransference. Special issue: psychotherapy and religion. *Psychotherapy*, **27**, 98–106.

Gaskell, E. (1976) *Cranford and Cousin Phillis*, Penguin, Harmondsworth, Middlesex.

Gilbert, K. (1992) Religion as a resource for bereaved parents. *Journal of Religion and Health*, **31**, 19–30.

Gilligan, C. (1977) In a different voice: women's conceptions of self and of morality. *Harvard Educational Review*, **47**, 481–517.

Glock, C.Y. and Stark, R. (1965) *Religion and Society in Tension*, Rand McNally, Chicago, IL.

Gold, A. (1988) *The Marrano Prince*, CIS Press, Lakewood, NJ.

Golding, J.M., Burnham, M.A. and Wells, K.B. (1990) Alcohol use and depressive symptoms among Mexican Americans and non-Hispanic Whites. *Alcohol and Alcoholism*, **25**, 421–432.

Goldman, R. (1964) *Religious Thinking from Childhood to Adolescence*, Routledge & Kegan Paul, London.

Gonzalez de Rivera, J.L., de las Cuevas, C., Garcia-Marco, R. and Henry-Benitez, M. (1991) Age, sex and marital status differences in minor psychiatric morbidity. *European Journal of Psychiatry*, **5**, 166–176.

Goshen-Gottstein, E.R. (1987) Mental health implications of living in an ultra-orthodox Jewish subculture. *Israel Journal of Psychiatry and Related Sciences*, **24**, 145–156.

Gove, W.R. (1972) The relationship between sex roles, marital status, and mental illness. *Social Forces*, **51**, 34–44.

Grant, L. (1992) A fistful of rupees. *The Times Saturday Review*, **28 Nov**, 10–14.

Greenberg, D., Witztum, E. and Pisante, J. (1987) Scrupulosity: Religious attitudes and clinical presentations. *British Journal of Medical Psychology*, **60**, 29–37.

Greenberg, D., Witztum, E. and Buchbinder, J.T. (1992) Mysticism and psychosis: the fate of Ben Zoma. *British Journal of Medical Psychology*, **65**, 223–235.

Greene, S. (1989) The relationship between depression and hopelessness. *British Journal of Psychiatry*, **154**, 650–659.

Greven, P. (1991) *Spare the Child: the Religious Roots of Punishment and the Psychological Impact of Physical Abuse*, Alfred A. Knopf, New York.

Grossberg, S.H, (1979) Ethnic identification and use of social service agencies. *Journal of Psychology and Judaism*, **4**, 78–86.

Gwinn, R.P., Norton P.B. and Gretz, P.W. (1989) *The New Encyclopedia Britannica*, Enclyclopedia Britannica Inc., Chicago, IL.

Hannah, T.E. and Morissey, C. (1987) Correlates of psychological hardiness in Canadian adolescents. *Journal of Social Psychology*, **127**, 339–344.

Harris, T.O. (unpublished) Unpublished material on religiosity in Hebridean women collected for the series of studies reported in Brown and Prudo, 1981.

Hay, D. (1979) Religious experience among a group of postgraduate students: a qualitative study. *Journal for the Scientific Study of Religion*, **18**, 164–182.

Hay, D. (1982) *Exploring Inner Space: Scientists and Religious Experience*, Penguin, Harmondsworth, Middlesex.

Higgins, E.T. (1987) Self-discrepancy: a theory relating self and affect. *Psychological Review*, **94**, 319–340.

Higgins, E.T., Klein, R. and Strauman, T. (1985) Self-concept discrepancy theory: a psychological model for distinguishing among different aspects of depression and anxiety. *Social Cognition*, **3**, 51–76.

Hill, E.W. and Mullen, P.M. (1992) Jungian psychology and pastoral care. *Religion and Health*, **31**, 287–295.

Himmelstein, J.L. (1986) The social basis of antifeminism: religious networks and culture. *Journal for the Scientific Study of Religion*, **25**, 1–13.

Hingley, S. (1992) Psychological theories of delusional thinking: in search of integration. *British Journal of Medical Psychology*, **65**, 347–356.

Hobfoll, S.E. (1991) Gender differences in stress reactions: women filling the gaps. *Psychology and Health*, **5**, 95–109.

Hollingshead, A.B. and Redlich, F.C. (1958) *Social Class and Mental Illness*, John Wiley, New York.

Holm, N.G. (ed.) (1983) *Religious Ecstasy*, Almqvist and Wiksell, .

Holm, N.G. (1987) Sunden's role theory and glossolalia. *Journal for the Scientific Study of Religion*, **26**, 383–389.

Hong, S.M. and Grambower, T. (1986) Do women still differ from men? *Psychological Reports*, **59**, 1332.

Hood, R.W., Jr. (1970) Religious orientation and the report of religious experience. *Journal for the Scientific Study of Religion*, **9**, 285–291.

Hood, R.W., Jr. (1977) Eliciting mystical states of consciousness with semistructured nature experiences. *Journal for the Scientific Study of Religion*, **16**, 155–163.

Hood, R.W., Jr. (1992) Sin and guilt in faith traditions: Issues for self-esteem, in *Religion and Mental Health*, (ed. J. Schumaker), Oxford University Press, Oxford.

Horney, K. (1939) *New Ways in Psychoanalysis*, Norton, New York.

Huizinga, J. (1960) *Men and Ideas: History, the Middle Ages, the Renaissance*, (trans. J.F. Holmes and H. Van der Marle), Eyre & Spottiswoode, London.

Hundert, G.D. (1989) Jewish children and childhood in early modern East Central Europe, in *The Jewish Family: Metaphor and Memory*, (ed. D. Kraemer), Oxford University Press, New York.

Hunt, R.A. and King, M.B. (1972) The intrinsic–extrinsic concept: a review and evaluation. *Journal for the Scientific Study of Religion*, **10**, 339–356.

Hunter, J.A. Stringer, M. and Watson, R.P. (1991) Intergroup violence and intergroup attributions. *British Journal of Social Psychology*, **30**, 261–266.

Jacobs, J. (1987) Deconversion from religious movements: an analysis of charismatic bonding and spiritual commitment. *Journal for the Scientific Study of Religion*, **26**, 294–308.

Jacobs, L. (1973) *What Does Judaism say about...?*, Keter, Jerusalem.

James, W. (1902) *The Varieties of Religious Experience*, Collier, New York.

Joffe, W.G. and Sandler, J. (1965) Notes on pain, depression and individuation. *Psychoanalytic Study of the Child*, **20**, 394–424.

Johnson, P.E. (1956) *Psychology of Religion*, 2nd edn, Abingdon, Nashville, TN.

Jones, L. and Cochrane, R. (1981) Stereotypes of mental illness: a test of the labelling hypothesis. *International Journal of Social Psychiatry*, **27**, 99–107.

Joyce, P.R., Oakley-Brown, M.A., Wells, J.E. and Bushnell, J.A. (1990) Birth cohort trends in major depression: increasing rates and earlier onset in New Zealand. *Journal of Affective DIsorders*, **18**, 83–89.

Jung, C.G. (1933) *Modern Man in Search of a Soul*, Harcourt Brace Jovanovitch, New York.

Jung, C.G. (1958) *Psychology and Religion: West and East*, Routledge & Kegan Paul, London.

Kallstad, T. (1987) The application of the religio-psychological role theory. *Journal for the Scientific Study of Religion*, **26**, 367–374.

Kaney, S. and Bentall, R.P. (1989) Persecutory delusions and attributional style. *British Journal of Medical Psychology*, **62**, 191–198.

Kehoe, N. and Gutheil, T. (1984) Shared religious belief as resistance in psychotherapy. *American Journal of Psychotherapy*, **38**, 579–585.

Kelley, H.H. (1967) Attribution theory in social psychology. *Nebraska Symposium in Motivation*, **15**, 192–238.

Kelly, G.A. (1955) *The Psychology of Personal Constructs*, Norton, New York.

Khan, H. (unpublished) Life-events and depression in Asian Moslem women in Britain. University of London. Ongoing research for PhD.

Khanum, S. (1992) Education and the Moslem girl, in *Refusing Holy Orders: Women and Fundamentalism in Britain*, (eds G. Sahgal and N. Yuval-Davis), Virago, London.

Kieren, D.K. and Munro, B. (1987) Following the leaders: parents' influence on adolescent religious activity. *Journal for the Scientific Study of Religion*, **26**, 249–255.

Kiev, A. (1964) Psychotherapeutic aspects of Pentecostal sects among West Indian immigrants to England. *British Journal of Sociology*, **15**, 129–138.

Kinderman, P., Kaney, S., Morley, S. and Bentall, R.P. (1992) Paranoia and the defensive attributional style: deluded and depressed patients' attributions about their own attributions. *British Journal of Medical Psychology*, **65**, 371–384.

Kirkpatrick, L.A. (1988) The Conway–Siegelman data on religious cults: Kilbourne's analysis reassessed (again). *Journal for the Scientific Study of Religion*, **27**, 117–121.

Kirkpatrick, L.A. (1992) An attachment-theory approach to the psychology of religion. *International Journal for the Psychology of Religion*, **2**, 3–28.

Kirkpatrick, L.A. and Shaver, P.R. (1990) Attachment theory and religion: childhood attachments, religious beliefs and conversion. *Journal for the Scientific Study of Religion*, **29**, 315–334.

Klein, M. (1932) *The Psycho-Analysis of Children*, Hogarth Press, London.

Kohlberg, L. (1968) The child as a moral philosopher. *Psychology Today*, **2**, 25–30.

Kohlberg, L. (1969) Stage and sequence: the cognitive–developmental approach to socialization, in *Handbook of Socialization Theory and Research*, (ed. D.D. Goslin), Rand McNally, Skokie, IL.

Kose, A. (1994) British converts to Islam. University of London. PhD thesis.

Krol, J. (1982) Wplyw posiodanego obrazu ojca na pojecie Boga u mlodziezy (Young people's image of father and its influence on their image of God). *Roczniki Filozoficzne Psychologia*, **30**, 73–103.

Kupferman, J. (1979) *The MsTaken Body*, Paladin, London.

Lannert, J.L. (1991) Resistance and countertransference issues with spiritual and religious clients. *Journal of Humanistic Psychology*, **31**, 68–76.

Larzelere, R.E. (1993) Response to Oosterhuis: empirically justified uses of spanking: towards a discriminating view of corporal punishment. *Journal of Psychology and Theology*, **21**, 142–147.

Larzelere, R.E., Klein, M., Schumm, W.R. and Alibrando, S.A. (1989) Relations of spanking and other parenting characteristics to self-esteem and perceived fairness of parental discipline. *Psychological Reports*, **64**, 1140–1142.

Leach, P. (1993) Should parents hit their children? *Psychologist*, **6**, 216–218.

Lee, R.S. (1948) *Freud and Christianity*, James Clarke, London.

Leff, J. (1993) Comment on crazy talk: thought disorder or psychiatric arrogance. *British Journal of Medical Psychology*, **66**, 77–78.

Lehtinen, V., Lindholm, T., Veijola, J. and Veisanen, E. (1990) The prevalence of PSE-CATEGO disorders in a Finnish adult population. *Social Psychiatry and Psychiatric Epidemiology*, **25**, 187–192.

Lerner, M.J. (1980) *The Beliefs in a Just World: a Fundamental Delusion*, Plenum Press, New York.

Lerner, M. (1991) The belief in a just world and the 'heroic motive': searching for 'constants' in the psychology of religion ideology. *International Journal for the Psychology of Religion*, **1**, 27–32.

Levin, T.M. and Zegans, L.S. (1974) Adolescent identity crisis and religious conversion. *British Journal of Medical Psychology*, **47**, 73–82.

Levine, S.V. and Salter, N.E. (1976) Youth and contemporary religious movements: psychosocial findings. *Canadian Psychiatric Association Journal*, **21**, 411–420.

Levitz, I.N. (1992) The impact of the marriage imperative on Jewish life. *Journal of Psychology and Judaism*, **16**, 109–122.

Lewis, H.B. (1971) *Shame and Guilt in Neuroses*, International Universities Press, New York.

Lewis, I.M. (1971) *Ecstatic Religion*, Penguin, Harmondsworth, Middlesex.

Lewis, J.R. and Bromley, D.G. (1987) The cult withdrawal syndrome: a case of misattribution of cause? *Journal for the Scientific Study of Religion*, **26**, 508–522.

Littlewood, R. and Lipsedge, M. (1989) *Aliens and Alienists: Ethnic Minorities and Psychiatry*, 2nd edn, Unwin Hyman, London.

Loewenthal, K. (1967) How are first impressions formed? *Psychological Reports*, **21**, 834–836.

Loewenthal, K.M. (1988a) Religious development and experience in Habad-hasidic women. *Journal of Psychology and Judaism*, **12**, 5–20.

Loewenthal, K.M. (1988b) Marriage and religious commitment: the case of hasidic women. *Religion Today*, **5**, 8–10.

Loewenthal, K.M. (1988c) The strictly orthodox Jewish community and the helping professions. Federation of Jewish Family Services (now Jewish Care) Seminar, July 1988.

Loewenthal K.M. (1989) Marriage and religious commitment: the case of hasidic women. *Religion Today*, **5**, 8–10.

Loewenthal K.M. (1992) Depression, melancholy and Judaism. *International Journal for the Psychology of Religion*, **2**, 101–108.

Loewenthal, K.M. (1993) Religion, Stress and Distress. *Religion Today*, **8**, 14–16.

Loewenthal, K., Amos, V., Goldblatt, V. and Mullarkey, S. (in press) Some correlates of wellbeing and distress in Anglo-Jewish women, in *Religion, Personality, and Mental Health*, (ed. L. Brown), Springer-Verlag, New York.

Loewenthal, K.M. and Cornwall, N. (1993) Religiosity and perceived control of life events. *International Journal for the Psychology of Religion*, **3**, 39–46.

Loewenthal, K., Eames, K., Loewenthal, C.S. *et al.* (1993) Levels of wellbeing and distress in orthodox Jewish men and women. *Journal of Psychology and Judaism*, **16**, 225–233.

Loewenthal, K.M. and Goldblatt,V. (1993) Family size and depressive symptoms in orthodox Jewish women. *Journal of Psychiatric Research*, **27**, 3–10.

Loewenthal, N. (1990) *Communicating the Infinite: the Emergence of the Habad School*, University of Chicago Press, Chicago, IL.

Loewenthal, N. (1991) Early Habad publications in their setting, in *Hebrew Studies*, (eds D. Rowland Smith and P.S. Salinger), The British Library, London.

Lofland, J. and Skonovd, N. (1981) Conversion motifs. *Journal for the Scientific Study of Religion*, **20**, 373–385.

Long, T.R. and Hadden, J.K. (1983) Religious conversion and the concept of socialization: integrating the brainwashing and drift models. *Journal for the Scientific Study of Religion*, **22**, 1–14.

Lovinger, R.J. (1984) *Working with Religious Issues in Therapy*, Jason Aronson, New York.

Lovinger, R.J. (1990) *Religion and Counselling: the Psychological Impact of Religious Belief*, Continuum, New York.

Lowe, C.R. and Garratt, F.N. (1959) Sex pattern of admission to mental hospitals in relation to social circumstances. *British Journal of Preventive and Social Medicine*, **13**, 88–102.

Lowe, D.W. (1986) Counselling activities and referral practices of ministers. *Journal of Psychology and Christianity*, **5**, 22–29.

Luria, A.R. (1961) *The Role of Speech in the Regulation of Normal and Abnormal Behaviour*, Pergamon Press, Oxford.

MacIsaac, D. (1993) Personal communications.

MacLeod, A.K., Williams, J.M.G. and Bekerian, D.A. (1991) Worry is reasonable: the role of explanations in pessimism about future events. *Journal of Abnormal Psychology*, **100**, 478–486.

MacNamara, P.H. and St George, A. (1979) Measures of religiosity and the quality of life, in *Spiritual Wellbeing: Sociological Perspectives*, (ed. D.O. Moberg), University Press of America, Washington, DC.

MacPhillamy D.J. (1986) The personality effects of long-term Zen monasticism and religious understanding. *Journal for the Scientific Study of Religion*, **25**, 304–319.

Mahler, M.S. (1971) A study of the separation–individuation process and its possible application to borderline phenomena in the psychoanalytic situation. *Psychoanalytic Study of the Child*, **26**, 403–424.

Maimonides, M. (1967) *The Commandments (Sefer Ha-Mitzvoth)*, (trans. with foreword, notes, glossary, appendices and indices C.B. Chavel), Soncino, London.

Marcia, J.E. (1966) Development and validation of ego-identity statuses. *Journal of Personality and Social Psychology*, **3**, 119–133.

Margolin, J. and Witztum, E. (1989) Supernatural impotence: historical review with anthropological and clinical implications. *British Journal of Medical Psychology*, **62**, 339–342.

Masson, J.M. (1984) *The Assault on Truth*, Penguin, Harmondsworth, Middlesex.

Maton, K.I. (1989) The stress-buffering role of spiritual support: cross-sectional and prospective investigations. *Journal for the Scientific Study of Religion*, **28**, 310–323.

Maton, K.I. and Pargament, K.I. (1987) The roles of religion in prevention and promotion. *Prevention in Human Services*, **5**, 161–215.

McIntosh, D.N., Silver, R.C. and Wortman, C.B. (1993) Religion's role in adjusting to a negative life event: coping with the loss of a child. *Journal of Personality and Social Psychology*, **65**, 812–821.

McMinn, M.R. (1991) Religious values, sexist language and perceptions of a therapist. *Journal of Psychology and Christianity*, **10**, 132–136.

McPherson, A.S. (1979) *Aimee: The Life Story of Aimee Semple McPherson*, Foursquare Publications, Los Angeles, CA.

Mead, G.H. (1934) *Mind, Self and Society*, University of Chicago Press, Chicago, IL.

Meadow, M.J. and Kahoe, R.D. (1984) *Psychology of Religion: Religion in Individual Lives*, Harper & Row, New York.

Meier, L. (1991) *Jewish Values in Jungian Psychology*, University Press of America, Lanham, MD.

Meissner, W.W. (1984) *Psychoanalysis and Religious Experience*, Yale University Press, New Haven, CT.

Mester, R. and Klein, H. (1981) The young Jewish revivalist. *British Journal of Medical Psychology*, **54**, 299–306.

Milgram, S. (1974) *Obedience and Authority*, Tavistock, London.

Miller, L. (1972) Mental illness. *Encyclopaedia Judaica*, Keter, Jerusalem.

Moody, R.A. (1975) *Life After Life*, Mockingbird Books, Atlanta, GA.

Mordechai, T. (1992) *Playing with Fire*, BP Publishers, New York.

Mowrer, O.H. (1961) *The Crisis in Psychiatry and Religion*, Van Nostrand Reinhold, New York.

Moyers, J.C. (1990) Religious issues in the psychotherapy of former fundamentalists. Special issue: psychotherapy and religion. *Psychotherapy*, **27**, 42–45.

Murphy, J.M. and Leighton, A.H. (1989) Repeated investigations of prevalence: the Stirling County study. *Acta Psychiatrica Scandinavica*, **79**, 45–59.

Newman, J.P. (1986) Gender, life strains and depression. *Journal of Health and Social Behaviour*, **27**, 161–178.

Noam, R. (1992) *The View from Above*, CIS Publishers, Lakewood, NJ.

Nolen-Hoeksema, S. (1991) Responses to depression and their effects on the duration of depressive episodes. *Journal of Abnormal Psychology*, **100**, 569–582.

Oakley, A. (1981) *Subject Women*, Fontana, London.

O'Connor, K.V. (1983) The structure of religion: a repertory grid approach. University of New South Wales. PhD thesis.

Oden, T. (1967) *Contemporary Theology and Psychotherapy*, Westminster Press, Philadephia, PA.

Olson, D. (1989) Church friendships: boon or barrier to church growth? *Journal for the Scientific Study of Religion*, **28**, 432–447

Oosterhuis, A. (1993) Abolishing the rod. *Journal of Psychology and Theology*, **21**, 127–133.

Pahnke, W.N. (1966) Drugs and mysticism. *International Journal of Parapsychology*, **52**, 295–324.

Paloutzian, R. (1979) Spiritual wellbeing, loneliness and perceived quality of life. Symposium chaired for the American Psychological Association, New York, September 1979.

Paloutzian, R.F. (1981) Purpose in life and value changes following conversion. *Journal of Personality and Social Psychology*, **41**, 1153–1160.

Paloutzian, R.F. (1983) *Invitation to the Psychology of Religion*, Scott Foresman, Glenview, IL.

Pargament, K.I. and Hahn, J. (1986) God and the just world: Causal and coping attributions to God in health situations. *Journal for the Scientific Study of Religion*, **25**, 193–207.

Parker, G.B. and Brown, L.B. (1982) Coping behaviours that mediate between life-events and depression. *Archives of General Psychiatry*, **39**, 1386–1391.

Parker, G.B. and Brown, L.B. (1986) Coping behaviours as predictors of the course of clinical depression. *Archives of General Psychiatry*, **43**, 561–565.

Paykel, E.S. (1991) Depression in women. *British Journal of Psychiatry*, **158**, 22–29.

Pescosolido, B. and Georgianna, S. (1989) Durkheim, suicide and religion. *American Sociological Review*, **54**, 33–48.

Peterson, C. and Seligman, M.E.P. (1984) Causal explanations as a risk factor for depression: Theory and evidence. *Psychological Review*, **91**, 347–374.

Pettigrew, T. (1979) The ultimate attribution error. Extending Allport's cognitive analysis of prejudice. *Personality and Social Psychology Bulletin*, **5**, 461–476.

Piaget, J. (1967) *Six Psychological Studies*, Random House, Vintage Books, New York.

Pinter, R. (1990) No guilt feelings. *Jewish Tribune*, **18 Oct**, 5.

Potts, M.K., Burnham, M. and Wells, K.R. (1991) Gender differences in depression detection: a comparison of clinician diagnosis and standardized assessment. *Psychological Assessment*, **3**, 609–615.

Power, M., Champion, L. and Aris, L. (1988) The development of a measure of social support: the Significant Others Scale (SOS). *British Journal of Clinical Psychology*, **27**, 349–358.

Prasinos, S. (1992) Spiritual aspects of psychotherapy. *Journal of Religion and Health*, **31**, 41–52.

Pressman, P., Lyons, J.S., Larson, D.B. and Gartner, J. (1992) Religion, anxiety and fear of death, in *Religion and Mental Health*, (ed. J. Schumaker), Oxford University Press, Oxford.

Pressman, P., Lyons, J.S., Larson, D.B. and Strain J.J. (1990) Religious belief, depression and ambulation status in elderly women with broken hips. *American Journal of Psychiatry*, **147**, 758–760.

Proudfoot, W. and Shaver, P. (1975) Attribution theory and the psychology of religion. *Journal for the Scientific Study of Religion*, **14**, 317–330.

Prudo, R., Brown, G.W., Harris, T. and Dowland, J. (1981) Psychiatric disorder in an urban and a rural population. 2: Sensitivity to loss. *Psychological Medicine*, **11**, 601–616.

Prudo, R., Harris, T.O. and Brown, G. (1984) Psychiatric disorder in an urban and a rural population. 3: Social integration and the morphology of affective disorder. *Psychological Medicine*, **14**, 327–345.

Purpura, P. (1985) Catholicism and psychoanalysis. Washington Square Institute Friday Evening Conference, New York. *Issues in Ego Psychology*, **9**, 63–65.

Quackenbos, S., Privett, G. and Klenz, B. (1986) Psychotherapy and religion: rapprochement or antithesis? *Journal of Counselling and Development*, **65**, 82–85.

Rabinowicz, L. (1960) *A Guide to Hasidism*, Yoseloff, Jerusalem.

Rayburn, C.A. (1992) Counselling depressed female religious profession-als: nuns and clergywomen. Special issue: depression and religion. *Counselling and Values*, **35**, 136–148.

Richardson, J.T. (1985) Psychological and psychiatric studies of new reli-gions, in *Advances in the Psychology of Religion*, (ed, L.B. Brown), Pergamon Press, Oxford.

Rizzuto, A. (1974) Object relations and the formation of the image of God. *British Journal of Medical Psychology*, **47**, 83–89.

Robbins, T. (1988) *Cults, Converts and Charisma: the Sociology of New Religious Movements*, Sage, London.

Roberts, C. (1988) Imagining God: who is created in whose image? *Review of Religious Research*, **30**, 375–386.

Rogers, C.R. (1951) *Client-Centred Therapy: its Current Practice, Implication and Theory*, Houghton Mifflin, Boston, MA.

Rogers, C.R. (1959) A theory of therapy, personality, and interpersonal relationships, as developed in the client-centred framework, in *Psychology, the Study of a Science, vol. 3: Formulations of the Person and the Social Context*, (ed. S. Koch), McGraw-Hill, New York.

Rogers, C.R. (1980) Client-centred psychotherapy, in *Comprehensive Textbook of Psychiatry*, 2nd edn, (eds A.M. Freedman, H.T. Kaplan and B.J. Saddock), Williams & Wilkins, Baltimore, MD.

Rorsman, B., Grasbeck, A., Hagnell, O. and Lanke, J. (1990) A pros-pective study of first-incidence depression: the Lundby study (1957–1972). Special Issue: Cross-Cultural Psychiatry. *British Journal of Psychiatry*, **156**, 336–342.

Rosenfield, S. (1992) The costs of sharing: wives' employment and husbands' mental health. *Journal of Health and Social Behaviour*, **33**, 213–225.

Rotenberg, M. (1986) The 'Midrash' and biographic rehabilitation. *Journal for the Scientific Study of Religion*, **25**, 41–48.

Rotter, J.B. (1966) Generalised expectancies for internal versus external control of reinforcement. *Psychological Monographs*, **80** (whole number 609).

Rumke, H.C. (1952) *The Psychology of Unbelief*, Rockliff, London.

Ryckman, R.M. (1993) *Theories of Personality*, Brooks/Cole, Pacific Grove, CA.

Sahgal, G. and Yuval-Davis, N. (1992) *Refusing Holy Orders: Women and Fundamentalism in Britain*, Virago, London.

Sandler, J., Dare, C. and Holder, A. (1992) *The Patient and the Analyst: the Basis of the Psychoanalytic Process*, 2nd edn, (rev. and expanded by J. Sandler and A.U. Dreher), Karnac Books, London.

Sanua, J.D. (1969) Religion, mental health and personality: a review of empirical studies. *American Journal of Psychiatry*, **125**, 1203–1213.

Sayal, A. (1990) Black women and mental health. *Psychologist*, **3**, 24–27.

Scarnati, R., Madry, M.A., Wise, A. and Moore, H.D. (1991) Religious beliefs and practices among most dangerous psychiatric inmates. *Forensic Reports*, **4**, 1–16.

Schloss, O. (1993) Counselling the right way. *Jewish Tribune*, **21 Oct**.

Schneersohn, Y.Y. (1990) *The Principles of Education and Guidance*, Kehot, Brooklyn, NY.

Scobie, G.W. (1975) *Psychology of Religion*, John Wiley, New York.

Seligman, M.E.P. (1975) *Helplessness: on Depression, Development and Death*, Freeman, San Francisco, CA.

Shaffer, D.R. (1985) *Developmental Psychology*, Brooks/Cole, Monterey, CA.

Shain, R. (1992) *Dearest Children*, Feldheim, Jerusalem.

Shams, M. and Jackson, P.R. (1993) Religiosity as a predictor of well-being and moderator of the psychological impact of unemployment. *British Journal of Medical Psychology*, **66**, 341–352.

Shapira, K.K. (1991) *Chovat HaTalmidim (A Student's Obligation)*, (trans. M. Odenheimer), Jason Aronson, Northdale, NJ.

Shaver, P., Lenauer, M. and Sadd, S. (1980) Religiousness, conversion and subjective wellbeing. *American Journal of Psychiatry*, **137**, 1563–1568.

Silverstein, B. and Perlick, D. (1991) Gender differences in depression; historical changes. *Acta Psychiatrica Scandinavica*, **84**, 327–331.

Singh, G. (1986) Violence against wives in India. *Response to the Victimization of Women and Children*, **9**, 16–18.

Snow, D. and Machalek, R. (1984) The sociology of conversion. *Annual Review of Sociology*, **10**, 167–190.

Solomon,V. (1965) *A Handbook on Conversions*, Stravon.

Sorenson, S.B., Rutter, C.B. and Aneshensel, C.S. (1991) Depression in the community: an investigation into age of onset. *Journal of Consulting and Clinical Psychology*, **59**, 541–546.

Spero, M.H. (1980) *Judaism and Psychology: Halakhic Perspectives*, Ktav/Yeshiva University Press, New York.

Spero, M.H. (1985) *Psychotherapy of the Religious Patient*, Charles C. Thomas, Springfield, IL.

Spero, M.H. (1992) *Religious Objects as Psychological Structures: a Critical Integration of Object Relations Theory, Psychotherapy and Judaism*, University of Chicago Press, Chicago, IL.

Spilka, B. (1986) Spiritual issues: do they belong in psychological practice? Yes – but. 93rd. Annual Convention of the American Psychological Association: Spiritual issues: do they belong in psychological practice? *Psychotherapy in Private Practice*, **4**, 93–100.

Spilka, B., Hood, R.W. and Gorsuch, R.L. (1985) *The Psychology of Religion: an Empirical Approach*, Prentice Hall, Englewood Cliffs, NJ.

Spilka, B. Shaver, P. and Kirkpatrick, L.A. (1985) A general attribution theory for the psychology of religion. *Journal for the Scientific Study of Religion*, **24**, 1–20.

Spilka, B. and Werme, P. (1971) Religion and mental disorder: a critical review and theoretical perspective, in *Research on Religious Development: a Comprehensive Handbook. A Project of the Religious Education Association*, (ed M.P. Strommen), Hawthorn Books, New York.

Stace, W.T. (1960) *Mysticism and Philosophy*, J.B. Lippincott, Philadelphia, PA.

Stack, S. (1992) Religiosity, depression and suicide, in *Religion and Mental Health*, (ed. J. Schumaker), Oxford University Press, Oxford.

Stanley, G.S. (1964) Personality and attitude correlates of religious conversion. *Journal for the Scientific Study of Religion*, **4**, 60–63.

Staples, C.L. and Mauss, A.L. (1987) Conversion or commitment? A reassessment of the Snow and Machalek approach to the study of conversion. *Journal for the Scientific Study of Religion*, **26**, 133–147.

Starbuck, E.D. (1899) *The Psychology of Religion: an Empirical Study of the Growth of Religious Consciousness*, (with a preface by William James), W. Scott, London.

Stark, R. (1971) Psychopathology and religious commitment. *Review of Religious Research*, **12**, 165–176.

Stark, R. and Bainbridge, W.S. (1980) Towards a theory of religion: religious commitment. *Journal for the Scientific Study of Religion*, **19**, 114–128.

Steer, R.A., Beck, A.T. and Brown, G. (1989) Sex differences on the revised Beck Depression Inventory for outpatients with affective disorders. *Journal of Personality Assessment*, **53**, 693–702.

Steinitz, L. (1980) Religiosity, wellbeing and *Weltanschauung* among the elderly. *Journal for the Scientific Study of Religion*, **19**, 60–67.

Stouffer, S.A. *et al.* (1949) *The American Soldier, vol 2: Combat and its Aftermath*, Princeton University Press, Princeton, NJ.

Strayhorn, J.M., Weldman, C.S. and Larson, D. (1990) A measure of religiousness, and its relation to parent and child mental health variables. *Journal of Community Psychology*, **18**, 34–43.

Strommen, M.P. (1972) *A Study of Generation*, Augsburg, Minneapolis, MN.

Suls, J. and Mullen, B. (1981) Life events, perceived control and illness: the role of uncertainty. *Journal of Human Stress*, **7**, 30–34.

Switzer, D.K. (1976) Considerations of the religious dimensions of emotional disorder. *Pastoral Psychology*, **24**, 317–328.

Szasz, T. (1993) Crazy talk: thought disorder or psychiatric arrogance? *British Journal of Medical Psychology*, **66**, 61–68.

Talbo, T. and Shepperd, J.A. (1986) Self-righteousness: cognitive, power and religious characteristics. *Journal of Research in Personality*, **20**, 145–157.

Tan, S.Y. (1991) Religious values and interventions in lay Christian counselling. Special issue: religious values in psychotherapy. *Journal of Psychology and Christianity*, **10**, 173–182.

Thomsen, M. (1965) The culture shock of sudden death. *San Francisco Chronicle*, **25,26 April**.

Turner, J.C. (1975) Social comparison and social identity: some prospects for intergroup behaviour. *European Journal of Social Psychology*, **5**, 5–34.

Ullman, C. (1982) Cognitive and emotional antecedents of religious conversion. *Journal of Personality and Social Psychology*, **43**, 183–192.

Valentine, E.R. (1989) A cognitive psychological analysis of meditation techniques and mystical experiences. *Ethical Record*, **April**, 9–20.

Valentine, E.R. (1992) *Conceptual Issues in Psychology*, Routledge, London.

Vergote, A. and Tamayo, A. (1980) *The Parental Figures and the Representation of God*, Mouton, The Hague.

Vredenburg, K., Krames, L. and Flett, G.L. (1986) Modifying the B.D.I.: a rejoinder to Steer and Beck. *Psychological Reports*, **57**, 903–906.

Vygotsky, L.S. (1962) *Thought and Language*, MIT Press, Cambridge, MA.

Watson, P., Morris, R. and Hood, R. (1989) *Journal for the Scientific Study of Religion*, **28**, 337–347.

Watts, F. and Williams, M. (1988) *The Psychology of Religious Knowing*, Cambridge University Press, New York.

Wearing, A.J. and Brown, L.B. (1972) The dimensionality of religion. *British Journal of Social and Clinical Psychology*, **11**, 143–148.

Weiner, B. (1979) A theory of motivation for some classroom experiences. *Journal of Educational Psychology*, **71**, 3–25.

Wikler, M. (1979) Fine-tuning: diagnostic techniques used by orthodox Jewish clients. *Journal of Psychology and Judaism*, **3**, 184–194.

Wikler, M. (1986) How orthodox Jews enter therapy. *Social Casework*, **67**, 113–118.

Wikstrom, O. (1987) Attribution, roles and religion: a theoretical analysis of Sunden's role theory of religion and the attributional approach to religious experience. *Journal for the Scientific Study of Religion*, **26**, 390–400.

Williams, L. (1992) Torture and the torturer. *Psychologist*, **5**, 305–308.

Winnicott, D.W. (1958) *Collected Papers: Through Paediatrics to Psycho-Analysis*, Tavistock, London.

Witztum, E., Dasberg, H. and Greenberg, D. (1990) Mental illness and religious change. *British Journal of Medical Psychology*, **63**, 33–42.

Zales, M.R. (1978) Mysticism: psychodynamics and relationship to psychopathology, in *Expanding Dimensions of Consciousness*, (eds A.A. Sugerman and R.E. Tarter), Springer-Verlag, New York.

Zimbardo, P.G. (1969) The human choice: individuation, reason and order versus de-individuation, impulse and chaos, in *The Nebraska Symposium on Motivation*, (eds W.J. Arnold and D. Levine), vol. 17, University of Nebraska Press, Lincoln, NE.

Index